The Sound of Hope

The Sound of Hope

A True Story of an Adoptee's Quest for her Origins

Anne Bauer

iUniverse, Inc.
New York   Bloomington

The Sound of Hope

A True Story of an Adoptee's Quest for her Origins

iUniverse books may be ordered through booksellers or by contacting:

iUniverse
1663 Liberty Drive
Bloomington, IN 47403
www.iuniverse.com
1-800-Authors (1-800-288-4677)

ISBN: 978-0-5955-2030-5 (pbk)
ISBN: 978-0-5955-0936-2 (cloth)
ISBN: 978-0-5956-2118-7 (ebk)

Library of Congress Control Number: 2008939980

Printed in the United States of America

iUniverse rev. date: 11/13/2008

For Michael, Shali, and my three little angels.
Their love and support has been the inspiration
behind this memoir.

Author's Note:

The following story is a true account of my life as an adoptee. In order to protect the privacy of those still living, certain names, locations, and events have been changed.

Contents

Part One

"Earth has no sorrows that heaven cannot heal." —Irish Proverb

One

Split In Half

The day I realized I had two mothers, I was cut in half. One mother had had me in her belly and brought me to the special nursery, while this mother I called Mommy took me home from the nursery to live. One half of myself resided here with my family, and the other half was lost, lost to a shadowy woman floating somewhere out there in the world.

You see, I'm adopted.

You'd never know it if you saw me beside my adoptive family. On the outside, we look very much alike. We have the same eye color, the same fair complexion—yes, the adoption agency did its job well. The difficulties lie on the inside, deep beneath the outer layers—where the heart and soul reside. Here, they did a dreadful job.

My parents, like other adoptive parents of their generation, were urged by the social workers to tell their children about their special status as early as possible. It was imperative that we be told about coming from somewhere else, our biological parents. It was considered to be in our best interest, most likely an attempt to thwart the accidental *spilling of the beans* by a close friend or relative. In any case, there was just one problem with the social workers' advice: We weren't allowed to know anything more. This strange woman's name, where she lived, what she looked like—such information was taboo.

Even when I turned eighteen, the information available remained the same. I was cut off from my origins, emotionally and legally. A part of me, deep within the depths of my soul, felt incomplete. This was the very thing my adoptive family could never come to understand.

As I look back now, I wonder how I ever weathered growing up with so little information, knowing only that I was adopted, and how I endured the guilt thrown at me whenever I inquired about my origins.

My grandmother, bless her soul, used to tell me about the day my family went and *picked* me out from the adoption agency's nursery ward. It became one of my favorite stories, though the story was incomplete. It lacked the beginning—where I came from and how exactly I came to be at the nursery ward.

Still, Grandma told a great story, keeping me at the edge of my seat. I'm sure she embellished some of the details, as was her nature, but one thing I'm certain of is that it had to have rained. According to Grandma, it poured like cats and dogs that cold and dank day in November 1966.

I've been told that the morning they came to get me, Grandpa drove my parents' light blue station wagon with Grandma in the front next to him, my mom, dad, and two brothers in the back. Rain started to come down in sheets. After a forty-five-minute drive, Grandpa pulled up in front of a large Victorian mansion. Everyone stared at the vastness of the house that loomed over them as Grandpa carefully parked the car across the street. Grandma explained that the once grand house had been converted into a home for unwed mothers. As told in Grandma's dramatic storytelling fashion, the next scenes always kept me at the edge of my seat.

"Annie, we had only one umbrella with us. I told your grandfather that he ought to bring several by the look of the clouds before we left, but he wouldn't listen. No siree. Anyway, we each hopped out of the car—me first, and I huddled under the umbrella along with your mother and Grandpa. Poor Thomas and Brian, they dashed across the street with your father and were soaked through within seconds. You know your father; he couldn't wait his turn for the umbrella." Grandma threw her hands up in exasperation. "And you know what?" she asked, widening her eyes. Mine widened too. "We looked like a bunch of refugees by the time we arrived at the front door. Thomas's and Brian's clothes, those beautiful checkered blazers and new wool pants, were clinging to their bodies!" Grandma took a deep breath as if to shake off the memory of her grandchildren looking less than impeccably dressed. "We all stood there huddled under the awning, and you know what? The door was locked. Can you believe that? They knew we were coming. We rang the doorbell, and by that time, the rain was coming in sideways and my feet were soaked! I had *had* it and was ready to get back in the car." Whenever Grandma got to this point, I worried each time that they'd change their minds and instead return home—without me. But Grandma quickly continued her story, saving me every time. "Finally," Grandma said, leaning forward, "the door swung open and a tall, skinny nun dressed in a dark habit motioned for us to come inside. Oh … she was mean-looking. We followed her through a spotless, long hallway and into a small office. And you know what, that nun never even bothered to look our way; she rummaged through some papers on an old desk in the corner, while we all paced the floor, smelling some stinking Pine-Sol they must have just used to clean.

"I always hated that nun. Why couldn't she at least smile?" Grandma shook her head before she went on. "The nun finally found your papers and your poor mother … why she was as white as a sheet standing there. I think she thought the nun had lost them! She asked if everything was all right, and that nun just looked at her for the longest time and then said, 'Yes, the girl's papers are in order. She's all yours.'"

Grandma would always pause at this point and look up in deep thought. I imagined she was reliving the moment when she knew I'd be her granddaughter.

"Your mother was so relieved. Finally, a little girl in the family! You know, Annie … you're my very first granddaughter." A wide smile quickly blossomed across her face, and then, just as quickly, she turned serious. "Don't get me wrong, I love my three grandsons, but there's nothing like a granddaughter."

Grandma then would go on. "'Do you want to see the child?' that angry nun asked. Her face looked as solemn as the clouds outside. She led us into another room, and our ears were instantly bombarded with your shrieking cries. All the other babies were silent … all but you," she added chuckling.

"The nun on duty was the sweetest little thing. She had red hair, and she looked relieved that you were going. Finally some quiet! Thomas and Brian went over to see you, and Thomas asked, 'Can't you pick out a quieter baby?' Your father didn't want to hear that, and when Thomas cupped his hands over his ears, your father nearly blew a gasket!"

"What about Brian?" I always asked.

"Brian was only two. He didn't understand. Grandpa took Thomas out of the room while I told your mother to pick you up. 'Why, Erin,' I told her, 'she's probably hungry. Come pick up your baby. The poor thing needs soothing.'"

But as the story goes, Mom lifted me out of the bassinette, and a loud wail erupted from my mouth. She began rocking me back and forth in her arms, taking turns with Dad, but the cries persisted and even grew louder with each passing moment. It wasn't long before my parents were at their wits' end. There was nothing they could do to quiet me, that is, until I landed in Grandma's arms.

"I really don't know what the big deal is," Grandma would tell me. "You only needed to be in *my* arms."

Grandma ended the story with how she carried me to the station wagon, and Grandpa drove off, cruising slowly through the hovering mist, in honor of the new vulnerable cargo.

During the car ride home, I eventually conked out, whereupon Grandma reveled in the fact that only *she* could stop my crying.

*   *   *

Grandma was Anna Marie, and I was her namesake. Even though she stood barely two inches over five feet, her rigid, upright stance coupled with her piercing blue eyes and strong disposition demanded attention from anyone in her presence. In a way, she was the matriarch of the family, our own Rose Kennedy. Nothing was decided without first consulting Grandma. Her opinion mattered. She weighed every decision between church doctrine and her own. Although highly devoted to the Catholic faith, especially to Saint Jude, her vocabulary broke any restrictions the church imposed about using God's name in vain. But she reserved her most colorful language for family and close friends. Grandma maintained her status within the community by attending church every Sunday and ensuring that her six children were always impeccably dressed no matter what the family budget.

Grandma couldn't help herself. Clean and well-dressed children were a sign of respectability. She learned this from her grandparents, who emigrated from Ireland to the United States in the late 1800s after the great potato famine. They made sure they were clean, even if it meant washing the same clothes and wearing them again the next day.

Grandma knew a lot about her grandmothers, including their maiden names and the Irish counties in which they were born. Family history was one of her favorite topics. "My mother's mother was named Molly Devine. I always liked the name Molly," she told me with a wide smile, showing off her perfect gleaming teeth. Grandma was proud of her dentures. "Molly was from County Louth. My father's mother's name was Bridgett Courtney, and she was from County Longford."

Grandma was also proud of her hair, which she had done every Tuesday morning at the beauty shop. Her stark white hair, currently curled and styled attractively around her face, made her smile even more striking. Everyone in the family agreed: Grandma was an extremely attractive woman.

Grandma, the firstborn daughter of the Dolans and named after her mother Anna, grew up in an all-Irish neighborhood on the lower east side of Manhattan. In 1937, when she turned eighteen, she married my grandfather, James Murphy. He was raised in the same Irish neighborhood, and they had attended grammar school together. When they decided to marry, they were afraid to ask permission from their parents, so they eloped. After the ceremony, they went home to their own families and kept the marriage secret for a week. When Grandma finally worked up the courage to tell her folks, her mother beat her with a broom on her backside for doing such a stupid thing.

"Jimmy's father's a drunk," Great-Grandma Anna scolded. "He works in a tavern, for goodness sakes. Your father works in a bank. Which is more respectable, Anna?"

It didn't matter to Grandma where Jimmy's father worked—she refused to have the marriage annulled. They remained married and the following week moved into a small apartment of their own in the same neighborhood. My adoptive mother, Erin, arrived a year later, followed by my Aunt Brenda and twins, Patrick and Marianne. Marianne died during the delivery, but this unfortunate experience didn't deter them from having more children. After my grandfather returned from serving in the navy during World War II, three more arrived, Lorraine, Cecilia, and Teddy.

It was a tough childhood for Erin. Being the eldest of six children and a daughter, not only was she responsible for the majority of the chores around the house, she did the lion's share of child-rearing. The youngest, Teddy, born when Mom was fourteen, was an active boy and Grandma lacked the energy to keep up with him. Progressive obesity, which plagued every female in the family, made it especially difficult for Grandma. That wasn't Grandma's only problem, though. Her husband routinely came home drunk.

Mom's early responsibilities taught her endurance, but it came with a price. She lacked the capacity to give affection. I'm sure the emotions were there, but they were buried deep beneath her granite surface. Perhaps she was just plain worn out. Who had the time to hug or kiss family members when there were so many chores to do in the house?

By the time Teddy was born, my grandparents had bought a large split-level home in the northern suburbs of New Jersey. Grandma gave each one of her children routine chores. "Many hands lighten the load," she'd say. Mom had the most. Besides cleaning up after dinner, twice a week, she'd vacuum the entire house, dust all the furniture, and clean the bathrooms. When her youngest three siblings started school, she made sure they were up and ready in the morning and made their bagged lunches. She juggled her responsibilities with maturity and resilience. Her only outlet, her one true love, was reading books. She'd read anything she could get her hands on, everything from mystery novels to the classics. She was a regular at the local library. At times, she could be found reading three or four books at the same time, one for each room in the house, as Grandma would say. Reading was her mainstay and her escape, the one activity that saved her soul.

After high school, Mom went to a Catholic nursing school in New York City; she was the only one in her family to pursue higher education. Grandpa, who managed to work his way up to being a director within the longshoremen's union, arranged her first job as the head nurse of a clinic. At twenty-one, she married Bob Willoughby, my adoptive father. Like other young newlyweds, my parents wanted a family right away. After trying for two years, they learned the news: They were unable to conceive a child.

It was the 1960s, a time with no surrogate mothers or in vitro fertilization, and their only option was to adopt.

Most adoptions were handled by private adoption agencies. My parents were directed by their parish priest to contact the agency affiliated with their church located in Newark. After undergoing several months of interviews and home inspections by the social workers, they were approved and a baby was selected for them.

My older brother, Thomas, the first addition to the family, came along in 1962, at the age of three months. In 1964, my other brother, Brian, followed. Soon after, my parents wanted another child, a daughter. The agency selected me for my parents.

When it came to telling us about our adoptive status, my parents waited until we were at least four years old and initially used a book to explain the situation. The small hardcover volume was a present from the agency after they adopted Thomas. The cover featured a picture of a five-year-old blond-haired boy named David with his parents. Inside was the story of how David's parents *chose* him to be their son.

A few days after my fourth birthday, I first encountered the book, which, having passed through both my brothers' fingers, had seen better days. Still, it was nonetheless one of my favorites, and Dad would read the tattered pages to me at least once a week, while sitting comfortably in his oversized recliner in the living room corner.

We had just moved into a two-family house with my grandparents. They lived on the second floor, and my family lived on the first. It was a modest, aluminum-sided home situated on a cul-de-sac along with other two-family homes on tiny lots in the town of Rochelle Park in northern New Jersey.

At first, the story about how David and his parents became a family didn't seem *special*, the word the book used to describe their situation. They were like my family and all the other families in my neighborhood. David's parents wanted a baby so they decided to adopt David. Big deal.

Then, when I was nearly five years old, the world shook beneath my feet. It was a sweltering day in August 1970. I stood next to my Aunt Lorraine with my hand pressed firmly on her protruding belly. Aunt Lorraine, one of Mom's younger sisters, was nine months pregnant, a week past her due date and in no mood for the likes of me, an inquisitive little girl completely enchanted with the idea of a live baby inside her belly.

My mother and grandmother, each with her own expanded waistline, were sitting like bookends on the love seat. Each held a cold glass of iced tea in one hand and a lit cigarette in the other. Aunt Lorraine, whose belly stuck so far out she couldn't even tie her own shoelaces, was sprawled out on the couch across from them, fanning herself with a *Good Housekeeping* magazine while the only fan we owned oscillated in front of her. The three of them wanted nothing more than to be left in peace.

"Don't press too hard, Annie," Aunt Lorraine warned. "You might hurt the baby." The glare on her face showed it was clear she had reached her limits with me.

"There it is again!" I exclaimed, my eyes dancing with delight. "The baby just kicked. Did you feel that, Aunt Lorraine?" I kept my hand steady on her belly, but my legs were bouncing with excitement as I waited for another movement.

Aunt Lorraine smiled. "Of course. I feel it every time the baby kicks, but I feel it from the inside."

"So is a baby really there?" I asked, not fully believing it.

"Yes."

"How come you don't need to pick out your baby? Mommy and Daddy went to the special nursery and picked me out. They said there were lots of babies that needed to be adopted and ..."

"Annie! Stop talking so fast," Mommy scolded.

I covered my mouth with my hand.

"Oops ... I forgot." Ever since I could talk, the words came out as fast as lightning; in fact, I did everything super fast. I possessed an endless amount of energy and was forever running, shouting, and moving. I drove everybody crazy. By the time I turned three, my parents had had enough. Where was the sweet, quiet little girl who was supposed to sit nicely all day and play with her dolls? Mom, after reaching her wits' end, asked my pediatrician for medication to calm me down. He refused and instead told her to enroll me in ballet classes to help release the excess energy.

Aunt Lorraine still hadn't answered my question, and I remained with my hand cupped over my mouth with wide eyes, waiting.

"No." Aunt Lorraine sighed. "We don't need to pick out our baby."

My legs stopped bouncing. "Why not?"

Aunt Lorraine glanced inquisitively at Mommy, who shrugged her shoulders as if to say, *You're on your own with this one.*

"No," Aunt Lorraine answered, turning back to me. "It's already here in my belly. Hopefully, the baby is going to come out soon." She adjusted the pillow behind her back. "Then the baby will stay in the nursery until we both come home."

"Like the nursery I was in, like Thomas and Brian too," I told her.

"Annie," Mommy interrupted. "You know what I told you before. When your father and I decided that we wanted a baby, we called the adoption agency and they told us to come to the special nursery. That's how you, Thomas, and Brian were adopted." She told me in a brisk, matter-of-fact way, as if she were referring to picking out a dog at the pound.

I looked at Mommy.

"But how did I get to the special nursery?"

She puffed deeply on her cigarette.

"Another woman gave birth to you. She brought you to the special nursery, and then we came and took you home."

"So I was in someone else's belly?" I asked, for the first time realizing that not everyone was adopted. Up till then, in my fleeting thoughts, I always pictured parents going to a big room where newborn babies, wrapped securely in receiving blankets, were all lined up, waiting patiently. I never thought about how the babies actually got to the nursery, having only pictured the parents arriving, then looking over all the babies like slabs of meat arranged in a deli counter.

"Yes, you were inside another mother's belly," Mommy muttered, as if she hated to admit this fact.

"So Aunt Lorraine's baby won't be adopted?"

"No!" Mommy, Grandma, and Aunt Lorraine said in unison.

Another piece of the puzzle slid into place.

"Not all babies are brought to the nursery to be adopted?" I asked, tilting my head to the side. It wasn't so much a question but a statement needing confirmation.

"No, not all babies. Only the ones whose original mothers decide they can't keep them," Mommy said, stressing this fact. "Only Thomas, Brian, and you are adopted."

My vision of everybody being adopted exploded. Trembling and feeling sick to my stomach, I slid down to my knees on the floor.

"After we saw you, your father and I decided to keep you."

"Oh yes!" Grandma smiled, reaching toward the ashtray on the coffee table. "You were so tiny." She tapped her cigarette, and a long ash dropped off. "And you cried so much and so loud that Thomas asked if we could pick out a quieter baby." She cackled.

I looked at Mommy, then at Grandma.

"Why can't I see the mother who had me in her belly? Where is she?"

"We don't know where she is, Annie," Mommy said, shaking her head and glancing at Grandma.

Grandma shrugged. "After she decided to give you up, she wasn't allowed to see you."

I rested my back against the couch, reflecting on this revelation, then jumped back to my feet.

"Why not?" I demanded. "Why can't she see me?"

I tried to picture what she looked like, but only a picture of a woman veiled in dark gray formed in my mind. Immediately, an aura of mystery formed about this phantom mother of mine—my other mother. I wanted to see her.

My urgent question met with silence. The women just sat there watching the smoke from their cigarettes drift toward the fan.

No valid answer existed for my question. When I was adopted in 1966, the adoption process was kept closed in most states. My state, New Jersey, sealed the original birth certificate containing my birth name after the adoption became legal. From that day on, history was rewritten and I was considered to be the natural child of my adoptive parents. Nobody, not even a court of law could unseal or view the original document.

I glanced at Aunt Lorraine on the couch, still fanning herself with the magazine.

"Oh, this heat is unbearable," she moaned. "Why can't this baby be born?"

"The baby will come when it's good and ready. You can't rush these things," Grandma said knowingly. "You were born late, Lorraine, eleven days past your due date."

"Was I born late?" I immediately asked.

Mom rolled her eyes.

"Oh, I think they told me you were born right on time." She gulped the remainder of her iced tea.

The story about how I became a part of my family finally sank in. I truly understood what it was to be adopted, and this realization entered like a charging bull, taking hold of my naïve preconceptions and throwing them to the wind. It left me feeling half naked, as if I was missing some part of myself. But the lasting impression was as clear as a bright, sunny day: My brothers and I were different from everyone else. We were adopted.

Little did I know, at such a tender age, that I had only scratched the surface of the mystery of my origins. But deep inside, I was sure of one thing: No secret could be kept forever.

Two

Family Matters

Dad easily fit in with the Murphy clan. As for his own family, he rarely saw them. Dad had a tough childhood. He was an illegitimate child born in 1933, during the Depression. From the things he told me about his family, I gathered his mother, Helen, was a loving and affectionate person.

"She would have loved the three of you, especially you," Dad said almost every night as I squirmed on his lap, his warm arms wrapped tightly around me. "You would've been her favorite."

Unfortunately, I never got to meet my paternal grandmother. She died in 1949, when Dad was only sixteen years old.

It must've been very hard, losing a mother just a few years shy of adulthood. Maybe this was the reason Dad loved talking about her so much; it was his own way of sorting through the painful memory. I never tired of hearing him go on about how she loved to keep a spotless house, cook fabulous Polish dishes, and was the Rock of Gibraltar for everyone in the family. I only minded that I wouldn't be able to meet her. She almost sounded too good to be true.

This grandmother was a reminder of my original mother, who was never to be seen in the flesh but vividly imagined in the mind. But with Dad's mom, there was a big difference: I had photos and stories to complement my imagination. There were only three small black-and-white, weathered pictures of his mother, just enough to keep her image real and not some distant shadow. I'd stare at the photos for hours, slowly taking in every inch of her—the roundness of her middle; her dark, narrow-set eyes; and the pudgy, lined cheeks that seemed to be smiling only for me. It was as if somehow, she knew someday her granddaughter would be staring at her image wondering what kind of a person she was, or could have been. My gut told me I would have loved her as much as Dad claimed she would have loved me.

After she died, Dad remained with his father in their tiny railroad apartment in the city of West New York. There were also siblings, if you'd call them that, three sisters and a brother, but they weren't much comfort to Dad after their mother's death, being that they were years older, married, and had lives of their own. What spurred the distance between them more than the age difference was the fact that Dad was technically only their half sibling.

My grandmother Helen's first four children resulted from an earlier marriage. The eldest was a son followed by three daughters. When the children entered their teens, their father one day simply failed to return home from work. Rumor has it that he probably passed out in some gutter. Ten years later, she met my grandfather, Robert Willoughby, and soon became pregnant with Dad. They moved in together but never married.

This especially irked Dad's half sisters, Sophie and Helen, who shook their head at their own mother for living in sin. These two sisters were large, round, pompous women who considered themselves the keepers of societal decorum within their circles. Their noses turned up so far and so often that Dad joked they permanently burned out their sense of smell.

Sophie and Helen never treated their half brother or his father as real family. The youngest sister of the three, Irene, was a lot different—night and day, as Dad liked to say. Irene was Dad's favorite. She welcomed the arrival of her new baby brother with open arms and treated him with love and affection, like she did her own son, born three months earlier.

My paternal grandfather, Robert Willoughby Senior, to use Dad's own words, was a nasty son of a bitch. I myself never met the man; he died when I was only three weeks old. I could only imagine the awful things that happened in the household where Dad grew up, things that embittered him deeply. Apparently, my grandfather drank too much and routinely berated everyone in the household. Still, he held down a steady job and came home every night, something my grandmother must have desired. To maintain a stable home, she tolerated the other side of my grandfather, the destructive side that cut deeply into Dad's personality.

After Helen's death, Dad remained in the apartment along with his father. The days grew longer and darker without the natural buffer his mother once provided. His father, quite callous and often ornery, quickly made life unbearable for Dad. After two long years, Dad, having graduated from high school, moved in with his sister Irene and her family in Queens. My grandfather soon replaced Dad with another woman, nearly twenty years younger, and they lived together until his death in 1966.

My grandfather wasn't just an old grouch, he also didn't support my parents when they decided to adopt.

"Why would you want on take on someone else's problem?" he told Dad, not quite understanding how they were so willing to take a chance with some unknown baby. He thought adopted children were going to have serious physical or ongoing emotional problems. "There has to be a reason nobody in their own family wants to keep them."

Mom and Dad just wanted children. Simple. Period. It should've been the end of the story. Only everyone didn't understand the plight of an infertile couple: being plagued with frustration and ongoing disappointment from trying to conceive over and over without any success. Adoption was their only salvation.

Dad shuddered every time his father made a derogatory comment regarding the upcoming adoption of Thomas. Never did Dad dare to challenge him when it came to his comments. Inside, Dad remained the same little boy who cowered in the presence of his father.

After Thomas came along, my grandfather tolerated the new arrival but lacked any of the warmth or appreciation that is typical of any first-time doting grandparent.

Dad's siblings weren't as vocal as my grandfather—though I'm sure they just kept their comments to themselves. Their disapproval showed in more subtle ways like forgetting to buy birthday and Christmas gifts for us. My parents clearly understood each overlooked occasion and whispered to each other how Dad's siblings never seemed to forget their other nieces and nephews. Was it because Dad had adopted children or because of Dad's illegitimacy? Most likely, it was a little bit of both. Not surprisingly, Dad slowly withdrew from his family. He preferred the Murphys who were more down to earth. He loved the way they all gathered together, friends and family, every weekend to drink and party into the wee hours of the morning. If Dad's family got together, it was either a holiday or a special event like a wedding or a funeral. Otherwise, they pretty much stayed in their own small circle, keeping to themselves.

Dad kept in touch with his favorite sister Irene, seeing her every so often, but it wasn't as often as he would have liked. Maintaining a strong relationship with her amongst the other sisters proved too difficult.

Mom too had problems with her own family, the Murphys. At first, it wasn't so easy introducing adopted children into this big Irish family. They were a lot more verbal with six siblings, four of whom were sisters that didn't always get along. They often squabbled over trivial matters as each vied for Grandma's attention. Brenda, the second born, always bristled when her sisters received praise for doing so much around the house during their childhood, and lately, it irked her that Grandma spent so much time with Mom. Soon after the arrival of Thomas, Brenda wasted no time brewing new trouble.

"He's not *really* your son so he's not *really* part of the family like my Terry is," Brenda taunted Mom.

Apparently, Brenda wanted her son, born a year earlier and Grandma's very first grandchild, to remain in the spotlight.

When Grandma got wind of Brenda's comments, she marched over to her apartment and punched her daughter in the face. It was not as subtle as Dad's Polish sisters, but then again the Irish did have their own unique way of handling problems. And it usually worked.

However, Brenda was Irish too, and the next day, she brought assault charges against Grandma. When the case came before a judge, he threw Brenda out of the courtroom, scolding her for having the nerve to file charges against her own mother.

After this incident, nobody in the family dared to breathe a word about our adoption status. Grandma would have taken their heads off right on the spot. It was obvious: Nobody messed with her. I'm not sure where Grandma's fighting spirit came from. It may have formed after being the wife of a longshoreman, the tough working Irish on the docks of New York City. Or maybe it was her Irish genes filled with spunk and vigor from her ancestors who survived the famine and made it across the Atlantic under horrid conditions. All I know is that if any malicious comments were made, they were done so far away from Grandma's or Mom's hearing range. Never again did Mom have to endure comments about how her children weren't really part of the family, and life amidst the Murphys went on.

However, Brenda's relationship with her parents and siblings never completely recovered. Grandma tried to patch things up; she wanted all her children around, even Brenda. As the months went by, Brenda started coming by the house less and less frequently until eventually we saw her and her family only on Christmas and Easter. Brenda's jealousy remained, and she frequently complained to Teddy about all the time their mother spent with my family. She wanted to be the one who lived with Grandma in the two-family house. She wanted her son to be Grandma's favorite grandchild—not her sister Erin's adopted kids.

Brenda's resentment toward my family only fueled Grandma's affection for us. We went everywhere and did everything together—shopping, the movies, and even vacations. All of Mom's siblings were a bit envious as well because everybody wanted to be close to Grandma and it was a dream come true to live with her.

And it was like a dream. Grandma soon became my own version of Maria from *The Sound of Music*, my favorite movie which I watched on television every holiday season. It was not that Grandma routinely skipped through the house, rode bikes through the valley, or sewed her own clothes like Maria; instead, Grandma had the music side, and if we weren't watching television together—Grandma's favorite pastime—we were listening to her collection of old records. Grandma would play her favorites, like *Music! Music! Music (Put Another Nickel In)* and *Making Whoopee*, and she taught me all the words and had me perform for her and Grandpa. They'd sit together, drinking martinis and chuckle, saying how someday I'd be a star.

The music and singing weren't the only things that drew me to the movie, *The Sound of Music*. For some reason, I related to the plight of the von Trapp kids. We had a lot in common. They too lost a mother who was only to be replaced by the wonderful singing governess who laughed, joked, and brightened their lives amidst the gloomy household of their strict father. I was no different. Grandma was my Maria, and Dad was the stern father, Captain von Trapp. Only at that time, I never fully understood how true the comparison was.

Three

Unanswered Questions

Every time I ventured upstairs to my grandma's section of the house, typically humming, "My Favorite Things," I'd imagine I was Brigitta, the youngest von Trapp girl, on her way up to Maria's room for a singing lesson. The thought alone had me skipping in delight as I entered Grandma's kitchen. Every day, I visited, and every day, Grandma had a cup of tea in the making.

One day, after I arrived home from kindergarten, it seemed like an ordinary afternoon. I could hear the hum of the kettle over the distant sound of the television as I reached the top stair. Apparently, today was going to be without singing.

"Hi, Grandma," I yelled, bursting through the door.

"Oh, hi, Annie," she answered with an air of surprise. She stood by the kitchen counter, dipping chicken breasts into milk before placing them inside a plastic bag filled with bread crumbs. "You're up here early," she said, shaking the chicken inside the bag. She wore her usual flowered housecoat, made of a stretch knit material that clung to every fold and bend of her overweight body.

Many people mistook us for mother and daughter because my features so closely resembled hers. My eyes, blue at the time, almost matched her blue-gray eyes. We even shared similarly shaped lips, which were naturally rosy and full. Her smooth, radiant complexion made her look younger than her age. Although she was as fair as I was, the abundant freckles on her arms and legs gave the impression of a year-round suntan. Her hair, once jet black, had turned pure white. My light brown hair contained lots of red highlights, and in the summertime, people often mistook me for a redhead.

"Mom fell asleep, and she won't wake up," I whined, rambling into her kitchen. "Can I have some apple juice?"

"She worked last night at the hospital," Grandma said, placing the chicken breasts on a foil-covered cookie sheet and popping it into the oven. "She needs her rest."

"But I want her to play Candy Land with me," I said, planting myself on the stool and swirling around.

"Annie!" she snapped. "Sit still."

Abruptly, I halted in the middle of a spin and slid off the stool onto the linoleum floor. Just then, the teakettle began to whistle. Grandma wiped her hands on a dishtowel and walked over to the stove to turn down the heat under the kettle.

"Get up," she said shaking her head. "We'll have our tea together now." She motioned for me to join her at the counter.

I climbed back onto the stool. Grandma passed by and opened the cupboard door over the counter. She smelled of Jean Nate body splash, her favorite. She took out the ceramic sugar bowl and placed it in front of me. I grabbed the spoon and took several heaping spoonfuls of sugar, spilling some on the counter.

Like in the previous year, I still was unable to remain idle, and my inability to sit still for even a minute along with my incessant chattering still remained. Mom had a hard time lining up family members to babysit while she slept during the day.

Grandma's eyes narrowed.

"Oh, Annie," she said, eyeing the spilled sugar. "Go and get the sponge."

I scurried over to the sink and retrieved it, stealing a quick glance at Grandma. She was looking right at me, and her eyes softened. I needed only to look beyond her steel shell to discover her tender, serene side. Sometimes I wondered if this woman could possibly be my first mother.

She turned to put away the milk, and following her movements, I caught a glimpse of my reflection in the shiny chrome toaster. I looked like a boy. My parents received numerous compliments whenever we went out. They had three such well-behaved young gentlemen.

"Why didn't God give me long hair?" I asked plaintively. It was unfair. All the other girls had long hair. They wore pigtails and ponytails. I couldn't because my hair was too thin and never grew much. Mom said it would eventually start growing, but I wasn't so sure. I was five years old, and still my hair didn't look anything like the hair of other girls who were my age. Mom couldn't use ribbons or even get a barrette to stay in place.

"Now, Annie, you know that your hair grows slowly. It's your own fault for always pulling it out when you were little."

"Did not!" I said, crossing my arms in defiance.

Grandma shook her head, grinning. She was right. I had been a habitual hair puller as a baby. My parents tried everything to get me to stop. They even went to the extreme of putting mittens and a hat on me at bedtime. None of their interventions worked. Somehow, I still managed to get my fingers to my hair. Until I replaced hair pulling with another habit of touching everything, I was continuously bald on one side of my head.

"I want hair like Aunt Cecilia and the other girls," I went on, turning down my lower lip. Maybe if I appeared as pitiful as possible, Grandma could perform magic and make my hair grow.

She stood there, hand on hip, looking sideways at me. It wasn't working.

"Even Maggie has longer hair than I do," I added, tears forming in the corner of my eyes.

Maggie was my Aunt Lorraine's daughter. From the moment I first saw my aunt and uncle Ron whisk her through my grandparents' door on their first visit when Maggie was two weeks old, I was infatuated with my cousin. She was now almost a year old and had the Murphy side of the family's fair skin, but her almond-shaped dark green eyes coupled with a headful of thick, wavy brunette hair, already at the length of her shoulders, mirrored my uncle Ron.

The thing that kept me so preoccupied with Maggie wasn't her hair, which I secretly envied, but the way she responded to me. She was full of smiles and giggles when we were together, and I regularly lavished her with kisses and hugs much to the chagrin of my Aunt Lorraine who wanted me to leave her baby in peace. The truth was I loved Maggie. We had a special bond between us, and it pained me to have brought up my cousin in the middle of complaining about my hair.

"Oh, come on," Grandma said. "Take your tea and let's go sit inside and watch TV together."

Begrudgingly, I followed her thinking about when Maggie was in Aunt Lorraine's belly last summer. When we reached the living room, I asked the dreaded question.

"Grandma, where is my other mother?"

She stopped dead in her tracks, almost spilling her tea.

"I have no idea."

"Why did she make me adopted?"

Her eyes briefly glanced upwards as if trying to remember the rehearsed answer.

"She … she wasn't able to take care of you so your mother and father decided to raise you instead."

"She couldn't take care of Thomas and Brian either?"

"No, Thomas and Brian had other mothers, not the same one as you."

"But why?"

"Annie, I don't know." She sighed deeply. "It's just the way it is."

Her answer, like Mom's, wasn't satisfying. I wanted to know exactly who this other mother was and why she couldn't keep me. Aunt Lorraine kept my cousin Maggie after she was born. Why couldn't mine have done the same? The notion of this other mother existing dangled in front of me like a piece of meat in front of a dog, tantalizing—but I wasn't allowed to bite.

"Maybe someday you'll find out, but for now, take your tea and let's go sit inside and watch TV."

The living room was my favorite place in her house. It looked like a page out of *House Beautiful* magazine. There were two sturdy oval tables made of cherrywood on each side of the velvet couch and a longer one in front of the bay window that overlooked the cul-de-sac. Grandma loved lace, and each table contained lace doilies, which matched the ivory curtains adorning the bay window. Framed photographs of her children and grandchildren were displayed on all the tables, along with crystal lamps and glass vases, which held painted ceramic flowers. On the coffee table, also made of cherry, sat three ruby glass bowls filled with glass candy. The real candy was kept in a secret hiding place in the kitchen, which prevented everybody else from eating it all. Grandma loved peppermint patties and had several bags as well as chocolate kisses and boxes of oatmeal cookies. Only I knew where this special place was—in the back of the dishwasher that Grandma never used because she preferred to wash by hand.

On the living room walls hung a series of pictures that Grandpa painted himself—by number. My favorite was of a young girl in a white flowing dress perched comfortably on a pine-needled forest ground. Her eyes, sad-looking, glanced up as if she were in deep thought. I believed this girl and I were somehow connected as I too had quite large cerulean blue eyes that were almond shaped. What made mine so distinct was the way they ever so slightly turned down at the outer edges, giving me my trademark sorrowful appearance. Everyone in my family loved to make comments about my eyes. Dad would routinely point to my eyes, and say, "So sad-looking."

Grandma never agreed with Dad. She thought my eyes looked mysterious and would joke to the rest of the family that "Those eyes were here before."

Mom only liked to point out that they looked tired all the time.

"And look at the bags under them," she'd add. "It looks as if Annie hasn't slept in a week."

It was true; I slept very little. Ever since I could walk, I'd awaken before the sun rose and go the entire day without taking any naps.

After hearing Mom comment about my eyes, I'd run to the bathroom, climb on top of the sink, and peer at my eyes in the mirror, but I never saw any *bags* under them.

Glancing at each item carefully as I set my cup of tea on the coffee table, I slipped one of my hands inside a ruby bowl, feeling the smooth surface of a piece of glass candy shaped like a gumdrop.

"Be careful, Annie, those are glass. You might chip one."

"Okay," I said, yanking my hand from the bowl.

Grandma and I settled onto the couch to watch *Hollywood Squares.* Usually, I loved to guess which way the tic-tac-toe line would form in the squares for the winner. But that day, I wanted to talk.

"Grandma, tell me about the day you took me home after I was adopted."

"What's there to tell, except you cried the entire time?" she snapped, annoyed that she'd missed the answer to the first question. "But of course you only stopped when I held you in my arms." Suddenly, a smile broke out and her dentures gleamed. Then she turned her attention back to the program.

I stopped pestering her and watched the show. Before the contestants had a chance to answer the next question, Grandpa came home from work. We heard the door slam behind him, and presently his tall, lanky body staggered into the living room.

"Hiya, Annie," he said heartily, his speech slurred. He wore a tweed sports coat, a crisp white button-down polo shirt underneath, and a matching tweed cap, which immediately slid off and fell onto the floor exposing his pale, bald head. "Where ya goin'?"

I slithered off the couch and sat on the floor behind the coffee table. His hat was lopsided, and I wanted to laugh, but I sensed Grandma's tension.

For the most part, my grandfather was a happy drunk. When my family gathered on the backyard patio for a party, he'd have a few too many. These were occasions for singing old songs, mostly off-key, and if she was in a playful mood, Grandma would join in. Today, however, she was in no such mood. Glaring at Grandpa, she stiffened like a lioness, and foolishly, he chose to enter her den.

"You've been drinking again!" Grandma hollered, waving her hand in disgust.

"Soo what?" His face fixed in a crooked smile, he made his way to the couch, bumping off every table and chair like a pinball in a machine. He held his thumb and forefinger together. "I only had a little one."

This enraged her.

"And in front of Annie! She shouldn't have to see you in this disgusting state." In a flash, she leaped off the couch, confronting him.

"I only wanna give her a big huug and kisss." Reaching out, he was thrown off balance and almost toppled over.

Grandma stood there with her hands on her hips and glared at him. When he'd regained his composure, he made an attempt to step around her, but she stood her ground.

For many years, I never considered that Grandpa had a drinking problem. Seeing him on a daily basis, I thought his behavior was normal. How was a child to know the difference?

When I was much older, it occurred to me something was amiss. Mom, who instructed me not to mention such things, especially not to anyone outside the family, validated my suspicions. She thought if you didn't mention problems, somehow they vanished.

"Annie, go on downstairs," Grandma ordered.

I jumped to my feet and scurried around the other side of the couch, heading straight for the kitchen door. I glanced back and caught a glimpse of Grandma smiling my way. We shared a special bond. Why she never formed this type of relationship with her own daughters eluded me. My mother and aunts commented years later that she was the typical Irish mother—strong, opinionated, and not too forthcoming with her affections. But I saw another side. There was something special about the time we spent together during these early years, the way we casually talked and joked with each other and the way she'd tell me stories late at night. She never established such a close relationship with any other grandchild—and she had twenty-one.

*   *   *

Back in my own part of the house, I found my mother half asleep on the couch in the living room. The television blared, the volume turned all the way up; still, she slept like a baby. I lowered the volume, turning the dial to channel thirteen. The echoes of Grandma's voice yelling at Grandpa started drifting down. Mom rolled over and slowly sat up.

She was a short, plump woman with straight black hair, which was currently rolled up in green plastic curlers. Her blue eyes were big and exhausted looking. She rubbed them and yawned.

"Annie, get my glasses from the kitchen table."

I trotted off and fetched the glasses. When I returned, I found her reaching for a book on the coffee table. She shivered even though it wasn't cold. She was aware of the sound of arguing emanating from above, uninviting yet unavoidable.

"Oh, and get my robe from the bedroom."

I quickly retrieved the robe, hurrying back to her side.

"What's adopted?" I asked, handing her the robe.

"Annie, you know your father and I explained this. Sometimes parents can't keep their babies so they decide to let other parents take care of them."

"I'm adopted?" I asked, pretending not to know the answer.

"Yes, so are Thomas and Brian. When we decided to adopt you, we went to a special place and took you home."

"But where are the parents that couldn't keep us?"

She shook her head. "I have no idea."

"Why can't we see them?"

"I don't know," she said, frowning. "You're just not allowed." She opened up her book and flipped to where she left off.

"Why couldn't they keep us?" I persisted.

She glanced at me briefly then returned to the book. A moment later, she looked at me again.

"They weren't able to take care of you so your father and I decided to raise the three of you instead."

I received the same answer no matter how many times I asked, and from the annoyed look on her face, it appeared as if she wished she'd never told me about my adoption status in the first place. I sat down in front of the television and waited for *Sesame Street* to start.

"Annie …" Suddenly, she stopped reading and looked over at me. "Did you fold your clothes and finish cleaning your room?"

"Yes."

"Let's go take a look." She put down her book, went into my bedroom, and opened the top dresser drawer. Her eyes widened with surprise. "They're folded," she said surprised, picking up a pink sweater. Then she saw the unfolded clothes beneath. "What do you think your father is going to do when he gets home and sees this? … Do you want him to yell?"

I shuddered at the very thought of provoking him.

Mom glanced around my room; the rest was neat. Everything put away in its proper place.

"I'm sorry." I started to cry. "It's too hard folding shirts."

The sound of brakes screeching outside distracted her.

"That must be the school bus." She looked over her shoulder towards the window. "Thomas and Brian are home." As she turned to leave my room, she shook her head in disgust. "Make sure you fold those clothes."

I took out all the clothes in my drawers and put them in a big heap on the floor. Slowly, I folded each piece and put it back into my dresser, wondering about my other mother, the one who wasn't able to keep me. Maybe she was tired and needed to sleep, the way Mom did. Maybe that was the reason she couldn't keep me.

Four

Jekyll & Hyde

Dad was quite unusual in that he had what is commonly known as a split personality. He was extremely outgoing, starting conversations with anyone, and easily made friends wherever he went. Only once people got to know him better, they either loved him or hated him.

It was fun watching Dad turn on his charm. He could walk up to complete strangers and within five minutes have them believing he was the nicest family man around.

One summer afternoon at the Jersey Shore, we were standing in line at a concession stand. Dad started a conversation with a woman standing behind us, poking fun at how long it took the employees to make the hot dogs and fries.

The deeply tanned woman dressed only in a leopard-print bikini and flip-flops was immediately taken by my father.

"Your husband is so funny," she commented to Mom. This made Dad's eyes light up, and he continued to crack jokes about the slow service. "You're so lucky to live with such a pleasant person!" the lady went on. Her own kids, all boys, were about my age and stood next to her eyeing me up and down.

Mom rolled her eyes. She hated it when Dad started conversations with strangers. To her, it was embarrassing.

"Erin," Dad said, turning to Mom. "Janice here has three kids just like us." Mom curtly smiled and adjusted her sunglasses. Dad turned back to Janice and placed his arm around her shoulders. "We're staying at the Seven

Days Inn over on Atlantic Ave. Stop by with your kids to swim, and we'll have a few drinks, and maybe by then our hot dogs will be ready." Dad stepped up to the concession counter. "Hey, it'll be Christmas soon."

There were two teenagers behind the counter. They handed Dad our hot dogs, fries, and sodas, and we made our way back towards our spot on the beach.

"You had to invite them to our hotel!" Mom snapped, trudging through the hot sand.

Dad stopped short in his tracks.

"Oh, Erin, come on. What's the big deal?"

"The big deal is that they're not staying at our hotel, and you can't ask total strangers to come for a swim."

Dad, noticing the fed-up look on her face, quickly turned his attention to me.

"Look, Annie," he said, pointing to the ocean. "I just saw a huge whale over that big wave."

"Where?" I asked, my eyes scanning the water, but all I saw were people swimming.

"Anything to change the subject," Mom muttered under her breath. "Annie, come on. There aren't any whales in the water." Mom grabbed my hand, and we quickly walked ahead of Dad, settling onto our beach blanket.

Mom hated the fact that there was no middle ground with Dad—and no boundaries. Rules applied to everyone but him. But what most irritated her was that he loved to hug, kiss, and touch everyone; he was quite Mom's opposite.

But Dad had another side, where his darker temperament resided, spawned from the many years under his father's roof. Dad was careful when it came to showing this side to his personality, saving the worst for those he knew fairly well. Unfortunately, those who live together also eat, love, and fight together, and nobody truly knows anyone until they sleep under the same roof.

It was no different with Dad. My brothers and I experienced all facets of his moods, dark and bright.

*   *   *

One day after school, late in March, I found Thomas and Brian sitting cross-legged on the floor of the basement playing a board game together.

"Can I play?" I asked, sitting beside them. It was too cold to play outside, and Grandma was out shopping at Bloomingdales.

"No, we're almost finished," Brian said as he moved his red game piece to the last finish spot, joining the other three. "Ha! I won!" he shouted triumphantly, his green eyes dancing with delight.

"Let's play something else," Thomas said sulking. He hated losing, which he often did when he played games with Brian. His eyes scanned the basement perimeter then settled by the laundry area. "Let's play in the laundry barrel."

Brian, brightening at the idea, ran over to the large plastic barrel, which caught the laundry from the chute above. He turned it on its side and began pulling out the dirty clothes. Thomas and I quickly joined him, and soon, all the clothes were in a heap on the floor next to the bottom of the stairs. Thomas crawled inside the barrel and began rolling around on the floor.

"My turn, my turn!" I squealed with excitement. Thomas stopped and pulled me in alongside him, and Brian started pushing. "Whee!" I screamed in delight. But suddenly, Thomas rolled on top of my chest, knocking the wind right out of me.

"Get off!" I yelled, immediately panicking. But Thomas only laughed, and Brian continued rolling the barrel. I felt like passing out. Enclosed spaces terrified me, and now with the weight of Thomas on my chest, it was just too much. "Stop ... stop!" I screamed at the top of my lungs.

It wasn't long before the door at the top of the basement stairs opened, and we heard stomping as Dad made his way down. Thomas and I scampered out of the barrel as Dad came over to us. I hurriedly brushed away the tears from my eyes and promptly as a seasoned soldier took my place alongside my brothers in a row in front of our father. He stood at least six feet tall. When I stood in front of him, it was like looking up at a mountain. He was mostly bald except for a thick ring of jet-black hair that matched his dark, bushy eyebrows. He took one look at the basement.

"There's shit all over the place!"

We all stared up at him, terrified.

"We were just going to clean it up," Thomas said in a small voice.

Dad's gaze fixed on the pile of dirty clothes. Compulsive about keeping the house spotless at all times, he forever hollered at us to pick up.

"Goddamn it, what the hell is this?"

The three of us followed his gaze to the heap of clothes.

"We were just playing ..." Thomas tried to explain, but his voice broke off, and he began to shake.

"And what was Annie screaming about?" His head snapped towards Thomas. "Were you hurting her?" he asked through clenched teeth.

"No, she's okay," he answered, starting to cry.

I stood straight up.

"I'm okay, see?" I said. "Thomas was on top of me by mistake. He didn't mean it."

"You were lying on top of her?" he growled.

Tears were streaming down Thomas's cheeks.

"We were only playing. We were rolling in the barrel, and he rolled on top of me, but I'm okay," I assured him, my heart pounding swiftly.

But Dad wasn't hearing my words; instead, a wild look flashed in his eyes as he moved and stood directly over Thomas.

"What the hell were you thinking? She's a lot smaller than you—you could have smothered her!"

"I'm sorry," Thomas said weakly.

"How would you like it if I lay on top of you?" Dad grabbed my brother by the arm and shoved him onto the floor. "Lie down! I'll lie on top of you. See how you like it!"

Brian and I started to cry.

"Lay still goddamn it!" he bellowed.

Thomas rolled over onto his stomach and protectively put his hands over his head.

"I'll show you what it feels like to hurt your little sister," Dad mumbled under his breath. He got down on his knees and placed his body on top of Thomas's.

My cheeks were hot with tears. Thomas didn't move or make a sound. He didn't have the strength to push him off. Dad, at least a hundred pounds heavier and a lot stronger, didn't budge. I wanted to yell for him to stop, but the words wouldn't come out.

After what seemed like an eternity, Dad slid off of Thomas.

"How'd you like it?"

Thomas didn't answer; he only whimpered as he lay crumpled on the floor.

We didn't hear her coming down the stairs, but suddenly Mom was in the basement. Her hands were on her hips, a disgusted look plastered on her face.

"Bob, can't you leave the kids alone?!"

Thomas rolled over and sat up. Dad leaned toward us.

"Clean up this mess right now!" he said through clenched teeth.

Mom took a step forward.

"Bob!"

"What's the matter with you, Erin? The basement's a mess."

"Come on," she said flinging her arm up in the air. "You know what I'm talking about." She turned and went back up the stairs. Dad followed behind.

Quick as rabbits, we began snatching up dirty clothes and shoving them back into the barrel. Tears filled our eyes. We kept wiping them away. The three of us grew to be submissive, yet impenetrable.

When we finished cleaning up, we went upstairs and found Mom and Dad at the dinner table waiting for us, as if nothing had happened.

"Annie, don't forget after dinner, we have dance class," Mom reminded me, taking a sip from her can of diet cola. The three of us slid into our seats to a plateful of chicken and brown rice.

Dad opened his mouth to say something, but before he had a chance to speak, I blurted out, "Yay! Dance class!" I bounced up and down in my seat, forgetting the scene that had just played out in the basement.

"Annie, don't butt in when we're talking!" Dad bellowed.

Mom flashed Dad a sharp glance. We finished our meal in silence.

*   *   *

That evening, the class had its desired effect because when we returned home, I felt sleepy. Mom took me there every Wednesday. Along with four other girls, I learned how to plié like a ballerina and how to shuffle in my black patent leather tap shoes. Even though I wasn't as graceful on my toes as the other girls in my class, I still loved the music and the sound the tap shoes made against the wooden floor. Mom made sure she brought me to class every week.

"Just following doctor's orders," she'd tell Grandma. "There's got to be a way to calm Annie down."

Once home, we found Dad already in his recliner, coffee in hand, watching television. Mom grabbed some coffee for herself, drank it half down, then plopped onto the couch and quickly fell asleep.

"Come sit with me, Annie," Dad said, pulling me onto his lap. "Oh, be careful of the coffee." He placed the mug on the table.

His face radiated delight. It was like living with Dr. Jekyll and Mr. Hyde. We never knew what to expect. His moods could change from scorn to delight in a matter of seconds.

"Sing me the song about the baby goat?" I asked, yawning.

"You mean 'Paddy's Baby Goat'?" Dad said smiling. "And only one song, Annie, you look exhausted."

"No, I'm not," I protested, wiggling to a more comfortable position.

Dad chuckled and in his rusty voice sang about the baby goat to the tune of "Ba Ba Black Sheep." When he finished, I snuggled closer.

"When can we adopt a sister for me?" I asked. Every night, without fail, I prayed for a sister. So far, my prayers hadn't been answered, but I wasn't without hope. I knew that if I prayed long and hard enough, eventually God would send me one.

"We already have a little girl—you." He leaned over and kissed me on top of the head.

"But I want a sister," I whined. "She can play dolls with me, and she can sleep in my room just like Thomas and Brian get to sleep together."

"Annie," Mom said, rolling over on the couch. "It's time for you to be going to bed."

I scurried off Dad's lap singing, "Good night, Mom. Good night, Dad." On the way to my bedroom, I overheard them arguing.

"You know, Bob, you never spend any time with the boys, only with Annie."

"What do you mean by that?" Dad's voice grew louder. "You shouldn't talk; you'd rather lie on the couch."

"Keep your voice down," Mom said in a hushed tone.

His voice only grew louder.

"I'll say whatever the hell I want!" A loud thud slammed against the wall; the vibrations followed me down the hallway. Looking back over my shoulder, I saw a fresh hole the size of a fist in the living room wall. Dad stood, shaking his hand in agony while white dust circled the air around him.

"Damn! Look what you made me do!" Dad roared.

Shutting my bedroom door behind me, I crawled into bed and snuggled into my blanket. Once settled, I prayed the Our Father, Hail Mary, and then asked God to please have the lady from the adoption agency call my parents and tell them a sister was ready to be picked up at the nursery. "And, God, please make sure she has long hair," I added.

Five

A New Place to Live

When I started the first grade, I attended Saint Matthew's school located adjacent to the church where we went to mass every Sunday morning. Mom, who had attended only parochial schools along with her siblings, wouldn't have it any other way. Grandma said it was pure blasphemy to even consider attending a school that wasn't run by the nuns—even though she never found anything nice to say about them.

As for me, I harbored high expectations for the nuns who taught at the school and couldn't wait to hear them play their guitars just like the famous Maria.

I was in for a rude awakening.

The nuns weren't anything like Maria. In fact, they were more like the von Trapp father! They never smiled. Instead, their mouths were frozen in an eerie expression coupled with down-turned brows. Their hands, always glued to their hips, completed the look as they towered over each and every student. All the energy I possessed now needed to be kept bottled up inside. The nuns insisted we all sit quietly; otherwise, our knuckles were slapped with a ruler. My first-grade teacher, Sister Margaret, not only rapped knuckles with rulers, she also loved to grab our ears and vigorously shake our heads. The threat of such actions heightened by the daunting glares of the nuns was enough to scare any child out of her mind. So, from the first grade on, determined to avoid the wrath of the nuns, I learned to keep my pent-up energy at bay.

Each day, my brothers and I took the bus to and from school. We arrived home at three o'clock sharp, whereupon we changed out of our school uniforms, sat at the kitchen table, and hurriedly did our homework. Mom would be fast asleep on the couch, having worked the graveyard shift the previous night at Englewood Hospital. Thomas and Brian always finished their homework before me and joined the neighborhood kids playing in the cul-de-sac. It took me a lot longer. For some reason, I couldn't do the math and my writing was atrocious. After struggling for almost an hour each afternoon, I'd eventually scribble anything on my homework ditto sheets and dash upstairs to my secret haven with Grandma. We still spent time together like before; the only difference was it started a few hours later.

On the afternoons when Grandma shopped for clothes or visited her friends, I'd play outside with Thomas and Brian and the neighborhood children. All the kids who lived on the cul-de-sac could be found romping about in each other's yards or in the street playing kickball.

We loved our two-family home in Rochelle Park, but Grandma and Grandpa had different ideas of the ideal place to live. They detested the cold winters and wanted to live in a more temperate environment. Grandma and Mom started taking mini trips down to Florida, and by the time I finished the first grade, after my grandfather semi-retired from the union, my grandparents had made the decision to move to Florida.

They encouraged my parents to move too. Why my parents ever agreed to go along with them is beyond comprehension. They were nowhere near retirement age and knew nothing about the economy in Florida. This time around, my parents and grandparents bought single family homes in a town called Lantana located less than five miles from the beach. Our new neighborhood looked like a picture postcard. Palm trees lined the streets, and all the houses were made of cinder and cement and painted white or beige with Spanish-style adobe roofs. There was a canal across the road. Banana and mango trees grew wildly along the banks, and an occasional alligator could be seen roaming.

My grandparents' house, a stone's throw from ours, proved too far away, and the distance was enough to put an end to the daily visits that once brought Grandma and me so close together. We still saw each other most days, but it was usually me fetching items back and forth between the two houses. Mom needed to borrow some orange juice. Dad needed Grandpa's saw, or Grandma wanted me to give Mom some books she had finished reading. The errands were endless while they busied themselves with painting walls, arranging and rearranging furniture, and cleaning up the yards in their new homes.

At first, I missed Grandma terribly. I wanted my days to be exactly the same way they were in Rochelle Park, our afternoon teas, singing, and watching TV together. The first month, I waited patiently in Grandma's kitchen each day, but she never had time to sit and relax, let alone pull out her old records so we could sing together. There were too many things to do in a new house.

"Anne, I'm sorry but maybe tomorrow," she'd say, surveying her new kitchen cabinets. "Go and tell Grandpa that he needs to run out and buy some liners for the cabinet shelves."

Eventually, I gave up trying.

Mom was busy too. After a week, she easily found a job working the night shift at a local hospital. There were always openings for nurses. However, Dad wasn't that lucky. After six months of looking, he eventually found a position in sales at a glue company in Pompano Beach. With Dad working, we were able to settle into our routines and soon found ourselves loving the Sunshine State. Even Dad was more content, enjoying the slower pace of Southern living, and we rarely saw him fly off the handle when things weren't put away around the house.

Mom was happy too. She absolutely loved the warm weather and our close proximity to the beach. Every day, she'd pack a book or two and some snacks and round up my brothers and me to spend the entire day soaking up the sun and swimming in the waves. Her new passion ended once school started. We attended Saint Bartholomew's Elementary in Lantana, so she compromised, and the beach days were reserved for the weekends.

Every day after school, we'd pretty much do whatever we pleased. Study time immediately after school wasn't enforced, so I rarely did my homework. Instead, I went immediately outside in the yard or over to a friend's house to play. Brian could be found in the street playing stickball or riding his bike, and Thomas usually played baseball at the town fields with his friends.

Before too long, our adoption status became known in the neighborhood. For Brian, telling others about it became an amusement. He loved to see the shocked expressions on people's faces. It couldn't be true; we looked too much alike. We all had fair skin, light brown hair, and bluish-green eyes. We resembled each other more closely than some biological siblings we knew. This made the game more fun. His friends finally believed him, but they were still bewildered. Girls reacted to the news differently than boys.

"At least my parents wanted me," a girl named Natalie sneered at me one day.

She lived in the house next door, and we sat in her front yard arguing over what game to play. She wanted to continue playing with her new Barbie townhouse on her front lawn, and I wanted to go swimming and play Marco Polo. The air was hot and sticky, and her new in-ground pool looked so refreshing.

"What do you mean by that?" I asked, surprised.

Natalie was normally shy. Up until then, I'd never heard her raise her voice above a whisper. Slightly overweight, she was the type of kid who was routinely tripped in the halls, robbed of her lunch money, and ridiculed to the point of tears.

"Your real mother didn't want you. That's why she gave you away."

The words spit out of her mouth like sharp razors and tore through my skin. *Of course my real mother had wanted me*, I thought. *She just couldn't keep me because ... because ...* No answer came to mind.

"That's not true!" I blurted out, pulling myself up and standing over her. Although short and a good two years younger, I pulled myself up to my fullest height trying to intimidate her in hopes she would stop saying those terrible things.

"My parents didn't do that to me." She laughed, not threatened in the least.

I glared down at her, fists clenched at my sides. My face filled with blood, and a piercing rage ignited within—a familiar reaction, except I was usually on the receiving end. For a split second, it completely consumed me, and finally a frightened look came over Natalie's face.

"I'm going home," I announced, fighting back tears. Even though my stomach ached from her words, it wasn't worth getting this upset over. "You can play with your stupid old Barbie dolls by yourself!" With that, I stuffed my own Barbie dolls into my pink carrying case and marched straight home.

Mom, asleep on the couch, awoke when I came through the door. I told her what Natalie had said. She shook her head in disgust.

"Tell her your father and I chose you over many other babies. Her parents had no choice but to keep her."

"Okay, I will," I said, sinking into the couch. It felt good having Mom come to my defense. She reminded me of Grandma. "Tell me again how you adopted me."

I could barely remember the last time we had discussed this and prepared for the usual dark glares and abrupt answers, but this time, she hesitated as though deep in thought.

"Well," she said rather genially. "The agency called and said they had a newborn baby for us and that we should come by the nursery to see you." She grabbed the package of cigarettes in front of her, turned it upside down, and tapped the bottom until a cigarette popped out. "If we liked you, we could take you home." She stopped talking as her eyes searched the room. "Hand me the matches over there on the table."

I retrieved the matches.

"What if you didn't like me?" I asked, sucking in my breath.

"Then we didn't have to take you. Our caseworker told us that we could change our minds and return the baby if it didn't work out."

What's not to work out? I thought, horrified.

She lit her cigarette and released a whirl of smoke.

"But we never would've done that." She shook her head with a small smile. "We thought it was a silly thing to say because once each of you were in our arms, we knew we could never return you."

Wow, I thought, *they really did get to choose.*

"Anyway, there's no reason to be telling people that you're adopted."

"Why not? Brian tells everyone."

"It's nobody's business but ours. He shouldn't be telling anybody. Only we need to know." She reached down for the newspapers on the floor by her feet. By the rigid look on her face, I thought she had returned to her usual aloof demeanor. "Oh, and don't forget to straighten up your room. I don't want to hear your father holler about it later."

All that week and into the next, Natalie's words echoed in my head. Up until then, I had thought there was a perfectly good reason why I'd been given up for adoption. Now, for the first time, I considered the possibility that maybe my real mother didn't want me.

In bed, snuggled up in a ball deep under the covers, I drifted in and out of sleep, fantasizing about my first parents. No longer were they poor and living in a cardboard box on a city street. Now, in my mind's eye, they were a young couple—teenagers, strolling along a white sandy beach, holding hands. Her pregnant belly—the swell where I once resided—protruded through her long white sundress. The smell of the salty air and a warm breeze wafted through my senses as the waves crackled and crashed near the teenagers' feet. They continued walking, her head resting gently on his shoulder. All was serene, when suddenly a large wave crashed, and their hands dropped to their sides. She turned toward the young man; her face was now stern, not soft anymore. He tried to take her hand again, but she pulled away and walked back down the beach, alone, her stomach flat. The young man went the other way, and there in the sand, screaming at the top of its lungs, was an abandoned baby.

Natalie's voice rang out. "Your real mother didn't want you ... didn't want you." Her words rose over the sound of the baby's cries and over the roar of the waves.

Six

Stormy Skies

We soon learned Florida was notorious for its daily late afternoon thunderstorms. After enjoying a cloudless, sunny day at the beach, we'd return home only to be met with thick gray clouds quickly rolling in. Within an hour, the once-blue sky turned black, and the pounding rain, thunder, and lightning took over for an hour or two.

Our time spent in Florida mimicked the weather pattern. Our first year, like the bright, warm days spent at the beach, was illuminated. We felt blessed to be living in such a splendid and beautiful state. The second year mimicked the clouds rolling in. The vacation atmosphere was over. We stopped going to the beach so much. Grandma and Grandpa complained about missing the foliage, and Dad started noticing the condition of his house: It was a mess, and we never put anything away. Now we unwittingly entered the third year, the dark, late hours of the afternoon, when lightning cracked and thunder roared.

Dad lost his job.

After nearly a year and a half at the glue company, Dad, along with twenty other workers, wasn't needed anymore. It took him months to find work again, this time for a company specializing in fire alarms, and then that company went bankrupt. As time went by, Dad grew angrier and more discontent. His only recourse was to seek odd jobs. He started coming home later in the evening, between ten and eleven, and after raiding the refrigerator for leftovers, he'd plop himself in front of the television in his favorite black leather recliner and fall asleep. Mom slept on the couch till ten thirty, then got dressed in her white nurse's uniform, and flew out the front door minutes before eleven.

One night after Mom left, Dad awoke and blew into a rage.

"Thomas! Brian!" he bellowed, pushing open their bedroom door. "Wake up!"

"Anne!" My bedroom door flew open next, crashing against the wall. "I want to see the three of you immediately!" He aimed his finger at me then whirled around and headed for the kitchen.

It was past midnight. This was not a unique event—lately, we were often roused like this from sleep. I met up with Thomas and Brian in the hallway, and we trudged to the kitchen and lined up next to each other like toy soldiers. Dad stood over the kitchen sink scrubbing a Mr. Coffee kettle with a scouring brush. Our stances tightened when we saw Dad's gaze shift down to his feet.

"Thomas!" Dad's voice roared.

Thomas looked up, his bottom lip slightly quivering. Brian and I slithered closer together. We stole a quick glance at one another, knowing what the other was thinking. *Please hurry up, Dad, and get this over with.* We only wanted to get back to sleep.

"Come ... here!" Dad said firmly. Each word came out slowly, hissing through gritted teeth. Thomas took a few steps forward, and Dad pointed to the floor below the kitchen sink. "What the hell happened here!?"

Some cookies lay crushed in the corner under the cabinets, a reason for him to start on us. Actually, it was my fault. I'd swept the kitchen floor after dinner and missed the spot.

Thomas looked at the mess on the kitchen floor. His eyes were wide and terrified.

"Well?" Dad demanded.

Thomas lifted and lowered his shoulders while the color vanished from his face. He stepped back into line with Brian and me.

Dad bent over, flung open the white cabinet door beneath the sink, and took out a spray bottle of Fantastic, his favorite cleaner, and some paper towels. He squirted the gray linoleum floor with the spray, got on his knees, and wiped up the mess. But he didn't stop there; his eyes wildly looked around, and he sprayed the entire floor along the perimeters of the cabinets.

"Look at this shit. There's dirt everywhere!" he bellowed, a bead of sweat running down his cheek. "We don't live like pigs!" he ranted, fervidly wiping the floor until it sparkled. "Anne!"

"Yes," I said, stepping forward.

"Get me more paper towels!"

I grabbed more and leaned over, handing them to him, then quickly returned to my spot next to Brian.

"I don't want to see the floor like this again!" He squirted more spray. The mist from the cleaner permeated the air and burned my nostrils.

When he finished, his attention shifted to the counter. He wiped his hand across the entire length and then slammed it down hard, shaking the ceramic canisters.

"There's something sticky here!" He rubbed his fingers together, trying to determine the source of the stickiness.

"I cleaned the counters," I spoke up, hoping to take some heat off of Thomas. He received the lion's share of Dad's wrath, maybe because he was the oldest, the strongest, and the one who wasn't supposed to cry. It was rare to see Thomas cry anymore; he was twelve, and when he did cry, it was a disheartening sight.

Brian and I, however, cried every time Dad yelled. We couldn't help ourselves. It scared us to see a big man rant and rave, hurling toys that hadn't been put away. None of us dared argue with him or offer an explanation. It would only infuriate him more.

Clean, clean, clean, like our mom when she was a child, the three of us each had daily and weekly chores. Mine were to set the table for dinner and clear it then sweep the kitchen floor. Thomas washed the dishes, and Brian dried and put them away. Every morning, our beds had to be made. Never were clothes or toys allowed to be on the floor anywhere in the house, including our bedrooms. On Saturdays, I vacuumed the entire house. Brian cleaned the bathrooms, and Thomas dusted all the furniture. Before we reached adolescence, my brothers and I cleaned so professionally, we could have been considered for a housekeeping job at the most luxurious hotel. We didn't mind doing the chores—we knew it helped Mom—but in Dad's eyes, our efforts were never good enough. He always found something wrong with at least one of our chores every day. He'd scream and carry on for at least an hour then order us back to bed with tears in our eyes.

My brothers and I were bound by a common sense of fear. To survive and not provoke his anger, we covered for one another, making excuses and sometimes even blaming Mom.

"Those are Mom's socks in the corner," I offered one time. Dad had slept straight through the night and routed us out of bed early in the morning rather than late at night. This time, the sun hadn't even come up, yet here he was, shaking a pair of white sweat socks in front of our eyes.

"Put them in the dirty wash!" he ordered, throwing them my way. He turned toward the kitchen sink. "You're not supposed to leave dirty dishes in the sink all through the freakin' night!" he hollered, turning on the water and squirting Palmolive liquid soap onto his yellow sponge. Tears were rolling down my cheeks.

"Those are Mom's dishes in the sink; she ate a snack before going to work."

"Go on, get dressed for school."

Maybe it was wrong to blame Mom, but sometimes it worked and took the heat off of us.

I couldn't understand why Dad thought our house was such a mess. If he had ever gone into the house of one of our friends, he'd have had a heart attack right on the spot.

The three of us scurried away to our rooms. There I threw myself down on my bed and sobbed uncontrollably. "I hate him! I hate him!" I said over and over into my pillow, thinking he only wanted to adopt us in order to have cleaning servants. Though deep down I knew Dad loved us in his peculiar way, the thought frequently passed through my mind.

Nothing we did was ever right; everything was our fault. And we never knew when his overly bright mood would suddenly turn exceedingly dark. As for Mom, she was fully aware of his behavior and warned us never to talk about what went on in the house to others. Grandma knew too. Many times, I overheard her telling Mom about seeing our kitchen lights come on in our house late at night. Unfortunately, Mom rarely had the opportunity to intervene because she worked at the hospital when Dad busied himself waking us up at one in the morning. There wasn't much she could do at night, but when at home, she made sure my brothers and I ate three meals a day, went to school, and had clean clothes.

Every morning, Mom arrived home just in time to drive us to school. She wore all white, from her nurse's dress and stockings to her soft-soled shoes that she needed to paint each week with white shoe polish. She greeted us with tired, red eyes and an ample supply of yawns.

"Why were you crying?" she asked Brian one morning.

We just piled into the station wagon with our backpacks and lunchboxes. Dad had already left for work a half hour earlier.

Brian only shrugged. Thomas spoke up.

"Dad was yelling about the family room. I left my orange peels there from last night."

"Dad was even madder about the bathroom," I piped up. "He said Brian didn't clean the bottom of the toilet, but I saw him do it. Dad's always yelling."

Mom pressed her lips together.

"That's how it is in some families," she said firmly.

"I know, but ..."

Mom cut me off. "He's your father," she said, turning to look at me in the back seat. "Doesn't he buy you things and take you to the movies?" Her tired eyes widened, waiting for me to confirm her statement.

"Yes." I sighed.

Mom returned her eyes to the road.

Silently, we rode to school. Along the way, I considered what Mom had said and agreed with her; he did do a lot for us, and he could be fun and loving. I thought about the weekends when Mom worked. He'd take us to a movie and then out to lunch, and sometimes afterwards, we went to the mall. Then his angry face flashed in my mind, the tired and cranky face he wore by the end of the day. No, the good times didn't make up for the other half of the time spent in his company, when she wasn't around.

I folded my arms in front of myself and glared at the back of her head, furious with Dad for being so mean and doubly furious with Mom for not doing anything about it. I wanted to scream at her but knew it wouldn't help matters; she'd only side with Dad, and I'd be in loads of trouble and probably have to do extra chores around the house.

Thomas, sitting next to me, nudged me on the arm.

"What?" I said annoyed.

"Let it go," he said in a low voice, obviously sensing my brewing anger. Only I ever dared to argue with our parents, especially our father—the one person neither one of my brothers ever dared to venture to even talk to.

For our mother's sake, my brothers and I dutifully maintained the illusion of a close family. We never mentioned our father's behavior to anyone, and we didn't even discuss it among ourselves. We followed Mom's unspoken rule: Don't talk about it and it won't exist. Eventually, we even stopped telling her and kept whatever fear or disappointment we had deep inside, buried away where no one could see it.

But people knew, especially those who lived close by. Dad didn't need a bullhorn to make his presence known. Some of the neighborhood kids poked fun at me, saying my father was a lunatic and beat the three of us.

"He does not," I argued. "Look," I said holding out my arms and pointing to my legs. "Do you see any bruises on me?"

The bruises and scratches weren't visible. They resided inside the heart. These injuries hurt the most and take the longest to heal.

Brian, who played with the same group of kids, was lured into many a fistfight defending our family. He didn't like the teasing, especially when it was directed at me. However, we all silently agreed with the taunts we heard from the neighborhood kids.

Seven

Lost At Sea

As I grew in stature and in years, so did my curiosity about my original family. Who were they, and, more important, why did they decide to give me away? I was told my mother couldn't take care of me, but what about my father? He was never mentioned, never referred to. It was always, "Your mother couldn't keep you."

There had to be a father, too.

I started imagining my birth parents as street people living in a cardboard box. I saw a woman dressed in tattered clothes, sitting on the sidewalk next to a tall office building, with serious blue eyes like mine. Being poor, of course she had no other recourse than to give me to the special nursery.

Although this fantasy made me grateful to be living in a house and not on the streets, I still yearned to know more about this woman and her husband. At times, I felt like a sailor on a lost ship, abandoned by the captain and the rest of the crew. I was left to navigate on my own without a map or a compass, and I didn't know which direction to sail. I was lost to these other people, the ones who took me to the nursery, and they were lost to me.

Another possibility soon came to mind: Maybe my original parents were somehow related to the Murphys. The idea sprang after reading the comic book about the orphan with the curly red hair named Annie. In the end, Annie turned out to be "Daddy" Warbucks' niece! Everybody said I looked so much like Grandma, with our big blue eyes and fair complexions. Maybe one of her relatives gave me to the adoption agency. The possibility seemed likely, but Grandma put an end to that fantasy.

"No, Anne," she said, smiling. "It would be nice if it were true, but there's nobody in my family who gave away a baby. Believe me, I'd know," she added with a twinkle in her eye.

Of course Grandma would have known, I thought, slumping in my chair. It irked me that Little Orphan Annie was related to her adopted family. I wished Grandma and I were related too. I put the Annie comic books aside and instead, turned to the pile of books Mom had bought me recently on one of her weekly visits to the bookstore, the *Little House on the Prairie* series and *Anne of Green Gables*. I was instantly hooked. First, I consumed each and every page of the Laura Ingalls Wilder series as quickly as a fire rages through a forest, and then I read *Anne of Green Gables*.

Another orphan! *What is it with the name Anne and originally being an orphan!* However, I enjoyed the life of Anne Shirley and thought living in Florida's hot tropical climate was almost as exotic as living on the Avonlea farm on Prince Edward Island. This book only spurred my imagination further, and I started to write little stories about my beginnings. I was a princess given away to hide my true identity from a wicked relative, a poor girl whose parents were killed and who had a fortune waiting in the bank—the possibilities were endless. My stories always ended with me being reunited with some biological relative.

Brian too wondered about his original family, but he made it clear to me that he'd never try to find his original family.

"Why should I try to find them?" he asked, flipping a clump of his chestnut hair out of his eyes. "They haven't bothered with me."

"But don't you want to know anything?" I persisted.

"Yeah, but ..." He hesitated, taking a sigh. "Don't you see how Mom looks every time you mention your first mother?" He appeared uncomfortable, sitting cross-legged on the floor next to me. A board game, Stratego, was spread out between us. Brian was winning as usual. I only shrugged my shoulders.

"Yeah, I do wonder," he said looking up into my eyes. "I'd like to know who she is and see what she looks like. It would be kinda neat if we resembled each other." He leaned over and rolled the dice, then as smooth as a fox, swept up my army game pieces in Northern Africa. "Anyway, did you ever think about Dad and how he'd react? I think he'd just yell."

I shuddered at the thought. Brian was right. Dad wouldn't take this well. Maybe he'd see it as a betrayal.

"No, I never thought about that," I slowly admitted.

Brian raised an eyebrow, his green eyes studying my face.

"What are you planning to do?" he finally asked.

I shrugged my shoulders, looking away.

"Tell me!" his voice cracked. There was a definite edge to his tone; he was somewhere on the border of hysteria. Brian, who was careful not to do anything to set Dad off, seemed to think I wanted to start trouble.

I stared into his eyes and sighed. No, I couldn't let him worry like that. Lately, Brian seemed to be walking on eggshells, retreating to his room whenever Dad was home. And he rarely talked to any of us, only me when I played board games with him.

"Nothing," I finally answered, glancing down. "What *can* I do? Only Mom and Dad can find out anything, and so far, they've told me nothing."

The reality of my own words sank in. There wasn't anything I could do on my own. At that moment, I wanted to be alone, alone to face the possibility that I'd never know them. I'd never see the two people who were responsible for giving me life. It felt as if a hot metal rod pierced through my stomach. I wanted to throw up.

Brian didn't seem to realize how upset I'd become. He appeared more relaxed once I extinguished the possibility of trying to locate my birth mother. He rolled the dice again, this time taking over my last army in Brazil.

Game over. I'd lost. Again. In so many ways, I felt like I'd lost so much more than a silly board game—I'd lost me. Where was the original me? I needed to know right now, but deep inside, I knew it would be years until I'd be in any position to find out.

"Just wait, Anne," Brian said gently, as if he'd just read my thoughts. Surprisingly, he'd forgotten to rub it in that he'd beaten me again. Instead, an ample amount of sincerity laced his words. "Don't go asking too many questions and get yourself into trouble. If it means so much to you, I'll help you search for your mother when we're older, like in our twenties. We can figure it out then, okay?"

I nodded. Never before had I recognized the compassion Brian possessed. He really did care.

∗   ∗   ∗

If Thomas wondered about his own birth relatives, Brian and I were none the wiser. He never brought up the subject, and we didn't mention the topic around him.

Thomas had his own life, attending his first year at Atlantic High, playing for the school's junior varsity football team and hanging out every night with his group of friends.

Mom never knew where Thomas went or what he did each night he went out. So far, nothing out of the ordinary had happened that would spark her curiosity. He always came home on time, so she never inquired. But his activities were crystal clear when one night, he came staggering in through the front door, just as Mom opened it up to leave for work.

Lucky for Thomas, Dad wasn't home. He had an interview for a new job two hours north and was spending the night at a hotel in the area.

"Jesus Christ! You've been drinking!" Mom yelled.

The commotion jolted me awake, and I crept out of my room, slowly making my way down the hallway. I saw Mom bent over Thomas, who was slumped against the dining room wall.

"Get up!" Mom screamed, yanking his arm. "Get up this instant!" She glanced my way. "Anne, get back to bed," she ordered, bending down and placing her arms under his armpits. In one swift motion, she pulled Thomas to his feet.

I didn't want to go back to bed. Instead, I wanted to make sure Thomas wasn't going to die! He looked so pale and could barely stand on his own. Recently, I'd seen on the news a story about how some college students drank themselves to death. Alcohol intoxication, the newscaster had called it, and now it looked as if Thomas had done the exact same thing.

"Anne ... get going!" Mom ordered. I think she saw the scared expression on my face because she added more gently, "Don't worry, he'll be all right."

Despite Mom's avowal, tears sprang to my eyes. I quickly returned to my bedroom, slid under the covers, and listened to their voices echoing in the distance.

"Where'd you get the liquor from?" Mom demanded. Her voice had returned to its usual stern tone.

"No, no ... it wasn't liquor ... wasn't," Thomas stammered.

I shivered, frightened at the sound of his voice. He was way too young to be so drunk, only fourteen! I buried myself far beneath my covers, but their voices remained audible.

"Where'd you get it from?" Mom demanded again. "Tell me!"

"It's nothing ... Joey got it from his ... uhhh ... uncle. It was on ... only wine."

I heard flesh being smacked, probably his face.

"Did you drink the entire bottle?" Mom screamed, followed by another smack.

Peeking from under the covers, I could just barely see them both shuffle by through the crack in my door; Mom's arm was around his shoulder, and she pulled him along as he still vehemently denied that he'd done anything wrong.

Mom didn't go to work. Instead, she sat in the living room and cried for the longest time. I didn't sleep either. Instead, staring up at the ceiling over my bed, I listened to Mom. It crushed my spirit—Mom never cried. Her typical unemotional response to everything was what I expected— what I needed. The image of Thomas drunk and slumped against the wall wouldn't go away. I kept seeing his pale face, hearing his slurred speech, and remembering Mom's reaction. Typically, when Mom got upset, she'd either speak up calmly, stating her concerns, or she'd keep her mouth shut, ignoring the situation as if all was okay in the world.

Tonight was different. Her obvious devastation made me ache to go and wrap my arms around her, for her comfort and for mine. But I never left my room, knowing fully she'd only send me back to bed.

It seemed like hours before her sobs gradually ebbed and the house fell silent.

Eight

Grandma's Decision

Like Grandma, Grandpa too missed living up North and decided to return to work at his job with the union. He started flying to New York every other week. Grandma went with him for the first trip but then stayed home and instead complained about his drinking to Mom. Grandma started having problems walking; she had been recently diagnosed with a genetic neurological condition called ataxia, which left her balance and coordination very poor. Coupled with her obesity, the ataxia left Grandma unwilling to walk more than she had to. If we were out somewhere, she'd quickly find a seat and plant herself firmly until we were ready to leave.

During this time, Aunt Lorraine and Maggie started visiting on a regular basis. Every couple of months, they flew down and spent a few weeks with us. I looked forward to every visit and like always, marveled at Maggie's beautiful long, wavy hair. She now possessed big, round freckles on her arms and legs, in similar fashion as the rest of the Murphy woman, whose fair skin burned terribly in the sun. My skin, like Brian's, tanned to a beautiful bronze that lasted year-round.

Having Maggie around was like having a sister, and it felt like heaven when she was here. Maggie loved to sing and dance too; she was even more of a ham than I ever had been back in Rochelle Park. Even though I'd given up dance classes, in spite of Mom's protests, I still enjoyed dancing, and we'd dress up and perform in similar fashion to the *Donny & Marie* show. I'd dress up as Donny and Maggie as Marie, and we'd sing "I'm a Little Bit Country" much to the amusement of Grandma.

We went everywhere and did everything together while Mom, Aunt Lorraine, and Grandma sat around the cast-iron table on the patio in their polyester housedresses, smoking their cigarettes and complaining about everything from their foul-mouthed drinking husbands to the gloomy state of Florida and its economy.

"My paycheck hardly pays for a week's worth of food," Mom said dolefully. A cigarette half hung out of her mouth, and her bare feet lazily perched on the empty seat next to her.

Aunt Lorraine, who'd been sitting with a glass of iced tea in one hand, a lit cigarette in the other, nodded her head as if she understood and felt Mom's pain.

But not Grandma, she got a smug look on her face and said in a dry voice, "I'll tell you, Erin—it's a sad day when a family has to depend on a wife's wages to feed the family."

Something in the tone of her voice made Maggie and me, crouched down behind a chalkboard in the corner of the porch playing school, suddenly look up and listen.

Grandma went on. "Bob should be thanking God he married a woman willing to work like you," she said wryly, never missing an opportunity to take a jab at my father. From the look on Mom's face, Grandma's words had sliced a layer of skin off her back. Many times, I'd overheard Grandma telling Mom it was deplorable that Bob couldn't support his family on his own.

"Well," Mom said, looking over at Aunt Lorraine for support that didn't come. "It's not because of Bob. The jobs here are scarce … And it's not his fault companies don't pay as much as in New York," she added defensively, the color rising in her cheeks.

Grandma took a long puff on her cigarette.

"Really, Erin," Grandma finally said, flicking a long ash onto the ground. "The reason Bob can't hold down a job for more than a year is because of his own irritable demeanor."

Mom looked away. She didn't want to hear any more even though her tight expression showed that she knew Grandma was right.

"Isn't it peculiar that every company he works for seems to go out of business?" Grandma asked, shaking her head. "Erin, that husband of yours has got some real problems."

Mom winced and looked away.

Grandma nodded to herself seemingly proud of her sage wisdom. She lit up another cigarette, looking our way, where Maggie and I sat behind the chalkboard. Feeling Grandma's eye turn in our direction, we both instinctively jumped making the chalkboard fall over.

Aunt Lorraine quickly got up from her seat and came over. Her angry eyes scanned from me to Maggie and then to me again, where they remained.

Mom let out a long sigh, cast a dark look our way, and shook her head from side to side.

"Look, the kids are listening."

Of course we'd heard. Though Maggie and I hardly understood their conversation, we easily understood the tone, and even Maggie, only six years old, must have realized that my father was being criticized.

Aunt Lorraine kept her eyes on me, not faltering for even a second as I sat next to Maggie shaking.

"We didn't mean to listen," I apologized, pulling the chalkboard back up in front of us. "We were just playing school together." I pointed to the scribbling on the board.

"Get out from behind there!" Grandma said furiously, waving her arm in our direction. "Go and find something else to do," she barked.

Maggie and I scurried out from our hiding place behind the chalkboard and made a beeline for the front of the house while Aunt Lorraine could be heard muttering aloud.

"Imagine if that was us, Erin? Momma would've whipped our backsides till they were raw! … Now, Momma, do you mind if I borrow your car and take Maggie to the beach? We'll be leaving for Jersey soon, and we should at least take advantage of the weather here. Erin, do you wanna go?"

"No, I've got work tonight."

Mom hadn't yet slept today after working through the night. Her eyes were tired looking, and it was from a lot more than a lack of sleep. The battering she just took about Dad wasn't helping.

"Well, how about tomorrow?" Aunt Lorraine asked.

Mom nodded, and they agreed to spend the next day at the beach along with me and Maggie.

Lately, Mom didn't spend as much time lounging at the beach. Florida, with its sunny beaches and beautiful sunrises which at first seemed full of splendor, had lost its luster. The palm trees, once so new and different, now swayed monotonously in the warm breezes. They never changed to brilliant colors of fuchsia and gold like the trees in the Northeast. The summers were brutally hot and unbearably long, and we began to crave, especially Grandma, the grandeur of the changing seasons. I especially missed the snow. Meanwhile, my parents were practically bankrupt.

*　　　　*　　　　*

A few days later, after Aunt Lorraine and Maggie had flown home, Grandma made a decision that affected all of us. She finally decided she had had enough of Florida and started to prepare for her and Grandpa's return to New Jersey. Mom didn't take it seriously until she saw the *For Sale* sign on their front lawn. The real estate broker sold the home within a week.

It all happened so fast, and Mom and Dad were initially in shock. They couldn't believe my grandparents had made such an important decision without them.

Grandma and Grandpa packed up everything and were out of the house by the next month. The day they left, my family stood at the curb, waving good-bye with mournful faces. My grandparents drove away in their silver Cadillac, heading north without us.

Within a week, my parents decided they too wanted out of the state, and our house went up for sale. The decision wasn't based on my grandparents' moving, even though Mom always itched to stay close to her parents. The real need rested solely with Dad. He still couldn't find a full-time job, and while we waited for our house to sell, he went back to New Jersey and found work buying parts for a radio manufacturing company.

The rest of us stayed in Florida. We were not as fortunate as my grandparents when it came to finding a buyer. Once a month, we held open houses, but seven months passed and still we hadn't received a single bid.

With Dad gone, we all got a taste of living in peace—and we savored it fully. However, Dad flew home to be with us every other weekend. On Saturday mornings, before his expected arrival, we made sure the house sparkled. Sinks were scrubbed, floors mopped, and garbage cans emptied in addition to our usual chores. He especially loved to check the base of the toilets, so Thomas made sure they were sparkling.

One weekend, Dad surprised us. He took an earlier flight and arrived home in the wee hours of the morning. When we awoke, before we had a chance to clean, Dad called for us and we begrudgingly entered the kitchen, thinking we were surely in for it. We had to be; there were unwashed dishes in the sink and toys scattered on the living room floor.

But as we lined up, we were met with an astonishing sight: Dad singing Elvis's "Hound Dog" along with the radio while washing the dirty dishes in the sink. He was in a good mood!

"Kids, I have great news." He shut off the water, drying his hands on the dishtowel draped neatly over his shoulder. "I don't need to live away from you anymore. Can you guess why?"

"Why?" I asked excitedly.

"You found a job here," Thomas answered. His eyes popped open wide as he waited for confirmation.

"Nope, even better." He looked at Brian, but Brian looked down at his feet. "We sold the house!"

"Really?" Thomas and I said in unison.

Dad grinned ear to ear.

"Yes, it's sold. We have to be out of here in thirty days."

"Thirty days?" Thomas repeated.

"Yep," Dad answered. "Ain't that great?"

I jumped and squealed with joy. I wanted nothing more than to move back to New Jersey where my grandparents, aunts, uncles, and cousins all resided.

Brian didn't respond to the news, he merely nodded his head. Thomas, on the other hand, looked furious. I saw his green eyes glower when the news sank in. He didn't want to leave Florida. He had loads of friends and often commented about how he loved his high school and planned on becoming a lifeguard at the beach. He wanted to stay. But by early October, we were in our station wagon, which was filled to the brim with suitcases, pillows, and toys, on our way back to the Garden State.

Nine

Bye, Bye, Sunshine

That fall, we moved into a colonial house in northern New Jersey, the place we considered our real home. Grandma and Grandpa were living in a townhouse in an adult community near the Jersey shore, about an hour's drive south of us. Grandma hated it there and constantly complained about all the grumpy old people in her development. She wanted to move up our way.

Mom enrolled me and Brian in the public middle school. I was in the sixth grade and Brian in the eighth. Thomas joined the sophomore class at Ramapo High. There wasn't enough time to investigate the Catholic schools in the area.

Our new neighborhood was full of children, and it wasn't long before my brothers and I made new friends. I met Sharon Compton right away. She lived only a few blocks away, and we became close since we both loved to play softball and ride horses.

Sharon, also adopted, had twin older brothers, James and Henry, natural children of her parents. The brothers were part of a group of boys who played football and baseball and especially liked to go out and party on the weekends. Not surprisingly, Thomas quickly befriended Sharon's older brothers and started drinking with his new buddies. Mom never faced him drunk again. Thomas made sure he arrived home well after midnight, after she left for work. And Dad never saw it either. By that time, he was fast asleep in his bed.

There was only me to face.

For some reason, I stayed up, waiting and worrying myself sick each and every time Thomas went out on the weekends. Maybe it was the scene I witnessed in Florida, Thomas plastered from drinking so much wine. He looked like death won him over that night, and the image of him never left my head. I still feared for his safety, thinking he'd drink himself to death or die driving home with one of his friends.

The parental roles were now reversed. Dad slept while I waited up for my big brother, hoping to God that he'd make it home safe and especially that he'd be quiet. All I needed was for Dad to wake up and see him in that condition. He'd flip out for sure if he caught Thomas staggering through the door reeking of alcohol.

Brian, unlike Thomas, never drank. He preferred a small group of friends. They played cards at each other's houses on weekend nights.

Too young to be going out like Thomas, I usually watched television or slept over at Sharon's house. There we'd meet up with her brothers also returning home drunk. Mr. and Mrs. Compton usually met them at the door, quickly escorting them up to their bedrooms. They never yelled at them—at least not in front of me.

I was so lucky to have Sharon for a friend. Aside from having common interests and brothers who were also friends, Sharon was the only person I knew other than my own brothers who was adopted.

Like me, Sharon seemed to blend right in along with her family. Nobody ever guessed her adoption status; they all looked too much alike. Her brothers had dirty blond hair and large round freckles all over their faces. Sharon's skin was fair like James' and Henry's but perfectly clear and milky white; her freckles were only on her arms and legs. She had a mane of thick mousy brown hair, similar to her Mom's, that she liked to put up in a big floppy ponytail.

Also like me, Sharon yearned for a sister. Whenever we were together and met someone new, we pretended we were sisters—twins, since our birthdays were so close. We had so much in common, and I was blissfully in heaven in my new town back in New Jersey.

*   *   *

Over the course of the next two years, I practically became a part of Sharon's family, sleeping over at her house most weekends and spending nearly every afternoon at their house. Her mother, a tall, slender woman, fair-skinned and even tempered, coached the softball team we played on, and most days after work, she liked to sit and play cards with us. She taught us how to play Uno, and it quickly became Sharon's favorite and mine.

Almost every day, we rode bikes together. One of our favorite spots, a large fenced in farmhouse a few blocks from our neighborhood, had several horses grazing in the front yard. We'd feed them chunks of apples and raw carrots and spend hours there most afternoons.

One late winter day after school, Sharon and I were perched together on my bicycle. We'd just finished feeding the horses and were on our way back to Sharon's house. The air had again turned cold, and the biting wind blew on my face and into my lungs.

She sat solidly on the seat, while I stood up, pedaling fiercely. We followed the street to the top of the hill and stopped at her house. No cars were parked in her driveway, and I assumed her mother would arrive home shortly. I steered the bicycle into her driveway, coasting right up to the front door. There, we were met with an overstuffed mailbox.

"Nobody's home yet," Sharon said, hopping off the bicycle and grabbing the mail. "Why don't you come in for awhile?"

"Okay, but only for about fifteen minutes. My mom will be mad if I'm not there when she wakes up for dinner."

Sharon began sorting through the mail. Halfway through the pile, she froze. She stared in silence at an envelope, and her hands began to shake.

"What's the matter?" I asked, peering over her shoulder. The letter was addressed to her mother.

"It's from San Francisco," she said in a low voice.

"San Francisco, so what?"

"It's where I'm from," she said slowly.

"Oh ..." I said, suddenly realizing what this letter meant. "It must be about your real mother," I cried. My heart started beating frantically inside my chest.

Sharon stood there in a trance, the letter clutched in her hand. She didn't say anything.

Finally, I couldn't take the suspense any longer.

"Are you going to open it?" I eagerly asked. "Or wait for your mom?" I said as an afterthought.

We looked at each other. Sharon turned the envelope over in her hands. She seemed to be fighting the impulse to immediately tear it open. She looked again at the envelope, then back at me, hesitated, then made up her mind.

"I'm opening it—I can't wait—I have to see what it says."

Feeling as though I had better give her a hand, I followed her into the kitchen. Sharon grabbed a knife, and although her fingers were trembling, she carefully slid it under the flap of the envelope and opened it neatly.

I assumed she wanted to try sealing the envelope after perusing the contents.

"Come on, let's go to my room," she said, leaving the kitchen with the letter still inside.

I followed her upstairs, and we sat on her bed. She unfolded the pages and carefully placed them on her lap. Dead silence prevailed as I leaned in close, and silently, we read the letter together.

It told the complete story of her birth and reasons for adoption. So much information! I couldn't believe it, and then I became completely flabbergasted when I read the next part about how her real mother tried to win her back in court when Sharon was only a year old.

"My God!" I said, breaking the silence. "She tried to get you back."

It never occurred to me that birth parents could change their minds and try to get back their child. I read further on and saw that Sharon's birth mother was unsuccessful during the court battle over Sharon. They fought over her!

The letter went on and explained all the details behind her real mother's decision to place Sharon for adoption. She'd originally given Sharon a name, Caitlin, and put her in foster care temporarily as she tried to get on her own two feet financially and emotionally. After Sharon's birth, she moved in with an aunt and found a job. But her efforts proved fruitless; she couldn't earn enough money to support them both, and the father was no longer in the picture. The letter made little reference to him.

I looked at Sharon. She was speechless. For the longest time, she sat there beside me, a faraway look on her face. I imagined she tried to picture the scenario we'd just read inside her head. After a couple of minutes, she looked up at me.

"She tried to get me back," she said solemnly, looking me straight in the eyes. "I wonder why my parents never told me about that," she murmured, her eyes returning to the letter.

I remained silent, pondering the same thing and wondering whether my parents received information about me in the mail as well. It would be a good idea to start checking the mail every day, just in case.

The last paragraph of the letter gave the name of the agency acting as the liaison. It stated that the biological mother requested the latest information about Sharon.

We were both astounded at having suddenly gained insight into such uncharted territory. We shared the same curiosity about our origins and often discussed the possible scenarios as to why we were placed for adoption. Sharon considered the possibility that her parents had died in a car crash shortly after her birth while I always said mine were very young and unmarried. The what-ifs, especially about if we had never been adopted, came up quite often. What would our lives have been like? Sharon pictured herself in an orphanage somewhere in the state of California. She couldn't fathom the possibility that her parents somehow survived and couldn't raise her. I saw myself dressed in rags and living in old, run-down apartments, my parents always one step ahead of the rent collector. They had to have been poor, I reasoned; otherwise, they'd have found a way to keep me.

Now we had some answers. A large chunk of reality suddenly smashed into our dream world built up around our adoptions. Even though the information regarded Sharon's situation, and not mine, there was still something about her mother trying to keep her that gave me some kind of peace. Her real mother wasn't some cold, unloving individual. She did want Sharon. She'd even gone to court along with her own lawyer and tried to win her back.

Finally, the contents of the letter sank in. Sharon's birth mother was a real person with feelings and a desire to keep her child. This letter proved that sometimes it's simply impossible for mothers to keep their babies. Maybe my own had a good reason too, I thought wishfully. Now my guesses that she'd been young and unmarried and poor, like Sharon's mom, seemed more real.

"What are you going to do now?" I asked, trying to catch my breath from this sudden onslaught of information.

"I don't know." Her eyes remained on the letter.

"Are you going to show it to your mom?"

Sharon gripped the letter in her hands, as if the information would suddenly disappear if she let it go. Her eyes breezed over the last two paragraphs about the court battle. I leaned over and read it again too, feeling the butterflies in my stomach.

Suddenly, Sharon sprang up.

"My parents can't know I opened this," she said, stuffing the letter back into its envelope. "I wonder if they were planning on letting me see it." She tried to seal the flap closed, but the glue had dried. "I bet they received others as well and never told me about them," she said rather disgustedly.

I thought exactly the same thing. But then I had a hard time seeing Mr. and Mrs. Compton deliberately keeping things from Sharon, especially something like this. Mrs. Compton often overheard us talking about our adoption status and typically joined in on the conversations saying how lucky we were to have each other and how someday we both would probably search and find our birth parents. But the letter made reference to the fact that this was a follow-up to an earlier contact, made a few years before. It was obvious Sharon's mother already knew a lot about the circumstances surrounding her adoption and kept this information secret.

A determined look marked Sharon's face as she dashed over to her dresser and scooped up a box of school supplies.

"Come on, Anne," she said impatiently. "We have to make it look like we never opened this envelope." She took some glue, and I helped her seal the envelope ever so carefully. When we finished, it looked as if it had been tampered with.

"It'll have to do," Sharon said halfheartedly, not seeming to care anymore if her parents saw it opened or not. We put it back in the middle of the pile of mail anyway, in hopes it would blend in with the other letters.

Five thirty approached, and I needed to get going. As I rode my bicycle home, the wind pounded my back, almost guiding me along. Resentment started to surface toward my best friend. Not only did she know about her real mother, but her real mother wanted her.

Again, I tried to convince myself that my situation was the same. My original mother, also young and poor with no family or support, shared similar circumstances. But then a disturbing thought flashed through my mind: Maybe I was an unwanted baby. As far as I knew, my real parents never tried to contact me or win me back in court. Certainly, I'd have known if that were the case, even though Sharon didn't.

Why hadn't my real parents tried to make contact? Clearly, they had no interest in me, I thought, recalling the haunting vision of the baby abandoned on the beach.

A profound sense of resentment settled within, but it mixed with gratitude because at least I was alive. If abortion were legal in 1966, most likely, I wouldn't be here.

*   *   *

Sharon's mother noticed the envelope had been opened. The very next day after school, she paid a visit to my house, along with Sharon. Mrs. Compton said she wanted to talk with my mother and me concerning what Sharon and I had done. My mother welcomed them in.

Sharon and I retreated to the kitchen while our mothers went into the family room. My stomach fluttered for a good fifteen minutes as we heard them whispering back and forth. I was convinced we were both in big trouble. Eventually, they called us in to join them. We reluctantly made our way to the couch and sat close together.

The smell of freshly brewed coffee permeated the air. Before anyone spoke, Mom rose from her recliner and went to the kitchen. She filled two ceramic mugs with fresh coffee and returned, handing one to Mrs. Compton. Our two mothers sat in the twin recliners with long, expressionless faces, like rigid bookends. Sharon and I slouched into the couch, bracing ourselves for the lecture.

Mrs. Compton sipped her coffee and then began to speak. There was something about the softness in her voice that calmed me. She told a tale about two prying young girls, and she seemed more amused than I'd have thought. Before she could finish, a news flash appeared on the TV.

President Reagan had been shot.

What perfect timing! Although shocked to see our president wounded, the news deflected the attention away from me and my fellow conspirator. The scenes of the shooting were replayed time and again. I saw the shots being fired, the president bending over and clutching his chest, and the Secret Service herding him into a limousine. In a matter of minutes, we watched it at least half a dozen times while reporters informed us that the status of his condition was unknown.

After about ten minutes, Mrs. Compton returned to her story, interjecting an occasional, "Oh my God, I can't believe he's been shot!"

Much to my surprise, instead of reprimanding us, Mrs. Compton began apologizing to Sharon.

"I should've told you about the contact with your birth mother all along," she said. "I can imagine how desperate you must have felt yesterday, when you saw that letter from San Francisco." She paused, then added, "I only wish you had come to me with the letter and we could have read it together." She hesitated again, as though unsure what to say next. "I wanted to spare you this woman's problems. I guess the fault is mine ... for thinking you'd have no interest." She appeared slightly embarrassed as she glanced down at the coffee mug in her hands. "I was the one who was wrong and not you two girls," she added, looking at both of us. "Of course you want to know about your beginnings. I had no right to try to keep any information from you." She focused her attention directly on Sharon. "Maybe we can plan a trip to San Francisco to visit her. But I think you should wait another year or two, when you're a little older."

Sharon said nothing. She nodded her head in agreement and looked over at me, bending her head toward the other room, trying to tell me that she wanted us to go to my bedroom. But I didn't budge yet. I was dying to bring up my own adoption. Never before had this opportunity presented itself. I glanced over at my mother. Her eyes met mine.

"Can we try to find my real mother too?" I asked, thinking maybe she might have changed her attitude about this subject, especially after hearing what Mrs. Compton had to say.

My hopes were quickly extinguished. Mom threw me a sharp glance. Her expression said she wanted to be anywhere but here talking about this subject.

"Can't we at least try?" I persisted.

"That's for you to do when you're older. I want no part of it," she said, starting to get up from the recliner.

Sharon's mother glanced at her with an inquisitive look.

Mom suddenly looked embarrassed.

"What I mean is," she said, changing her tone and sitting back down on the edge of her seat, "there are organizations to help people find each other."

"I've heard you can sign up with special databases where they match names and dates to see if someone is looking," Mrs. Compton offered.

"I've had no contact with her or the agency," Mom replied. "I don't wish to get involved. If Anne wants to find her, then she can contact those places when she's older."

Mrs. Compton, sensing her uneasiness, sighed heavily and shifted the conversation to the fate of the president.

Apparently, Mom would never support me when the time came to begin my search. Brian had been right. Hopefully, he'd help me when the time came; otherwise, I'd have to do it myself. There was one thing for sure; one day, one way or another, I planned to discover the identity of my real parents.

Ten

All That Tumbles Eventually Falls

The subject of my birth mother wasn't mentioned. Mom didn't bring it up and neither did I. Instead, over the next couple of years, I tried my best to forget about my other mother.

Starting high school helped. I kept busy with schoolwork—which finally got easier for me—part-time jobs, and more friends to do things with. I met Janine Richardson during my freshman year, and she became my new best friend.

Janine, an only child, had a small, round face and a cute freckled nose that she complained turned up too much. Her family, like mine, boasted an Irish upbringing although her mother, also an only child, didn't have the family dynamics like the Murphys. There was no quarrelling, family feuding, or large family gatherings where everybody drank and sang old songs into the night. Janine got a kick out of my family on the holidays. She loved watching them all together, and I just got a kick out of Janine. For one thing, she made me laugh. She forever told jokes, was quick with her wit, and loved to make fun of everybody—including herself.

"Just look at me," she'd told me the first day we met. We were in line in the school cafeteria, waiting to buy a slice of pizza. We'd started talking during second period math where she told me to sit with her for lunch.

"I look like Pippi Longstocking," she whined, reaching up and holding her hair into two ponytails on each side of her head. "All I need is some red hair dye and I'd be set."

I imagined her brown hair red and burst out laughing.

"And my mother forced me to wear my hair this way all through grammar school," she went on, a disgusted look on her face as she let her hair fall back down over her shoulders.

"At least it's long," I pointed out, thinking about my own hair. It still grew slowly and remained paper thin. My current style, a slightly longer version of the Dorothy Hamill cut, delighted Mom. She loved me in short hair, urging me each time I visited the beauty salon to keep the length way above my shoulders.

I saw Sharon across the lunchroom and waved. She waved back. Every now and then, I hung out with Sharon, but she had a new group of friends. Janine and I spent most of our time at the mall, the movies, or just hanging out at each other's houses watching TV.

Thomas left for college, attending the University of Delaware, where he lived in a dorm room on campus. Unfortunately, he only lasted two years, never finishing his education. Partying seemed to be a bit more important than his studies. He moved back home just when Brian left for Stockton State College in southern New Jersey. Brian too lived on campus, and much to the surprise of everyone, he followed in his brother's footsteps. Brian discovered beer and partying and only lasted six months before failing out.

My parents were distraught. They tried to encourage their sons to either try college again locally or enroll in a trade school. They both tried, taking courses in computer technology, but dropped out after three months. Instead, Brian found a job as a bank teller, and Thomas in sales at a car stereo installation store.

"At least they're working," Mom liked to point out.

As for me, I trudged through the first three years of high school swearing I'd never drink away my education. Even though I wasn't an honor student, bringing home mainly C's with the occasional B or D, I knew college had to be an option for me. I loved kids and had a part-time job at a nursery school as a teacher's aide. I wanted to get a degree in early childhood education. So I studied even harder, and by the time I finished my junior year, I brought home mostly A's and B's.

But Mom and Dad never noticed. They were too wrapped up worrying about their sons and what their futures held.

*   *   *

I was determined to be different from my brothers. Eagerly, I looked forward to my senior year of high school. And on the first day back, I should at least have been a little excited. After all, I'd waited and waited for this year, the time when teachers typically went easy on us. They'd let up on the work and allow the seniors some privileges, like the option of leaving the school grounds during lunch and study hall.

Instead, I felt absolutely miserable. My first day back felt more like a nightmare. Mom called to say she'd be late getting home in the morning and couldn't give me a ride, and Janine, who drove, had already left. It was too late to call someone else, and I couldn't drive. My seventeenth birthday, which would make me the legal age to drive was only two months away. This proved just as annoying. I was the only senior who didn't yet have a driver's license.

I begrudgingly walked the two miles to school by myself, fuming the entire way. *This is no way to start off my senior year,* I thought as I kicked a stone.

Luckily, my schedule wasn't too bad, just the usual courses: American history, biology, British literature, Home Economics II, Algebra II, and an elective course in creative writing. There was also gym and lunch period. Janine and I, along with some other girls, took advantage of our newfound freedoms and drove to Burger King for lunch.

After school, the sight of Janine waiting for me—in her parents' new silver Volvo—made me smile. *The day was getting better,* I smirked to myself.

Janine's hands were tightly wrapped around the leather steering wheel. Her round, brown eyes danced with delight when she saw the expression on my face.

"Wow! Are they letting you keep this?" I asked, excited, slipping into the front passenger seat. Her father had bought the Volvo a month before Janine got her license, wanting something extra so there would be a car for everybody. Her mother already drove a year-old shiny black Nissan Maxima, and her father, a stockbroker in New York, had his Mercedes. The Richardsons, unlike most other families in town, had money—and lots of it.

"They're only letting me drive it today, 'cause it's the first day," Janine explained when she saw the astonished look on my face. "Mom's going to keep this and sell the Maxima."

"You mean they intend to make you drive that old brown boat?" I asked, mouth hanging half open in disbelief. According to my standards, Mr. and Mrs. Richardson were cool parents. Janine didn't think so. She thought they were too fuddy-duddy, especially when they insisted on keeping an old, dark brown four-door Ford sedan. It was so wide and long that Janine nicknamed it "the boat."

"Yeah … they're keeping the boat," she sneered. "They think it'll be safer in case I get into an accident," she said, shaking her head.

"At least you'll have something to drive," I said, wondering what my prospects were come November. So far, Mom and Dad hadn't mentioned a car for me, and I knew I'd be asking to borrow theirs like most other kids in my class.

Janine dropped me home in time to be met with a sinkful of dirty dishes and a pile of dog poop in the middle of the living room. *Just wonderful,* I thought as I spied Shannon, our Irish setter, sulking in the corner. She cowered when I approached, but I went over and patted her head and shooed her outside to the backyard.

"It's not your fault," I mumbled as I began washing the dishes.

Mom's snoring echoed through the house. She slept soundly on the couch in the family room. When I finished the dishes, I saw clutter everywhere— the house was a mess! It had to be cleaned before Dad got home. Thomas and Brian lived here too, but I'd never wait for them to help straighten up. They used the house like a hotel, for eating and sleeping only; otherwise, we rarely saw them.

I washed the dishes, straightened up the counters, and threw in a load of laundry before settling onto the leather recliner in the living room, a hot mug of tea in my hands.

The phone started ringing. I jumped out of my skin. For some reason, it wasn't the typical sound heard each time the phone rang. This sound made the hairs stand on end over my entire body as if someone had just scratched their nails on a chalkboard.

Mom woke up and rolled over.

"Aren't you getting that?"

I just stood there, frozen. There was something wrong. I couldn't pick up the receiver.

Mom shook her head and answered the phone. Her face turned serious.

"Uh-huh … okay … I see," she mumbled, the color draining from her cheeks.

I rushed to her side with expectant eyes, but she brushed me aside.

"Oh my God!" she said going even paler.

"What's wrong?" I asked, practically pleading.

"Hold on … Anne, please. Give me a minute," Mom said waving me away.

I stared straight ahead, perplexed, waiting.

After a moment, the conversation ended. Mom slowly hung up the receiver, falling back into her seat on the couch. She looked over at me.

"Grandma had a very bad stroke today, this morning," she stated, matter-of-factly.

I sucked in my breath.

"They think she was on her way to answer the phone when it hit, and she fell backwards onto the kitchen floor. Her hip and leg are broken as well."

I could barely breathe. Poor Grandma. Lately, her balance had been horrible when she walked, and she'd taken a few spills, but nothing like this. I didn't know what to say or how to respond so I just stood there.

Mom went on. "Apparently, she was lying on the floor the entire day, soaked in her own vomit and urine. That was the nurse on the telephone. She's at Hackensack Hospital. I have to call your grandfather at his hotel; he'll have to come home right away," she said more to herself.

Grandpa was in Miami for a union convention. I didn't want to see his face or hear his voice when he learned the news. The scene of Grandma lying on her kitchen floor all day wouldn't form in my mind.

Mom quickly began dialing numbers, and I went and slumped onto the recliner with my heart pounding in my chest. I couldn't help but think about how this might change things between us. We only saw each other once or twice a month when she and Grandpa drove up to go out to dinner with us, but I didn't want to give that up. I loved Grandma and wanted her alive and well, like she'd always been.

"Will she be okay?" I quietly asked Mom after she made the call to Aunt Lorraine looking for Grandpa's number at the hotel.

"I don't know," she said slowly. "I'm going over to the hospital now. Stay home in case one of your aunts or uncles calls."

*   *   *

Grandma needed surgery on her hip. The day after, Mom took me over for a quick visit, and I could see, looking at Grandma's sunken eyes, that this would be her hardest fight yet. There were even more problems. Besides suffering from the stroke, the doctors discovered Grandma also had severe osteoporosis throughout most of her body. It was so advanced that the only treatment was prevention of further bone loss and to protect against further trips and falls. Her body, so vulnerable and fragile, wouldn't be able to withstand the slightest bump. It could leave her with more fractures.

After five weeks in the hospital recuperating, Grandma went to rehabilitation at Helen Hayes, located in Upstate New York. She remained there for nearly six months trying to learn to reuse her atrophied muscles. In the end, she would be mostly confined to a wheelchair. She could walk, with the aid of a walker, but only ten to twenty steps at a time. It was enough to get her from room to room in her house. But it was all too much for Grandpa. He needed help. He asked my parents to consider buying another two-family house. Grandpa explained he couldn't take care of her on his own.

Mom wanted to sell our house and look for something right away, but Dad flat out refused. Grandpa then turned to Aunt Lorraine and Uncle Ron, and within a year, they were all living in a newly built mother-daughter house in Chester, New York.

It was now Aunt Lorraine's turn to live with her parents. After a year, she realized it was a bit more than she had bargained for. Driving to the local bar several times a week in order to retrieve my grandfather was also part of the job besides helping out with Grandma. It all began to take a toll on her, and several times, I overheard her telling Mom about all the difficulties she faced. Aunt Lorraine couldn't fathom how we put up with the two of them all those years living together in Rochelle Park and then again in Florida. From the expression on Mom's face, it was obvious she'd trade places with Lorraine in a heartbeat. I knew my cousins were having the times of their lives. At every family gathering, they boasted about all of Grandpa's jokes and his funny sayings when he drank.

Maggie especially loved being so close to her grandparents. She got a kick out of seeing how dapper Grandpa dressed each morning before leaving for the train that took him into New York. He wore the finest tweed and wool suits with matching cap and made sure his shirts were always freshly pressed. Like Grandma before her fall, Grandpa liked to dress smart and wore only the finest clothing.

Maggie, unlike me, continued with her love of singing. She recently formed a band with her friends doing gigs in each other's garages. Even though Maggie had a few more years before graduating high school, Aunt Lorraine wanted her to concentrate more on her studies and less on music. She wanted Maggie to attend college, but Maggie told me she'd never go.

"I'd rather die first!" she exclaimed with enough exaggeration to surpass any drama queen. "What and leave this house? I'm having too much fun. Living with Grandpa is a blast!"

Nobody disagreed on one matter: The residence of my grandparents was the center of the universe for the family.

Eleven

The Child Within

Just as my last year in high school came to an end, a different relationship developed between my father and me. It began the day I saw with sudden clarity that my brothers and I never did anything so bad that we deserved such abuse from him. My cowering finally turned to anger.

The incident sparking this new revelation occurred one Saturday morning before I left for my new part-time job as a cashier at a supermarket. After showering and coming downstairs for something to eat, I found Dad and Brian at a standoff in the center of the kitchen.

"That goddamn bedroom of yours is a pigsty!" Dad said leaning forward into Brian. "How many times do I have to tell you to keep your clothes off the floor?" he bellowed, spit coming out of his mouth.

Brian desperately attempted to avoid eye contact with him and wouldn't say a word. I looked at his thin chestnut hair dangling over his eyes and wondered why my brothers and I were given this fate. Did we have to just stand still, taking it all in stride, over and over? I didn't think so.

Dad raged on, cursing and slamming kitchen cabinet doors, and at one point, Brian turned away, a smug look on his face. Dad must have noticed, because he started pushing Brian.

"Come on," he taunted. "Hit me! Go ahead! I know you want to." Brian steadied himself after each shove, but refused to respond.

"Goddamn it, look at me when I'm talking to you!" Dad screamed at the top of his lungs.

It was early June, and all the windows were open. Like my Mom, I thought about what the neighbors must be thinking. Brian, on the other hand, didn't seem to be thinking of anything. He stood there expressionless as if Dad's words were simply passing through him.

Brian's defiance only infuriated Dad all the more. His face scrunched up, and his fists clenched at his sides. I thought for sure he'd strike Brian, but instead, he turned toward the kitchen wall and drove his fist through it. When he pulled his hand out, pieces of white plaster fell to the floor.

"Son of a bitch!" He wiped his hand off and looked down at the mess beneath him. "Look what you made me do!" he screeched, pointing with his index finger first at Brian and then at the mess on the floor.

Brian wouldn't look. He stood there slightly hunched over, arms hanging loosely at his sides, keeping his eyes on his own feet.

"I said look!" Dad bellowed.

Dad seemed to be truly losing it this time, and my heart went out to Brian. He was such a quiet, sensitive boy and lacked the assertiveness to walk away. He clearly surpassed Dad in strength, recently having bulked up from weightlifting, and in height, but Brian would never strike our father. Gentle in his nature, Brian just didn't have it in him to do that sort of thing.

The horridness of seeing Brian abused over and over again my entire life seemed to have reached a culmination at this point. I couldn't take it anymore, and without thinking, I jumped between them and found myself standing in front of Brian directly face to face with our father. I took a deep, shuddering breath when the full realization hit of what I'd just done, but instead of panicking and recoiling, our typical reactions, I drew myself up to my full height and forced myself to look Dad straight in the eyes.

From the confounded look on Dad's face, I knew his shock matched mine. He stood rigid, studying my face and stance while I frantically tried to consider an alternate plan. What should I do now?

And then, as if an angel came and whispered in my ear and lovingly supported me by the shoulders, words effortlessly flowed through my lips in a resolute tone.

"Leave ... him ... alone."

It was a perilous road to travel, but I cruised along anyway, surprised that I possessed the strength. For the first time in my life, I was fearless in the presence of my father.

Dad looked as if I'd slapped him across the face, and his spiritless reaction only fueled me to venture even further.

"What the hell are you so mad about?" I screamed, the intensity of my voice matching his. Even in my defiance, tears still sprang to my eyes. "He did nothing wrong," I continued in the same steadfast manner. "Do you get your kicks yelling at us for stupid things?" The tears let loose. "You're *crazy*, absolutely nuts! There is nothing wrong with Brian's bedroom. It's the bedroom of a nineteen-year-old, for God's sake." I turned my attention to the plaster on the floor and shook my head as if to say this was unnecessary.

Dad looked at the plaster too, but he didn't say a word. It was as if he had suddenly lost all ability to speak. He seemed quite bowled over as nobody had ever dared to argue with him before in this manner.

I pointed my index finger directly into his face just as he had done to Brian only a minute earlier.

"You make a big deal out of the littlest things!" I said firmly then sucked in my breath, bracing myself for the worst.

Much to my surprise, the worst didn't come. How bizarre to see Dad standing so calmly, I thought. For once, he listened without cutting me off.

Then with a marked determination only found in the kitchen on that day, my finger still pointing at his face, I said in a steadfast manner, "You need to see a psychiatrist."

Dad winced and finally seemed to come back into the moment. "I see," he said in a small voice. He turned and grabbed the dust pan and mini broom on the counter, bent over, and began sweeping up the plaster from the floor.

Brian and I quickly exchanged looks, shrugging our shoulders at the same time. And then seizing the opportunity, Brian bolted from the kitchen without a word, going upstairs to his bedroom.

Dad finished with the floor and stood up with a smile on his face. His mood instantly brightened. He emptied the contents of the dustpan into the garbage can and turned on the kettle for tea as if nothing had happened.

It was a day of awakening. This man, our father, whose very presence could stir such fear within us, was vulnerable, exactly like a child. It seemed he didn't like a taste of his own medicine. My yelling instantaneously transformed him from a cruel man to a man full of diffidence and insecurity. Strangely enough, after that incident, I never felt threatened by his tirades again. In his humbled state, I saw a man full of cowardice and anguish, as much a little kid as the three of us had been throughout our childhoods. Perhaps his insecurities and lack of confidence drove him to lash out at the weakest people around him—his children. He knew we were too young and too weak to ever respond. Although his actions were wrong and had long-lasting detrimental effects, I felt sorry for him. My anger shifted to compassion, and after that day, whenever he tried to give me a hard time, I calmly told him not to take out his frustrations on me.

*   *   *

A few weeks later, Dad flew into another rage when he came home and found the kitchen a mess. Mom and I were sitting in the family room with our dinner plates on our laps. He couldn't understand how we could eat without first cleaning up the pots and pans. Later that evening, he summoned me into his bedroom. "Anne, come up here, I want to talk with you," he said in a stiff voice.

I reluctantly climbed the stairs going over my chores in the house that day. Vacuum, no it was Brian's turn to do that. The counters, no, they were cleaned already. Maybe I waited too long to wash the dinner dishes.

"Yeah, Dad," I said, entering his room.

He rigidly stood next to his bureau.

"Sit down." A somber look marked his face as if he were about to inform me that a family member had died.

I sat down on the bed and tucked my hands under my thighs.

He cleared his throat.

"I want to apologize to you about what happened earlier," he said, sighing deeply and running his hand over his bald head.

"I ... I was out of control. I'm sorry."

Not quite sure how to respond, I only sat there. He'd never apologized before, to me or to anybody. Dad never owned up to being in the wrong; the blame always rested with the other person.

"That's okay," I softly said.

He started pacing across the bedroom carpet in front of the door; clearly something bothered him. When almost five minutes had passed and he still hadn't said anything, I started to rise from the bed.

"No, wait a minute." He went over and shut the door. "You know your mother and I are not getting any younger," he said out of the blue.

I nodded thinking they weren't that old yet. Mom was only in her late forties and Dad in his early fifties.

"I know we fight a lot, but Mom means the world to me. The three of you do too, but she comes first. Promise me you'll take care of the both of us when we're older."

"Dad, why are you bringing this up now?" I asked confused. "You and Mom are nowhere near old age. Mom isn't even fifty yet."

"I know, but you never know what may happen. If I die first, please promise me that you'll never leave her alone or put her in some nursing home."

"I'd never do that," I said, picturing the episode of *Sixty Minutes* that had aired the week before showing deplorable conditions at a nursing home.

"Just promise me, please. I can't rely on Thomas or Brian. They only bother with your mother and me when they need something."

I nodded my head in agreement. Lately, between their jobs and their friends, they were only home to sleep and do their laundry.

"The two of them ... I don't know." He shook his head as if trying to figure them out.

"They're just busy," I said in their defense, still having that immediate reaction to stick up for them whenever needed. It became such an integral part of our childhood, and the habit wouldn't die.

"Just promise me," Dad asked. An expectant look lingered in his eyes.

"Okay, I promise," I said halfheartedly, not really sure what I was agreeing to.

"When we adopted the three of you," he said slowly, "we were so happy to have children."

I smiled, remembering the stories told so often about how they went and picked each of us up at the nursery ward. It was not the typical way most parents came by their children, but then again, this family was anything but typical.

"Dad, what do you think about me one day searching for my biological mother?" I asked. The desire to find my birth mother had receded somewhat, but it was still there, hovering in the background.

Dad tilted his head and considered my question.

"I wouldn't mind ... Actually, I'm a bit curious to know more about all of them, Thomas's and Brian's mothers too."

My eyes widened at his response, and I knew someday I'd find my birth mother.

"But I know your mother would mind," he said leaning in closer. "Please, if you decide to search, keep it a secret. It would hurt her terribly."

I looked up at him. His eyes met mine, and his eyebrows rose. He wanted me to agree with his request.

The thought that I might hurt Mom made me feel uneasy. It was the last thing I wanted to do. But still, I couldn't agree to keep my inevitable search a secret. I needed to know about my origins, about this other family of mine.

I shrugged my shoulders, not agreeing or disagreeing with his request, and stood up.

"I better get to bed. It's getting late," I said, turning towards the door. I heard Dad sigh heavily, but I left his bedroom without turning back. Why did there have to be so much secrecy surrounding my adoption? And if trying to find my birth mother was such a hurtful thing to Mom, then why did she even tell me about her in the first place? Knowing about her existence only strengthened the bond I felt deep in my gut. It was an attachment no one else seemed to understand—or no one wanted to understand.

Twelve

When The Tables Turn

After finishing high school, my attention shifted to college. My parents didn't expect much. They never realized that I'd taken home nearly straight A's during my last year in high school. Still, my SAT scores were low, and because of my poor prospects, I decided to live at home and attend a local college, William Paterson, which was only twenty minutes away.

I enrolled in their early childhood education program, but my interests starting leaning towards literature or biology. I still loved writing, never shying from any essay assignment in school, but couldn't see myself making a career out of it, so I switched my major to the field of public health. There were lots of biology courses to take, and most surprisingly, I aced every test that semester.

There wasn't a steady boyfriend yet. I had dated a few people in high school, but nothing went beyond the first date. My brothers, on the other hand, had no problem in that department. They were having the times of their lives.

Both Thomas and Brian finally moved out, getting apartments with their friends. Neither returned to college, much to the chagrin of Mom and Dad; instead, they continued working at their jobs and went out every night with friends and different girlfriends—at least a new girl every other month.

After working nights for more than twenty years, Mom decided to switch to days at the hospital. Although the night shift paid more, which was the reason she had worked those hours for so long, she wanted to sleep like normal people. Immediately after the change, she became a different person. For one thing, she was awake after arriving home at four o' clock in the afternoon. We started talking more since only the two of us ate at dinnertime.

And Dad busied himself selling coins during most evenings. He would arrive home around eight or nine. By that time, I had already left for my part-time job, and there was only Mom to fight with. Now the tables were turned—Mom complained to *me* about him.

"All he does is go on about the house and curse," she said one evening as we sat down together on the couch, coffee table pulled in as a makeshift table for our plates and cups, our usual dinner routine. Mom and I rarely sat in the kitchen anymore. We liked to watch the evening news and then old reruns of *Who's the Boss?* while we ate.

I had just started biting into my drumstick when Mom droned on about Dad.

"Who the hell asked him to clean up anyway? He makes me feel like I don't do a damned thing around here." She pushed her plate away.

It was hard grasping this new take on how things were in my household. It was especially odd that Mom was now Dad's punching bag. I quickly chewed and swallowed the mouthful of chicken and took a swig of iced tea.

"I'd be grateful for the cleaning," I pointed out, hoping maybe if she saw a positive side to Dad's obsessive nature she would just shrug it off as I learned to do. "Most husbands don't do a thing around the house," I added, picking up my drumstick again.

"I know ... but he has to be so mean about it." She sighed. "And what I really can't stand is that he lets everyone else know all the things he does around here. People must think I don't lift a finger," she added with a huff.

When Mom wasn't within earshot, Dad would complain to me about her.

"Jesus Christ, look at the dishes in the sink," he hissed, turning on the faucet. As usual, he flipped a dishtowel over his shoulder, grabbed a sponge, and started scrubbing a pan. "She should be cleaning these, not me. She doesn't do a damn thing around here."

"Just leave it," I said. "We'll clean it later. There's no rush."

"Anne, you don't understand." He sighed, scrubbing the pan harder. "When you leave these pans here for hours, it's impossible to get this gunk off." He pointed to the burnt residue from some pork chops cooked earlier.

"Whatever," I said, waving my hand and walking out of the kitchen. You couldn't reason with him.

Dad not only controlled the way the household had to be cleaned; he also personally did the laundry and shopped for all of the food. I think it was all a bit too much for him because the next month, he surprised us by hiring a professional cleaning lady. Not surprisingly, her efforts weren't good enough either, and Dad began complaining about her. He even purposely placed small pieces of paper under an area rug to see if she cleaned under it.

"You see, Erin," he said, peeking under the rug after the house was cleaned. "She didn't clean under here."

"See what?" Mom asked, annoyed. She didn't want to hear anything bad about the cleaning lady. She liked the idea of someone other than Dad being responsible for the cleanliness of the house.

"She missed these," he said showing her the bits of paper left behind.

"Then get rid of her!" Mom said in exasperation.

*   *   *

Dad fired the cleaning lady, and we all went back to our routine chores. With my brothers out of the house, I'd taken on even more things to do, and I wished Dad would have left the cleaning lady alone. But Dad went on to other problems. My brothers and their carefree way of living started encroaching on Mom's idea of family privacy. Both Thomas and Brian had been arrested for drunk driving, and this became a new topic for arguments between my parents. They both agreed, though, that they couldn't understand why their boys were having so much trouble.

Mom would say, "Boys are like that; they need more time to get themselves together." And Dad would criticize how they wasted all of his money for college on booze and girls. But many times, when Mom didn't know I could hear, I overheard her complaining to Dad.

"How can they do this to us? It's so embarrassing. I hope nobody sees Brian's name in the newspaper."

"Those newspapers have no business printing names just because people are driving drunk." He was in the kitchen cleaning, as usual. "Look at this shit in the sink. Who the hell left this here ...? Anne! ... Get down here, now!"

Part Two

"Secrecy is a Burden." (Isaiah 11:6)

Thirteen

First Love

It was late fall, freshman year, when Janine asked me to attend a fraternity party at Stevens College, located in Hoboken. The invitation stemmed from Jess, a girl Janine met at the Berkley Secretarial School they both attended. Jess's boyfriend, Mark, not only went to Stevens, but also lived on campus in one of the old Victorian fraternity houses located on Frat Row overlooking the New York skyline. This was my first experience at college partying since I commuted to school. It was there, at the Delta frat house, that I first saw him.

His name was Matthew. And he just happened to be in attendance with his own girlfriend. They were together in a corner, far from anyone else, arguing. Something about him caught and held my attention.

I watched silently, clutching a plastic cup filled with red punch, sipping slowly in case it was laced with grain alcohol, the tasteless substance used to spike drinks. Thomas had filled me in about it earlier when he saw me leaving the house dressed up in a new pair of pink denim jeans, a cropped V-neck sweater, and heavy midnight-blue eye shadow. He realized I was attending a party.

"Just be careful," Thomas warned, after I filled him in on my evening plans. "And watch what you drink," he added with a flash of worry in his eyes. He knew all too well about frat parties. "There'll be a keg there. Have one or two beers, but if there's any punch, it'll be laced, though it'll still taste normal."

Thomas was so sweet to care enough to warn me, and I was reminded how the three of us still had that innate need to protect each other. I made sure I didn't drink too much, for his sake and for mine.

My eyes remained on Matthew. He was average height, with a lean build and thick tousled brown hair. The girl, in whom he was presently engrossed, had her back to me. Her arms flailed wildly while he stood calmly, arms neatly folded over his chest. He looked over and held my stare.

"Who's he?" I asked Jess, who'd strolled over with Mark.

"Oh them," Jess said with a half laugh. "That's Matthew Bauer, Mark's best friend from high school. He's with his girlfriend, Lori."

I nodded, and we all turned, walking towards the dance floor. I could feel Matthew's gaze boring into my back, but I didn't dare turn around to look. Over the course of the evening, each time our paths crossed, our eyes met. It was only for a brief, fleeting moment, and yet, each time felt like an eternity, and each time made my heart skip a beat. *He has a girlfriend,* I reminded myself, *and even though they're arguing, they are probably very much in love.* Only then did I realize it would all be too complicated and instead of getting caught up with someone who was already taken, I dismissed Matthew and his gazes and returned my attention to my own group of friends for the remainder of the evening.

I didn't think of him again until three weeks later when he called asking for a date. He'd broken up with his girlfriend the previous week and gotten my number from Jess. He told me he couldn't keep the redhead he met at the party off his mind. It took a moment on the phone to realize he was talking about me. I was the redhead!

The next Friday night, Matthew arrived at my house to pick me up, and from the instant I saw him standing sheepishly at my front door, hands shoved in his pants pockets, I knew we were going to stay together. He looked deep into my eyes—again. Now that we were closer, I could see the brown, almost black color of his close-set eyes. Something about them made me feel déjà vu, like I'd seen them before that night at the frat house. I'd never felt this way before, almost giddy in his presence as my blood pulsed through my veins. It was obvious Matthew sensed my reaction by the lopsided grin on his face. And I couldn't be sure if he too felt this strange attraction. We stood there, mesmerized, staring at each other for the longest time as if a powerful spell had been cast over us.

"You look great," Matthew finally said, breaking his gaze and taking my hand. He gently led me to the passenger side of his silver Camaro.

I flashed him a smile as I slid into the seat. For some reason, I felt deeply content and perfectly at ease sitting next to him. Normally, I'd be awkward and nervous around someone I barely knew. I might have been loud and overbearing at home, as Grandma loved to point out, but when outside familiar territory, I was painfully shy and extremely quiet. However, the words now left my lips effortlessly.

"So what movie do you wanna see?" I eagerly asked.

"How about *Red Dawn*? It's playing over in Paramus?"

"Sure, I haven't seen it yet," I answered, glancing around the inside of his car. The seats were leather, and everything was impeccably clean.

"This was a present from my parents, a graduation gift for being at the top of my class."

"I love it," I said in awe. "I only have my parents' old yellow Volkswagen. Sometimes I fear it isn't going to make it up the steep hill to my college."

After graduation, Janine finally got that new silver Volvo. It turned out to be a graduation present after all. As for me, I inherited the Volkswagen, along with a thousand-dollar payment to my parents.

Matthew laughed.

"Do you use your feet like the Flintstones?"

I nodded, laughing along.

We caught an eight-o-clock showing at the theatre and afterwards, parked in the rear of the lot, our lips met for the first time. His kiss was soft and made my skin tingle. He kissed me again, this time with a bit more intensity, taking my breath away.

"Your eyes," he said with wonder. "There's something about them I just can't figure out."

I smiled inside. *He did notice it too!*

"Actually, my Grandma says I have the eyes of an old soul, whatever that means." I sighed, thinking about her sitting in a wheelchair. It seemed so unfair that she had no choice but to succumb to the illnesses of aging. I wished she'd stay fifty-five forever, her age when we lived in Rochelle Park.

"Does she live with you?" Matthew asked. His face was still close to mine, and I could hear him quietly breathing.

"No ... not anymore," I said sadly.

He must have sensed my uneasiness because he reached out with his hand and gently brushed my cheek. I looked up and smiled.

"She did when I was younger," I explained, thinking about our two-family house and our white cinder homes in Florida. "She had a stroke two years ago. Now she can hardly walk."

I looked down. That fact always made my stomach hurt.

Matthew didn't look too happy either.

"My grandfather, we call him Pop, also had a stroke, six months ago. He's still in rehab and should be coming home sometime this month." His eyes looked sad. It was obvious they were close. "And my grandmother died when

I was seven," he added with the same melancholy tone. "I never knew my dad's parents though; they died before I was born."

Maybe that was the attraction, I thought, wondering why I felt so comfortable in his presence. There were similarities with us both harboring sadness regarding our grandparents and their recent strokes. But there was more to it than that, something special drawing me to him. It wasn't his appearance though he was quite attractive in a Michael J. Fox sort of way—except Matthew had chubby cheeks, giving him the appearance of being younger than his nineteen years. I decided the attraction was in his voice, and in the way he looked at me, making my body quiver.

*   *   *

We saw each other again the very next night and practically every day thereafter. When Christmas approached, we spent Christmas Eve with my family at Aunt Lorraine's in Upstate New York. Matthew's parents invited me for Christmas Day dinner at their house. The Bauers, who lived in a modest expanded Cape Cod in Fair Lawn, were nothing like my family. For one thing, they all attended mass together every Sunday without fail and never ate a piece of meat on Fridays. As for us, gradually over the years, we weaned the weekly commitment, going to mass mostly on holidays. This earned us Janine's label, "A&P Catholics," those parishioners only appearing on Ash Wednesday and Palm Sunday in order to receive "their ashes and palms." That was certainly us—though we did attend mass on Christmas and Easter as well.

We also differed in the fact that Matthew's mother and father held traditional husband and wife roles. Mr. Bauer, the breadwinner, had owned his own landscaping business for twenty-five years. Mrs. Bauer stayed at home, cleaning and making sure there was food on the table every night for supper. Both parents always worked in my family, and everyone shared chores. Matthew never lifted a finger at home. His mother not only washed and folded his clothes each week, but she also put them away in his bureau drawers for him.

When I arrived at their house late in the afternoon, a gangly old man, gleefully swaying back and forth in an old wooden rocker next to the Christmas tree greeted me. *This had to be Pop,* I thought. He was exceedingly thin. A small potbelly protruded through his dull gray sweatshirt, and his left arm rested tightly against his chest in a sling. He was pale with wrinkly skin and clumps of white hair sticking up randomly over his head—It was easy to see where Matthew got his long, ski-slope nose from, although Pop's was much more pronounced.

"Whoa—what do we have here?" he practically whistled. "Hey, Matty, is she with you?" he hollered out, a wicked grin on his face.

"Yes, Pop, this is Anne," Matthew said, strolling in from the kitchen.

All throughout Matthew's childhood, Pop had been a presence. He visited every day, took his grandsons to dinner at Traci's restaurant every Friday night, and even accompanied the Bauers when they spent a week each summer at their rental house on Spring Lake.

I extended my hand, but instead of shaking it, he pointed to his cheek, smirking.

"Dama bushee," he cackled. "That means 'give me a kiss' in Polish."

Looking sideways at Matthew, I tried to see if this teasing was typical behavior for his grandfather or if he only did this to new girlfriends.

Matthew only smiled and nodded to say it was okay.

I leaned over and quickly gave Pop a kiss; my face flushed.

"There, are you happy?" Matthew teased him.

"Is he behaving himself?" Mrs. Bauer asked, appearing from the kitchen. "Hi, Anne," she said warmly, eying the tinfoil wrapped package in my hand. I'd just finished baking brownies, and the plate was still hot. "I'll take that to the kitchen for you."

I had met the Bauers the previous week. Mrs. Bauer was the exact same height as Matthew and had short, curly brown hair. She was wearing a cotton skirt, which hung just below her knees and a lamb's wool white sweater that accented her slim figure. She reminded me a lot of the typical 1950s style mother you saw on *Leave It to Beaver*, always home cooking in the kitchen, dishing out food as well as advice.

When dinner was ready, I slid next to Matthew at an oversized mahogany table complete with a red linen tablecloth, matching napkins, and Lenox holiday plates decorated with boughs of holly. Mr. Bauer, who was tall and burly, sat at the head of the table and dominated the conversation. He had deeply lined tanned skin, a result of working outside for so many years, and a headful of thick black hair. He talked a lot, mostly about his fishing trips he'd taken over the summer, but he also talked a lot about food.

"The one thing you have to know about this family," he said to me suddenly, looking me straight in the eyes, "is that we like to eat." His tone was serious, but everyone at the table, especially Matthew's older brother Adam, cracked up laughing when they saw him eye my plate and shake his head.

My plate was practically full. I looked around the table; every other plate was empty, completely clear of any trace of food having been there.

I tried to laugh along too, not quite sure if he was serious about being upset that my food was left uneaten. Matthew squeezed my leg under the table, giving me a look which told me not to worry.

"You have to excuse Pop and my father," Matthew told me later. We were sitting in his car outside my house; it was nearly ten o' clock.

I smiled. "It's okay; I've got quite colorful characters in my family too."

"My dad just really likes food. As you can see, everybody eats a lot in my family." Matthew patted his belly.

"I don't see anything there," I said, patting his belly too. "Well, maybe just a little bit," I teased.

"And Pop, he's always been like that, flirting with the pretty ladies. You should have seen him when he was at rehab," Matthew said laughing. "He had the time of his life. Never did his exercises though."

"My mom says she gets plenty of those at the hospital, but they don't pester her much anymore, only the younger nurses."

Matthew laughed, leaned over, and kissed me gently on the lips.

"I know if you were my nurse, I'd be flirting with you."

I chuckled and returned his kiss. It was so easy being with Matthew. He was soft-spoken, easygoing, and we never fought or argued. If there was something we disagreed about, we debated the issue and laughed later how I was the optimist and he the pessimist.

*　　　　　*　　　　　*

Over the next couple of months, we spent even more time together. On the weekends, we visited his grandfather at his house and my grandparents up in New York, and I even attended church several times along with his family on Sunday mornings. Sometimes we went out to a movie with Jess and Mark, or with Janine and her new boyfriend, Keith, but mainly Matthew and I liked to be alone.

One night, on our way home after eating out at a small Italian restaurant, we were caught in a downpour. We were in my little yellow Volkswagen, and the rain pounded the pavement, eventually making me pull over on a side street to wait it out. The strength of the wind rattled my little car as we huddled together, our arms entwined, like two lost souls on a deserted island.

"Let's wait till this completely passes," he suggested. "I don't want you driving in this rain. If you want, I can drive the rest of the way." Matthew cringed when I drove, claiming I was herky-jerky with the brakes.

"You just don't like my driving," I said with a sideways glance.

"No, no … it's not that," he pleaded, a wicked smile on his face. "I'm just better at driving in bad weather."

A crack of lightning jolted us upright.

"It's gonna pass over," he said, moving closer. His expression grew serious. "I don't know what it is about you." He squeezed me tightly; his strength mingled with his tenderness melted my insides. "But I think … oh, I don't know." He shook his head, all seriousness gone from his face.

"No, tell me," I prodded, not wanting to let him off this easy. Matthew wasn't romantic, preferring to sing theme songs from his favorite cartoon instead of singing along to a love song on the radio. Although I enjoyed his light, playful manner, I also wanted to see more of his serious, romantic side that he kept hidden. I persisted. "Tell me what you think."

"I think …" He drew me in closer. "… that I'm falling in love with you."

We kissed again, and without hesitation, but with slow, graceful movements, we climbed into the back of the car and dropped onto the rear bench seat, still entangled in an embrace. Matthew kissed me long and hard and pressed his body firmly against mine. When I didn't protest, he sat up.

"Are you sure you want to do this?"

I pulled him in closer. "Um-hum." I inhaled, smelling his light aftershave lotion, sweet and intoxicating.

"But don't you want to wait till you're married?" he murmured.

I shook my head, kissing him full on the lips.

"But …" He suddenly pulled back. "Are you really sure?"

"Matthew," I said gently, looking up at him, "I'm sure. I'm not waiting till I'm married. I love you, right here and right now. There's no reason to wait for marriage."

He looked at me curiously.

"Anyway, I've waited long enough. I was probably the only graduating virgin in my high school class," I said with a half laugh.

"So? That's actually a good thing," he said, tilting his head slightly to the side. "Why don't you think about it first? We can wait."

Instead of answering, I pulled him on top of me. His concern made me want him even more. That night, in my little yellow Volkswagen, we made love for the first time. Afterwards, as we listened to the storm settle down, there was an overwhelming feeling of contentment. I was so happy and at peace. His easy demeanor was so different from everybody in my family. There was one thing I was most certain of at that moment, more so than anything else so far in my life: I was head over heels in love with Matthew.

Fourteen

My Rock

Thomas, like me, entered into a serious relationship. That summer, he brought home Shelley Carter, a tall, slender girl with a pretty, heart-shaped face who worked as an x-ray technician in the same hospital as Mom. She lived in Franklin Lakes, the next town over, with her mother and older brother, her father recently deceased from an untimely heart attack the previous year. Their home was a graceful old Victorian, recently renovated and updated to meet modern standards. Her family, whose ancestry could be traced to the early Dutch settlers of Bergen County, owned a large textile company and kept active in the community, especially at their private country club.

Mom was thrilled with Shelley, although a bit overwhelmed by her pedigree and the fact that she only wore Ralph Lauren, smoked Pall Malls, and always carried the newest style Gucci handbag. These things Mom could get used to, especially in light of the fact that Thomas seemed to be getting his life together. He didn't go back to college and was still working at the same job but earned himself a promotion to assistant manager of the store. He talked about saving his money so that he'd have enough to put a down payment on a house in a couple of years. Mom credited his recent turnaround to Shelley and wished the same would happen to Brian.

Brian, however, received another DWI and this time lost his license along with his job. The branch manager learned of his arrest and fired him on the spot; it was company policy. Unable to keep up the rent for his apartment, he moved back home. Brian still kept to himself and rarely came downstairs to join us at the dinner table. The moment he came through the front door, he retreated to his room, his haven, where he had his own television and a snack tray for his meals.

"All he does is use this house like a hotel—and me as a bank!" Dad complained to Mom. Brian had been living at home for two months. "You'd think he'd at least come downstairs and talk to us once in a while."

Mom wouldn't respond. She hated to say anything negative about her sons, even when what Dad said was true.

Despite Dad's complaints, the next month, he helped Brian find employment as a janitor at a local Baptist church, and Brian rode an old ten-speed bike back and forth to work. It was a bit demoralizing for him to bicycle instead of drive, but then again, he made his own bed and had to sleep in it.

Mom and Dad started noticing that, unlike my two brothers, I remained in school. And Dad noticed the grades I earned—never taking anything lower than a ninety home. College work wasn't so hard after all. Matthew, however, struggled with the engineering curriculum at Stevens and dropped out, transferring to Seton Hall University, forty minutes away, to study accounting. It upset him at first when he couldn't keep up at Stevens, having been valedictorian of his graduating high school class, but he soon realized that keeping figures was more fun, and a lot easier. We'd spend most nights lounging on the couch at my house, studying—it almost became a competition between us of who could get the better grades.

*   *   *

The experience of dating Matthew maintained its dreamlike nature. The initial honeymoon period spilled over into the next year. We were always together with my breath still being taken away in his presence. But it wasn't until the following summer, July of 1986, when I was nineteen, that I realized just how lucky I'd been finding him.

I was convinced I was pregnant.

"Are you absolutely sure you're that late?" Matthew asked, a frown plastered on his face.

We were sitting together in my backyard on the patio, eating grilled hamburgers and slices of watermelon. I put my half-eaten burger on my plate; my appetite had suddenly disappeared. I didn't like that look. It was the first time anguish replaced his usual content expression.

"Yes, I'm pretty sure," I muttered. "Two weeks."

His body tensed, and I could almost hear him offering to pay for the abortion. How could I explain that abortion wasn't an option? Had it been legal in 1966, my existence would've been annihilated.

"Did you do one of those home tests?" he asked in a low voice, barely audible.

"Not yet. I'm going to buy one tomorrow. They're supposed to be pretty accurate."

We were both silent as rain started to gently drizzle over us. We didn't budge from our seats at the picnic table. The rain almost had a calming, hypnotic effect because suddenly, Matthew's expression changed.

"Don't worry. If you're pregnant, I'll marry you and we'll raise the baby together." He smiled, and his shoulders relaxed.

"You're not mad?" I asked, peering more closely at his face. "I thought you looked upset a minute ago."

"Just shock." He sighed, putting an arm around me. He stared intently into my eyes. "I pray every night that you'll only get pregnant once I put a ring on your finger," he said gently, taking my hand and slowly brushing it against his lips. "And so far, all my prayers have been answered. I have a good feeling the test will be negative."

"I hope so," I said, lowering my head. I wanted to believe him, but it was hard when I'd never been this late before.

"It'll be negative, don't worry."

*   *   *

After going through two home pregnancy kits, which I sneaked into the bathroom at five o'clock in the morning, and after tinkering with the confusing test tubes and droppers of dye, I still wasn't absolutely sure whether or not I was pregnant. I couldn't decide if the positive test color, a pale pink, was present—it looked as if each tube contained a hint of pink.

When another week passed, we were both convinced there was a baby on the way. *So much for Matthew's prayers,* I thought.

But Matthew wasn't cynical like me. He was happy.

"I hope it's a girl," he said. "That way, she'll have red hair like you."

I wanted a girl as well. For some reason, the idea of a baby wasn't so bad after all. And as much as I feared telling my parents about the pregnancy, not really knowing how they'd react, I craved this unborn child just as much. There was a large part of me that was thrilled to finally have a blood relative. Oh, how I hoped we would look exactly alike. The prospect of that wish kept me on a high, and then a week later, the world shattered—my long overdue monthly cycle returned. There was no pregnancy and no explanation, except that maybe I skipped a month, something I'd never done in the past six years.

Deep down, I grieved for my child that could have been, and surprisingly, it dredged up thoughts about my own birth mother. I started to grieve her loss too. She was the woman who carried me for nine months in her womb, and yet I wasn't allowed to know anything about her. Did she go through the exact same experience I just encountered, sneaking pregnancy tests and watching for every little physical sign of pregnancy? She must have—only in the end, she was pregnant and decided to give me away. Matthew knew about my adoption status and that one day I planned to search for my birth mother, but he suggested waiting until I finished college.

"We'll be done in less than two years," he reminded me. "By that time, you can decide what to do."

That was Matthew—always putting off to tomorrow what could be done today. I took his advice because quite honestly, I had no idea where to even begin.

Fifteen

Making Plans

After four years of college, commuting back and forth, studying practically every night together, Matthew and I graduated. He earned a degree in accounting, graduating summa cum laude, and I too achieved honor level, magna cum laude in community health education. We both had jobs by the summer's end. Matthew accepted a job as an auditor for a large accounting firm, and I decided to pursue a career in public health. Health inspectors were employed by the government at the local, state, and federal levels. It was an unusual career, mentioned casually by one of my professors, but something about it drew me in, carrying a sense of familiarity, a knowledge that this career would be both exciting and life-changing. Within a month after earning my college degree, I took additional classes at Rutgers in central New Jersey. The courses were in environmental health, which enabled me to sit for the state licensing exam.

That very same month, a sweltering Fourth of July day, Matthew presented me with a small black velvet box.

"What's this?" I asked sucking in my breath. Dusk was just approaching, and we were lounging on my backyard patio, dressed in shorts and T-shirts, waiting to leave for the firework show in Ridgewood.

"Go ahead and open it."

My hand shook as I slowly traced my fingers over the box then very carefully lifted the top, revealing a beautiful marquis-cut diamond ring. It sparkled, even in the dim lighting. It was breathtaking.

"Even though we've been dating for almost four years now, it feels as if we're married already," Matthew said taking the box from my trembling hands. He slipped the ring on my third finger of my left hand.

"It's beautiful," I murmured, tears filling my eyes.

He looked at me intently. "Will you marry me?"

His question painted a beautiful picture in my head. I saw us happily walking down the church aisle then painting walls together in the living room of our new little house, and then two light-haired children running past us, a boy and a girl, playing in the yard as we held hands, watching. Our life would be perfect.

I nodded, throwing my arms around his neck. How could I resist this mild-mannered, wonderful man? Matthew was a dream come true.

"Yes," I whispered, brushing my lips along his cheek. "Of course I'll marry you."

Matthew held me tight to his body. We remained perfectly still for the longest time as the sun sank deeper into the night.

*   *   *

We planned to marry the second of June, two years after our college graduation. The minute Mom learned of our engagement, she turned into a madwoman about the wedding details. We needed to book the church date and the reception place immediately. She was convinced we needed to start planning right away, two years wasn't enough time to ensure all the best details. As for me and Matthew, we honestly could care less about wedding details. A nice small ceremony with family and close friends would suit us just fine. We'd get a date, secure the hall, buy a dress, rent a tux, and show up in time to be married.

Mom shook her head angrily when I told her our ideas.

"Really, Anne," she sneered. "If you wait till the last minute and throw everything together then, you'll be eating your wedding dinner at McDonald's."

Wasting no time, within a month of my engagement, Mom began searching for a place to hold the reception. She dragged me to fancy hotels, restaurants, and catering halls. By late October, we'd made our decision, booking George's Restaurant in Moonachie. They had a grand, elegant dining room boasting a beautiful white wooden staircase for the bride and groom's entrance and floating minstrels to provide continuous music when the band was on break. I mentioned a DJ would be more fun, but Mom adamantly refused to even consider it.

"A band is much more traditional," she argued. "And who ever heard of a DJ at a nice place like George's?" she asked, shaking her head in disbelief.

Matthew and I agreed to George's house band. It really didn't matter much to us, and for some crazy reason, it made Mom happy.

In the meantime, I passed the state exams, earning my license, and settled into my new job working for the town of Edgewood's health department doing food inspections for retail outfits. This job earned me the utmost respect from Grandpa, who was quite impressed that someone in the family had earned a college degree.

"You know, she can walk into any restaurant in her jurisdiction, flash her badge, and see anything she wants," he told my cousins.

It was Christmas Eve, and we were all gathered in Aunt Lorraine's living room. Maggie sat next to me, her long dark hair pulled up in a bushy ponytail and a lit cigarette hanging out of her mouth. She had graduated high school in June and decided to work instead of attending college.

Her current job was waitressing at a local restaurant in Chester. She said her customers tipped well, and she planned to start bartending once she turned legal age in another year. She was already practicing her upcoming new trade and mixed everyone's drinks starting with a Bloody Mary for Grandpa and a martini for my dad.

Grandpa looked my way and said, "Case closed … Annie …" He waved me over.

When he was drinking, which he did at every family gathering, he called me by my childhood name. Lately, it took only two to three drinks for him to reach a deep state of intoxication. Mom said it was because his liver was probably broken down and that even one glass of wine would render him instantly drunk.

"I'll be right there, Grandpa," I replied, giggling along with Maggie. I got up and plopped myself next to Grandpa on the couch.

"I love ya!" he said, pulling me closer. "You know I love ya?"

"Yes, Grandpa, I know," I said, glancing at Maggie and shaking my head.

Maggie shook her head back. We both knew he'd never change.

"So what were you two whispering about over there?" he asked hiccupping.

"My wedding. Maggie is going to be my maid of honor," I said proudly.

The news of this made my mother glow with pride. She told me about how Brenda had been her maid of honor even though she didn't care much for her. Grandma had suggested she ought to ask the next eldest sister as it was the proper thing to do, and Mom, feeling the guilt Grandma was laying on her, conceded and asked Brenda to do her the honor.

"I really would've preferred my best friend Marge or even your Aunt Lorraine, but your Grandma said Lorraine, only fourteen at the time, was too young to be maid of honor," Mom explained.

"But, Mom," I had replied, exasperated, "I asked Maggie because she was the closest girl to me growing up. I adore her. I don't think it matters if the maid of honor is a relative or a friend."

"Well, I'm glad your cousin is your maid of honor and not one of your friends. It ought to be a family member," she added knowingly.

Grandma heard my news firsthand along with Grandpa about Maggie being in the wedding. I saw her looking my way. A smile spread across her face.

"Anne ... so ... nice ... having ... Maggie," she struggled to get the words out.

Grandma's speech worsened as each year went by. She could talk but the words came out painstakingly slowly. The stroke had weakened her considerably. She barely used her walker lately, relying more and more on the wheelchair.

"Yes, Grandma," I said, seeing the frustrated look on her face. "It's nice Maggie's going to be my maid of honor." I smiled warmly, finishing the sentence for her.

Grandma's deteriorating health took a toll on her strength and appearance. Her once-dancing blue eyes were now a stagnant dull gray, and her white hair that had enjoyed receiving weekly styling at the beauty parlor now was combed straight at the sides. However, she still maintained her spunk. It only came out more slowly.

"Anna ... Anna." Grandpa waved his arm. "Our Annie here ... getting married ... I love her!" He still had his arm around me and pulled me in closer again.

Then out of nowhere, taking everybody quite by surprise, Grandma said in a low but clear voice, "He'd step over ... ten ... naked ... women to get to a pint!"

"Momma!" Aunt Lorraine and Mom exclaimed together at the same time. Maggie and I pretended to be shocked at her comment. But we were trying hard not to burst out laughing.

Under Grandma's sunken eyes, there was still a small glint of her former self that became angered every time Grandpa got drunk.

*   *   *

We were all surprised when the next morning, while we were opening presents around the Christmas tree, Shelley waltzed into our family room with a brilliant round diamond sparkling on her left hand.

I noticed it right away and jumped up, my mouth half open ready to say something.

But Mom was way ahead of me.

"You got engaged!" she squealed, popping out of the recliner, still in her robe and slippers.

Shelley just smiled, flashing her perfect white teeth and held out her hand for us to see.

"When did Thomas propose?" I asked excitedly.

"Last night after we got home from Aunt Lorraine's," Thomas, who stood behind Shelley, explained.

"Two weddings!" Mom said, sitting back down again.

"We're not waiting as long as Anne and Matthew," Shelley started, sitting down on the couch. She tucked a piece of her blond highlighted hair behind her ear. "We don't want to wait that long. We're planning for sometime next December."

"This is so exciting. Congratulations!" I said, giving Shelley then Thomas a big hug.

"We want you to be in the wedding party," Shelley said, looking at me, and then her eyes found Brian, sitting on the floor next to the Christmas tree. "And you too."

"Thanks," Brian said, standing up. "And congratulations. Wow, another wedding?" he said disbelievingly. He proceeded to scoop up all his opened presents in his arms while Mom and Dad exchanged glances. They knew he was itching to return to his bedroom. They were right as Brian headed straight upstairs.

*   *   *

The day before New Year's Eve, I met Janine for lunch at a small cafe in Ridgewood. It was a new trendy spot known for gourmet salads and homemade breads. We hardly hung out lately, only getting together for a bite to eat or a movie every other month or so. Janine arrived wearing a tight velvet skirt in burgundy along with a white silk blouse that dramatically offset her recently dyed blue-black hair. I looked down at my outfit and sighed. I was wearing an old pair of blue jeans and a faded green cotton sweater. Nothing too dramatic, but then again I didn't have the job that Janine held. She worked as an executive secretary for the vice president of operations at IBM. She loved her job and was quite content that there wasn't a steady man in her life; she still preferred to play the field and had no intentions of settling down anytime soon. She was having too much fun in the corporate world, dressing up in skirts and suits, wearing high heels, and going out to power lunches.

"Oh ... I have news," I said, after we placed our orders for two chicken Caesar salads. I leaned forward. "Guess who got engaged?"

Janine's face lit up. She loved gossip.

"Who? Tell me, don't make me guess!"

"Thomas! He gave Shelley a ring on Christmas Eve."

"Wow, I never thought he'd settle down."

"What, like you?" I teased. "They're getting married next December. Oh, I almost forgot to ask you, do you wanna go bridesmaid shopping sometime next month? You know for dresses? I know it's early but my mother is driving me crazy!"

*　　　*　　　*

The following day, I asked Shelley to be a bridesmaid, along with Janine and Maggie. Brian and Thomas were ushers along with Matthew's older brother Adam. It seemed only appropriate to have Shelley in the bridal party. Soon she'd be my sister-in-law, the next best thing to an actual sister. It was a jolly holiday season for all amidst the cold, dank weather outside. My family happily discussed wedding details, especially Mom, who announced she was going on a diet. She wanted to lose at least fifty pounds before she'd even think of herself as the mother of the groom and then the mother of the bride.

"I think I'll make a trip over to Weight Watchers," she said casually as we sat down to a big New Year's feast prepared by Dad. Fresh shrimp with cocktail sauce, baked ziti parmesan, garlic bread, and cheesy broccoli sat tantalizingly in front of us.

"Well, after the New Year, of course," Mom added, taking a heaping portion of ziti and plopping it on her plate.

Mom remained in her glory for months at the prospect of two upcoming weddings.

Sixteen

Secrets

Everything in my life was running smoothly. I loved my new career, inspecting restaurants and ensuring the public's safety; it was both challenging and exciting. The wedding plans were coming along nicely. We continued with the details, finding a photographer and securing him for the wedding date. But there was something missing from my life, an emptiness gnawing from within. Even though I had a big Irish family filled with colorful characters, the deep yearning to know about *my* origins still existed. I wasn't even certain if there was any Irish blood in me. Grandma always said that everybody had a wee bit of Irish in them, but I wanted to be sure.

My relationship with Matthew, keeping up with college, our engagement, and recently the demands of my new job sidetracked me for quite some time. I'd practically forgotten about my need to search. Weeks, sometimes months flew by without so much as a single thought about my adoption status. I'd been too busy and much too happy to even notice the hole residing in my heart. Now that things were settling down, and there was more time on my hands, the urge returned in full force.

One Sunday, while visiting Grandma, we briefly discussed the possibility of me contacting my birth mother.

"Ahh … it's … a … good … boat … that … tries … to find … the … harbor … it … left," Grandma replied dreamily, citing yet again one of her old sayings. Her words came out slower than usual. "But … be … careful," she whispered. "Don't ... go ... loo ... king ... for ... someone ... who ... might ... not ... want ... to ... be ... found."

Her words shocked me. Never did it cross my mind that my birth mother wouldn't want to be found. No, Grandma's warnings didn't apply to me. I refused to even consider it a possibility. All I knew was I needed to tie up those loose ends in my life—my beginnings. And as my marriage date approached, this feeling intensified. I'd always known that someday the effort would be made to find my birth mother. Finally, the time felt right.

The bond between us couldn't be completely severed, as everyone seemed to want it to be. Another part of me existed somewhere in the world, a part I was once attached to and depended on for life. To me, the umbilical cord served a function that was much more than just physical. It was my essence, my origin, my connection to my biological ancestors. As far as I was concerned, the cord was still attached. Who were these people who were the cause of my existence? Did they wonder about me in the same way I often wondered about them?

Deep down, I was certain my birth mother was wondering too. The notion of her wanting to permanently end all ties after my birth was incomprehensible. Instinctively, she must be asking how her child was fending. No separation could completely wipe out the innate feeling a mother holds for her own baby.

There were lots of questions I needed answered about my ethnic heritage. Most important, however, was the question of why she decided to place me for adoption.

But exactly how did one go about searching? I knew no one who was adopted other than Sharon, and she didn't need to search since her birth mother kept contact through her parents.

I too was dependent on my parents to obtain whatever information they had about my adoption. It was the only way I could get started, and so I decided to begin with my father. One Saturday morning, while Dad was at his desk organizing papers, I summoned up the nerve to ask him the name and address of the adoption agency that placed me.

"Sure," he said, looking at me over his glasses. "Hold on a second." He began rifling through one of the desk drawers. Within a few minutes, he produced a large white envelope and pulled out three pieces of paper.

"These are the final adoption decrees for the three of you," he said. "I thought I had more." He looked back inside the envelope, shrugged his shoulders, and handed me the papers.

There was an individual sheet for each of us. I looked at mine. Before my eyes, for the first time, I saw my original last name: Female Cusack.

Cusack, I repeated to myself several times. I tried the name out with my first, *Anne Cusack,* but didn't like the way it sounded. Then I realized that the first name on the document was Female. Why in God's name was "female" put down for my first name? I shifted my eyes from the document to my father.

"Why wasn't I given a first name?" I asked with a hint of annoyance. I wasn't sure which was more insulting, never being given a first name or being referred to as a female. The document made no further reference to my birth mother's name or mine.

"I don't know," Dad answered, removing his glasses and cleaning them with his handkerchief. "I guess your mother didn't want to name you. Brian didn't have a first name either. Only Thomas was named."

"Yes, it says right here, Patrick Quinn," I said, switching to Thomas's document.

"There doesn't seem to be any more papers," he said closing the drawer. "I was sure there was more information about your nationalities." He looked perplexed at the notion of not being able to locate the documents.

Cusack, I thought. "Isn't that name in your family?"

"Yes, my aunt Rose was married to a Cusack."

"Did you ever think I could be related to them?"

My earlier fantasies about being related to Grandma flashed through my mind. Maybe it was Dad's family after all.

"No, you aren't. I thought about it at the time and even asked your cousin Sophie." He laughed. "But no, there's no connection. The name is just common."

"Oh." I sighed. "I wasn't aware they allowed you to see the original birth name," I said in disbelief, wishing I'd seen these much earlier.

"It has to be on the legal document, the one we signed," he explained. "For the court hearing. We don't know the parents' first names, though, only the background information they gave to us."

"That's the information you can't find?"

"Yeah … I think it said something like you were maybe part Irish or English and something else." He gazed at the ceiling, lost in thought. "To tell you the truth, I don't remember much."

"Oh." I looked down, full of disappointment.

"At the time, we were more excited to take each one of you home … especially you." His eyes sparkled. "You were so tiny, and we were afraid to pick you up and …"

"I know, I know, I was crying the whole time."

"Yes! And you still haven't shut up." He laughed, and I did too, hearing my favorite family story for the ten-millionth time.

"Can I make a copy of this?"

"Sure, go ahead. What are you going to do now, go and find your bionic mother?" he said with a teasing grin.

"Bionic?"

"You know what I mean," he said laughing. "Your real mother."

I looked up from the document.

"My *birth* mother. That's the politically correct way to refer to her."

"Birth mother?" he repeated, puzzled.

"Yes," I said, pausing. "And yes, I might try. I'd love to know who she was, but I think it'll be hard to find her with so little information."

Knowing her last name was a start, but if I knew her full name, I'd be able to thoroughly search records.

"I think I'll contact the agency that placed me and ask for background information, especially about my nationality."

"I can give you the name of the agency and the lawyer who handled the adoption." He offered, and without waiting for a reply from me, he began to look through the drawer again and located another envelope. Typed on the outside was the address for the adoption agency.

"The agency was in Newark?"

"Yes. The lawyer who handled the adoption was named Roberts, Jacob Roberts. He was very old at the time, about sixty. I'm not sure if he's still alive."

"Thank you," I said clutching the envelope. "The name of the agency should be enough to get me started."

"Anne." Dad's voice grew serious. "Just do me one favor?"

"What?"

"Promise me you'll keep this from your mother. She can't know that you're searching."

I looked straight into his eyes.

"Why not?"

"Just promise me."

I shook my head. There was no way I could've made that promise, thinking that maybe if Mom knew about my interest to search, she might decide to support me. Based on her previous reactions, it was a long shot, but one worth taking. I changed the subject.

"Do you think Thomas and Brian would be interested in seeing their adoption records?"

"I guess. They never asked."

"Thomas should at least be interested, since he's getting married in December. I'm sure they'd want this information, especially if they have children," I told Dad. "They'll at least need the medical history."

Dad got up from his chair and closed the door.

"You can show it to them if you want," he said, a serious expression on his face.

Here we go again, he's about to tell me to call off the search. I couldn't understand why he'd give so much information then expect me to just forget about all of it out of reverence for Mom.

"Actually," he said, lowering his voice, "Brian had two siblings. They were born a year after Brian. The social worker, Jane, called us at the time and asked if we'd be interested in adopting twins born to the same mother who had Brian."

"Twins?" I said with a puzzled look.

Dad drew a long breath and nodded.

"It was a boy and a girl."

"Why didn't you adopt them?" I asked, immediately trying to picture what Brian's siblings looked like. Did they share his sea-green eyes and thin chestnut hair?

"Your mother and I only wanted a girl, and they wouldn't separate the twins. They wanted to keep them together. We didn't have the money for two more children at the time so we told them no."

"But those were Brian's brother and sister," I stammered, trying to piece together the meaning of this. What if Mom and Dad had adopted them? What would've happened to me?

Dad's expression hardened.

"Hey, we're not responsible for that woman and all the babies she had."

"I know, but ..." Maybe Dad was right, he wasn't responsible for this other woman and her babies, but he *was* responsible for Brian. Didn't they realize that those siblings were also Brian's family?

Dad turned his attention back to his papers while I stood silently beside him.

"Dad," I said presently, "what if Mom, by a miracle, became pregnant at that time with twins? Would you've kept them?"

"Of course," he said, looking up. "But you know we couldn't conceive any children. That's why we adopted the three of you." He raised his eyebrows, waiting for me to confirm his statement.

I didn't reply. Clearly, adoption wasn't designed to protect children. The first priority was to create families for couples who couldn't have their own babies. We were like commodities, taken only if it was convenient for the adoptive parents. It didn't matter what was right for the children.

"Listen, Anne," Dad murmured, his eyes still on me. "Keep this a secret. You can never tell Brian about this or mention this to Mom. She'd kill me if she found out I told you."

*   *   *

Later that evening, I found Brian in his room sitting on the edge of his bed, a card table pulled up close as he ate his dinner.

"Brian, guess what I have," I said, waving the adoption papers in the air. "These are the legal adoption documents for the three of us. Our original surnames are on them ... look, here's yours," I said, placing his paper in front of him.

He looked, considered it, and without any emotion or comment, handed it back.

"Aren't you at least interested in knowing your birth mother's name?" It was surprising to see such complete indifference. I clearly remembered when he said he'd like to know, that he'd like to see a picture. And I especially remembered his promise to help me someday. The day had finally arrived.

"The name's right there on the paper," he answered matter-of-factly.

"I know ... but don't you want to find out more? Aren't you curious?"

He shrugged. "I could care less."

I'd expected him to at least show some enthusiasm, if not for himself, then for me.

"Gee, I've seen you get more excited about golf scores—and you hate golf." I shook my head. "I'm making copies of these. Do you want a copy?"

"Where'd you get them anyway?"

"Dad gave them to me."

Brian hesitated for a minute as if thinking this one over.

"He can hold on to my copy. I might lose it," he said, turning his attention back to his dinner.

A few days later, Thomas stopped by for a quick visit. He and Shelley planned to buy a new house, and Thomas had just finished giving Mom the rundown of the plusses and minuses of three they were considering. I met up with him on his way out in the foyer and told him about the documents.

"Why would I want to know anything about her? She gave me away!" With that, he stormed out, slamming the front door behind him.

For a moment, I stood dumbfounded in the foyer, staring after him. Why was he so angry? It was obvious he was bitter about his adoption, probably blaming his birth mother for all the problems he had in his life. But things were better for him now. He had a job, a fiancée, and soon he'd have a house. Shelley's mother was helping them with a down payment so their mortgage would be low and affordable. Things were going his way, for once, and I'd thought he'd want to know, like me, information about how he came to be a baby available and waiting in that special nursery ward. I felt that information was vital, a necessary component to complete our history before moving forward into marriage. It was obvious Thomas didn't share my sentiments.

After making copies of the adoption documents a day later, I returned the originals to Dad feeling confident with the knowledge of my birth mother's surname. It would be sufficient information to begin the search, but I was clueless about how to proceed. There had to be some way, I thought desperately, some way to get the ball rolling.

Seventeen

A New Hope

Remembering what Mom said to Mrs. Compton about there being search organizations, I first tried the local library. I thought they had to have some references located there, something that would guide me in the right direction, but the only resources related to adoption were a few books written for parents seeking to adopt. There was no other choice but to start combing through newspapers and magazines for any articles or advertisements related to adoption. I happened upon a small article in the *New York Times* that mentioned ALMA—the Adoptees' Liberation Movement Association. The article explained that the organization was founded by an adoptee, Florence Fisher, who sought out her own birth parents through walls of secrecy and sealed documents. The goal of ALMA was to try to unite people separated by adoption. They kept a reunion registry set up as a multilevel cross-file system containing information about adoptees and birth parents who had joined. A match occurred when both parties, adoptees and original family members, gave the same facts. Once the organization felt a match had been made, they notified both parties and planned a reunion. There was a higher chance for success when a lot of information was provided to the database, especially if you knew an original surname. But both parties had to belong to ALMA for it to work.

My hopes were high as I filled out my application to ALMA, including all the vital information: the date, time, and location of my birth and my original surname. Convinced that a match was inevitable, after mailing the application, I hurried home and poured over old family photo albums looking for pictures of myself from infancy through college graduation. The next day, I took about two dozen to a photo store to have copies made. I was sure my birth mother would want to see what I looked like as a child. I also added photos of all my major milestones—Communion, graduations— knowing she'd be grateful to get a glimpse of me growing up. She'd missed everything.

*   *   *

A package from ALMA came three weeks later. Inside was a guidebook, some pamphlets depicting successful reunion stories, and a one-page cover letter with the dreaded news: *Sorry, no matches at this time.*

It felt as if a nail had been driven straight through my heart. This proved she wasn't looking for me. Why wasn't she on this database? Didn't she want to find me?

These questions haunted me over the next couple of hours while I scoured every word of the pamphlets. A feeling of kinship instantly formed after reading through the many adoptee stories. We may not be blood related, but our lives were so similar, and many seemed to suffer in the same way I did—being cut off from their biological roots. And like me, they all yearned to be reunited with their birth parents. Each story was different in its own way, yet it seemed we each unwittingly carried an ugly scar deep within our souls made on the day we were separated from our birth families. There were also stories from the perspective of the birth mothers. In most cases, the shame from giving up a child was so great that they were afraid to search. They felt they didn't have a right to know their own children. Many of the reunions were initiated by the adoptees. *Maybe that's why she hasn't tried to contact me,* I reasoned.

The guidebook outlined various search strategies depending on the state where you were born. All states sealed original birth certificates and denied adoptees and birth parents any access to identifying information regarding each other, except three: Alaska, Pennsylvania, and Alabama. In New Jersey, my birth state, all records pertaining to adoption were sealed at the local, county, and state levels. My original birth certificate was no longer available; only the amended one with my adoptive name could be obtained. My hands were tied. However, ALMA had some search ideas, and one was to try to obtain the original sealed documents, because sometimes mistakes were made and the wrong document sent. There were several adoptees who had had success with this method and were sent their original names. I tried this maneuver first and simply sent a request to the State of New Jersey for a copy of my birth certificate. A week later, I received my birth certificate with my amended name only, Anne Marie Willoughby—I wasn't that lucky.

For those adoptees not initially matched through the database, ALMA recommended contacting the adoption agency to obtain background information. They had various suggestions for ways to maneuver through bureaucracies conditioned to conceal information from those who were searching for birth relatives. Sometimes adoption agencies also mistakenly gave out identifying information, like names or places of residence, with requests for background data. It felt so devious at first when I read how to word letters the right way in order to get information that wasn't supposed to be released, but then again, it was my own information. I had every right to data regarding my birth and my birth relatives.

Within a week, using the wording suggested by ALMA, I drafted a letter asking for background information and mailed it to the adoption agency. I'm not sure why, maybe it was the small glimmer of hope in the pit of my stomach, but I was convinced that this approach would be the key to my finding my birth mother.

Weeks went by without a response, and Saint Patrick's Day approached. The day unfolded with the aroma of corned beef simmering on the kitchen stove. The smell worked its way through the house, traveling up to my bedroom where it woke me up. I rubbed my eyes and remembered the need to wear something green. This posed a challenge. I wasn't particularly fond of the color; however, I did have a special pin depicting a leprechaun given to me by Grandpa. On it was an inscription: "I've got green roots." I fetched it from my jewelry box and laid it conspicuously on my dresser.

Having been raised Irish Catholic and more important, having been in my Irish grandmother's company for the majority of my life gave me a deep sense of pride about my adoptive family's heritage. This pride would shine brilliantly on Saint Patrick's Day when Mom insisted we celebrate the patron saint. It didn't matter if perhaps I wasn't truly Irish. This was the one day where I could be sure deep down within me was that wee bit of Irish Grandma always insisted was present.

I threw on my robe and followed the tantalizing scent downstairs. As I entered the kitchen, Dad greeted me.

"Good morning." He stood in front of the sink washing the morning dishes. An old dishtowel was draped over his left shoulder in anticipation of a quick wipe whenever needed. I'd taken to calling him our own Felix Unger, the anal-retentive character from *The Odd Couple*.

"Good morning," I replied, stifling a yawn.

Dad demanded a proper greeting every day, before anything further was said. "Happy Saint Patrick's Day," he said looking up, temporarily distracted from the frying pan he meticulously scrubbed.

I judged his mood by looking into his dark eyes. They sparkled, a rare sight when he cleaned.

"Why are you cooking so early?"

"Corned beef takes all day," he said, walking over to the stove. He lifted the lid on the stock pot and peered inside. There were three pots puffing out steam, keeping the kitchen warm.

I peeked in one pot and saw the bright red meat with white fat clinging to it and the water bubbling with white foam. Corned beef was the poor American Irishman's holiday food. As immigrants, the Irish could never afford a better piece of meat, and eventually, everyone mistakenly associated corned beef with Ireland and Saint Patrick's Day.

"It looks gross. Why does it have to be boiled?"

"Everybody boils corned beef, you dingy. That's how the Irish cook it."

I laughed. "How would you know? You're Polish."

"I learned a few things from the Murphys."

At my grandpa's home in Upstate New York, I knew Grandpa and Aunt Lorraine were also boiling corned beef on their stovetop.

I took another whiff and headed out of the kitchen. Eyeing the mail from yesterday resting undisturbed on the dining room table, I thumbed through it.

Still no response from the adoption agency.

*   *   *

Later, Matthew and I were upstairs in the spare bedroom which had been converted recently into a small office and den. Dad had his oak rolltop desk and a filing cabinet at one end of the room, and the remainder of the room housed a couch and a television resting on an old maple hope chest once belonging to Dad's mother, Helen. This was our haven where we spent many hours huddled together on the couch wrapped up in a big navy blue afghan watching television.

I'd eaten too many potatoes along with the corned beef and sat stuffed next to Matthew. He was up to his elbows in work. It was tax season, and his accounting firm, one of the big eight, drained every bit of blood from their newly hired college graduates, making them work into the wee hours of the morning. Matthew took his job seriously, rarely complaining.

Matthew's work papers were spread out in front of him, and I curled up into a ball with the afghan thrown over my lap, watching an old movie, *Jane Eyre*. It took him a good half hour before he realized what was on the television.

"How can you watch this stuff?" he asked with a half laugh. "I think *Die Hard*'s playing on channel seven."

"I'm not changing it," I said, grabbing the remote control and tucking it under the blanket. "You're doing work anyway."

Next to me was my notebook where I kept all of my adoption information collected thus far, including the search guide from ALMA.

"Look," I said when a commercial came on. I pulled out the copy of the adoption final decree and waved it in front of his face. "It has my original surname on it, Cusack."

"Anne, you're blocking my papers."

"I know what my original last name was," I repeated.

He looked at me without the slightest bit of interest, shrugged, and returned to his papers.

"Matthew!"

"What?" he said, looking at me and then at the paper in my hand. "Oh, I'm sorry. I was concentrating on an entry. I can't get it to agree. What'd you say?"

"I was trying to tell you something important. I know that my birth mother's last name was Cusack."

"How's that going to help you? She's probably married now with a different name."

"Knowing her last name, even if it's only her maiden name, will get me started." I was getting annoyed. Why couldn't he at least show some interest at my news? I picked up the ALMA guidebook and began flipping furiously through the pages.

"Why are you even bothering? You'll never find her," he said, after glancing at the cover of my guidebook.

"Yes, I will," I said with resolve. Although Matthew was easygoing, a quality I adored, his unceasing pessimistic views routinely came through, something I tolerated against my innate optimistic nature. It seemed his usual pessimism was trying to override my aspirations of a reunion. Did he really want to extinguish any hope I had of ever reuniting with my birth mother?

"I just can't understand why you need to find somebody who's a stranger to you."

"She isn't a stranger; she's my mother … the person who gave birth to me." My face flushed. Matthew's words stung, and I was preparing for an argument, but he was without emotion. "Regardless of whether or not she raised me, I don't consider her a stranger."

He considered my comment.

"Still … I think you're going to complicate things, especially with your mom. She doesn't even like it when you spend Mother's Day with my mother."

It was true; Mom insisted that I spend each Mother's Day only with her. Matthew preferred spending the weekend at his parents' new beach house at the Jersey Shore, but he made the sacrifice, and I appreciated it.

"Well, she certainly won't like the idea of you finding your birth mother," he snapped.

Why was he acting like this? Where was my faithful Matthew? Where was the one person who'd been my rock, my guiding light for the past four and a half years? I sighed. *He's probably all stressed out from working so much,* I thought, calming down. I tried explaining in a cooler tone.

"Matthew, I'm not trying to locate her because I want to complicate things or hurt my parents. I only want to make things less complicated for myself. I need to know why I was placed for adoption. You've always known who your parents are, so you can't begin to comprehend how it feels when you're clueless about how and why you came into this world." It seemed futile. Who could understand my desire but a fellow adoptee? Another point came to mind. "And I need to know my ethnic heritage."

"Why do you need to know that? What's the difference?"

"It must be a pretty big difference—because you're always bragging about being German, especially your father—that's all he ever talks about."

"Well, that and food," he added with a grin.

I could almost see inside Matthew's head, recounting all the stories told by his father about the delicious German food his grandmother once cooked. "So you can't say it's not important knowing your nationality when it's always a hot topic in your own family."

"Yeah … yeah," he muttered and then looked into my eyes. "I still can't see why you want to do this."

Our eyes locked until I suddenly remembered an important point.

"Another thing to consider is that I can find out my medical history. Look at your family and all their medical problems, like heart disease and cancer. Especially your dad—he has so many health problems. My God, he already had two heart attacks and at least you know to watch your cholesterol."

"The adoption agency should be able to tell you about any previous health conditions. You don't have to find her to know your medical history."

"Medical histories need to be updated when new things show up over the years. She might not have had anything at her young age."

"How do you know she was young?"

"That's just my point. I don't know. We want to start a family right away. Don't you think it would be nice to know if there are any genetic diseases on my side? Genetic tests are only done when family members have a history." I spoke with authority. With my degree in health, he couldn't argue with me on this topic.

"Yeah … but still."

"I know you hate to argue with me. But I can't let you off easy this time. I want you to be aware of my plans to actively search. Besides, I need your help. There's a section in the search guide about how to proceed when you know your original surname. They suggest looking through old telephone books from the year you were born."

"Old telephone books?"

"Yes, old telephone books," I repeated. "I found a library in Newark that has every phone book ever published in the United States."

"Really?" he asked, curiously.

"Yeah, really," I said with much anticipation. Maybe he was starting to take my search seriously. "Here's the address, but it's located in a pretty bad section of Newark. I don't want to go there by myself … And anyway, you know how I get lost so easily."

Matthew laughed. He always joked that I could get lost in my own backyard.

"Newark?" he said, shaking his head. "That's almost an hour away."

"I know, but it's the only place in this area with the telephone books I need."

"You're wasting your time looking at old phone books."

"No, I'm not wasting my time," I said defiantly. "I have a feeling she lived around here. And looking through old phone books will tell me where all the Cusacks lived back in 1966. I'm going to check the entire tristate area."

"I still think she was from another state, like California, and only came to Jersey to have you."

"Then if I can't find her name in New Jersey, I'll start checking other states. Anyway, the library has telephone books for the entire country," I explained. "And why do you think she wasn't from New Jersey?"

"I just have a hunch, and I'm usually right. You won't find her by looking through old telephone books," he said with an air of authority as if his statement were fact.

I closed the guidebook and placed it alongside my other things on the couch. There was no point arguing further with him. Whenever we reached a certain point in our few disagreements, we both knew it was useless to venture ahead. We were both stubborn enough that to concede to each other would feel as if we were surrendering a part of ourselves. While most couples would allow these minor impasses to eventually strain a relationship, they only strengthened ours.

But Matthew, on this occasion, conceded to my request.

"Okay," he said more gently. "I don't want you driving there by yourself. It's a dangerous neighborhood. If you want me to take you to Newark, I will."

Eighteen

Pieces of the Puzzle

We made the trip to Newark the Saturday after St. Patrick's Day. It was a warm, rainy day, and the clouds in the sky were dark and menacing, as if warning me to abandon my quest. However, there was nothing that could halt the burning desire within. Ignoring the dark sky, I popped a cassette tape into the car's stereo while we drove along the New Jersey Turnpike and began humming along to "Edelweiss."

"Not *The Sound of Music* again?" Matthew complained.

I smiled. "You know how I love these songs."

I settled back into my seat. The music had its usual calming effect and raised my spirits. He looked my way, shaking his head as if to say I was crazy.

The brownstone library, which housed all the printed telephone books in the history of the United States, was located a few blocks outside of the business district of Newark. By the time we arrived and found a place to park on the street, the rain began to let up. As we walked towards the library, the thick air laced with humidity entered my lungs, leaving an uncomfortable impression on my chest. The hazy sky above seemingly reflected the uncertainties residing within me. I feared Matthew's comments about my birth mother not being from this area might be true. What if she wasn't from New Jersey? What if I found her located in California or the state of Washington? It would be expensive to go there and search. How could I take the time off from my job? Maybe I wouldn't even be able to find her name. What would I do then? The questions tumbled over and over in my mind as we walked through the revolving doors and into the library. Matthew glanced at me smiling and motioned to the rows and rows of books that were spread out over a room almost the size of a football field. The vastness of the room and the amount of information it contained, coupled with the secure way Matthew was holding my hand, reassured me. Any doubts still hovering about faded away. If she wasn't from New Jersey, my search would simply expand. I'd tackle every state and travel there if necessary.

A librarian, seated at a large oak desk by the entrance, directed us to the second floor, last corridor on the right. The corridor was tall and dimly lit. At the far end was a metal rack shelving at least several hundred telephone books, maybe more. It was a gold mine.

Somewhere inside one of those old dusty pages was the name of my mother, the phantom other part of me. Those pages were like a tomb with her named sealed inside, waiting to be unearthed. I scanned the shelves and found the section containing the 1966 phone books.

"Look, Matthew," I said, holding up a 1966 New Jersey Bergen County phone book. "I found one." I also grabbed Passaic County and several other counties in central and northern New Jersey.

"What about the other states? I don't think she was from around here."

"Let's not get into that discussion again. I'm pretty sure she was from New Jersey," I said with confidence. I felt so much better now. The rain had stopped, and my mood brightened along with the sky, which was visible from a nearby window. I took a seat at the table. "Do you wanna help?"

"I might as well."

Matthew sat on the chair next to me and whistled the Frito Bandito tune from a commercial while copying down names, addresses, and phone numbers for every Cusack listed.

"And you have the nerve to make fun of my *Sound of Music* songs!" I said lightly, shaking my head.

"I know," he said smirking.

When we finished, we'd written fewer than two dozen names. I quietly thanked God that my birth mother's last name wasn't Smith or Jones.

*   *   *

A few weeks after my library trip, I returned home from work to find an envelope from the adoption agency. It sat waiting, undisturbed in a pile of mail on the dining room table. I looked around; there was nobody else home. Who had collected the mail and didn't notice this envelope containing a return address screaming the name of the adoption agency? Inside was a two-page letter:

The following is background information about you as taken from your birth mother's file. She was twenty years old when you were born. She was living with her parents; there is no mention of brothers and sisters. She was a high school graduate and trained to be a dancing instructor. She worked for the Steven Knightly Studios. She was of Irish/Spanish background. Her religion was Roman Catholic. She is described as 5'1½" tall, 101 pounds, with black hair, green eyes and a medium complexion. Her health history was good. Your maternal grandfather was forty-nine years old when you were born; he worked as a mechanic, completed grammar school, was a Roman Catholic, and was of Irish/Spanish background. He is described as having dark skin and hair. He had suffered one heart attack. Your maternal grandmother was all Irish, with red hair and blue eyes. She had completed two years of high school and was forty-three years old at your birth. She suffered with a gall bladder condition and stomach ulcer. There is very little information about your birth father, except that he, too, was a professional dance instructor. He worked with your mother at Steven Knightly's. His age was given as twenty-two. He was a high school graduate and had been in the army. He is described as 5'5" tall, a slight build, brown hair, green eyes, and a medium complexion. From his name, he could have been of a Scandinavian background. In addition to dancing, your mother was interested in swimming and horseback riding. She was seeing another young man at this time, who knew about her pregnancy and whom she married after you were placed for adoption, sometime in April 1967. She went to great lengths to hide her pregnancy. Her parents never knew she had you. She spent the latter part of the pregnancy in a maternity home and returned to her family from the hospital. Our records show the following dates: Date of birth, November 13, 1966, Surrender, November 17, 1966, Placed, November 21, 1966, and legal adoption March 3, 1968. There has been no contact from your birth mother since 1966.

My hands shook as I repeated the last sentence in my head: *There has been no contact from your birth mother.* My heart sank. It was true—she had no interest in being reunited. If she did, she would've made at least one inquiry about me over the years.

I retreated to my room with the letter and sat on the edge of my bed. I read it again and again, each time lingering on another part, trying to wrestle some meaning from the words. She was much older than I'd imagined, twenty—an adult, not some teenager! I was twenty-two now, only two years older than she was when she gave me up. When I was twenty, I was still in college and only worked part-time. What would I have done if I'd gotten pregnant?

For me, the answer was easy—I wouldn't give up my baby. Remembering the summer when we had the pregnancy scare and the fact that we had decided to keep our baby, I knew adoption or abortion wasn't even an option. And I'd been a whole year younger! Her situation wasn't much different from what mine had been. I had Matthew, who was going to stand by my side, and this letter said she got married shortly after my birth. So she had somebody too. She wasn't so alone!

The thought lurking in the back of my mind was suddenly overwhelming: *Maybe she hadn't wanted me at all.* This possibility had come up from time to time, but I had never accepted it as being the truth—until now. My naïve notion of her being a young girl of fifteen or sixteen and trapped was far from the truth. She wasn't young after all, but a woman of twenty years who worked and planned to marry someone soon after my birth. If she had wanted me, she could've kept me.

From this letter, I gathered she only wanted to get on with her life and marry this other man. It was obvious he didn't want a baby either.

For first time in my life, I felt betrayed. My existence was nothing more than a mere inconvenience, neatly tucked away in a maternity home and put to rest on the date of surrender, as the letter so blatantly stated.

Surrender.

What a cold term for giving up a baby. It sounded like the end of a long, dragged-out war, not a word to describe what you do with a child. The letter was so impersonal, referring to me as if I was a piece of meat hanging for sale in the butcher's window.

I leaned back against the pillow on my bed, clutching the letter to my chest. My thoughts scared me, and the explanation in the letter was unimaginable. Could this really be true? I wasn't sure. Closing my eyes tightly, I concentrated on my feelings. They were unsettled, shifting between offense at her actions and numbness from being casually tossed aside. But I knew the numbness stemmed from the gnawing thought that she didn't really want me.

Somehow, I couldn't accept this scenario. *No, I won't accept it!* There had to be more to the story. It made no sense that a mother could feel so little emotion toward her own child. *Of course she wanted to have contact with me,* I thought stubbornly. Rather than providing the answers I so desperately needed, the letter further kindled my curiosity.

I read the letter yet another time, hoping somehow I'd missed a name. But none was mentioned. My spirits flagged—I didn't know her first name, her married name, or any other name she might be currently using.

I was on the verge of losing hope, when I focused on the sentence about her marrying in 1967. And it came like a bolt of lightning: Somewhere filed away in a health department was her marriage certificate.

My job as a health inspector was a blessing in disguise. Besides the division governing retail food inspections, there were other areas of the health department, including the division that recorded vital records such as birth, marriage, and death. And I knew how to obtain these records in the state of New Jersey. When my birth mother decided to marry, she first needed to apply for a marriage certificate, and it had to be applied for in the town where the bride resided.

I scanned the letter again. My eyes rested on the information about her working for the Steven Knightly dance studio. There was a possibility she was still employed there, if it still existed. My heart raced inside my chest. I could call the studio and ask if someone knew or had once known a woman with the maiden name of Cusack. It seemed unlikely she'd be at the same location twenty years later, but it was certainly worth a try.

However cold and impersonal the letter, it did provide me with some important information. Along with her maiden name, obtained from the adoption decree, I knew the year and month she married. This new information could be compared to the list I'd gathered of every Cusack living in New Jersey in 1966 from the Newark library. They were spread out in exactly twelve towns. This should be enough information to send for her actual marriage certificate in order to learn her married name. She had to be from one of those towns.

My mind whirled, and I could feel some of the empty space within me start to fill with the new knowledge. It was comforting, if not surprising, to know there was some Irish in me—everyone always told me I looked Irish. But it was amazing to learn about the Spanish part. This threw all my preconceived ideas right out the window.

*   *   *

The next day, I worked up my courage and showed the letter to Mom. Deep inside, I hoped she would support me in the same way Mrs. Compton supported Sharon. She glanced at the letterhead and looked at me inquisitively.

"Go ahead and read it. It's from the agency that placed me for adoption. It has all my background information."

She quickly read the letter.

"Gee," Mom said, looking up. "Maybe you missed your calling to be a dancer."

"I know," I said with a small laugh. "They were both dancers, and I'm a restaurant inspector."

"I told you to stay with the tap and ballet after we moved to Florida," she said with annoyance. To this day, she still held a bit of resentment that her daughter never was a ballerina.

"It's too late now. Anyway, who is this Steven Knightly? I never heard of that dancing school."

"It's a popular school for ballroom dancing. Everybody's heard of Steven Knightly." She handed me the letter and turned her attention back to the newspaper, either uninterested or more likely wanting to avoid the subject altogether.

"I never heard that name before," I persisted.

"He was a famous dancer, like Fred Astaire."

"Well, of course I've heard of Fred Astaire." I pictured him dancing with Ginger Rogers; they floated on air when they danced together. "So what do you think of the letter?" I asked holding my breath.

She shrugged her shoulders. "I don't know," she answered, annoyed. Obviously, this conversation ventured into waters that she didn't wish to cross.

"I wanted to let you know what information I learned so far."

Mom nodded her head and returned her attention to the newspaper.

"Mom," I practically whispered. "Is there anything else you remember about my background that the agency told you?"

I was hoping for a little tidbit, something that might steer me in the proper direction.

She looked up from the newspaper and tilted her head, seemingly contemplating something.

"Like maybe something to do with my medical history. Maybe they forgot to include it in this letter but mentioned it to you at the time." I was also hoping for maybe something related to my actual birth. It was never mentioned, never referred to, only the day they came for me at the special nursery. My life began when I was ten days old.

"Hmm ..." she said, letting out a deep breath. "When you were an infant, you had a hemangioma."

"What's that?"

"It's like a birthmark, but it's red and it was on your private parts," she said motioning her head down towards her lap. "We had it removed."

I thought for a moment.

"Doesn't Maggie have something like that on her shoulder?"

Ever since I could remember, there was a large red patch in the shape of a figure eight on Maggie's shoulder. Intrigued by its unusual color and shape, I always yearned for a special mark on my body and now wished my mark was back. It felt like some sort of a special bond between my cousin and me.

"Yes, but Maggie's is a birthmark. It's flat. A hemangioma is raised."

I nodded.

"Aunt Lorraine was going to have Maggie's removed, but she never did. Yours was quite large."

"How did they remove it?" I asked, wondering what on earth this birthmark looked like.

"They used some kind of laser. It was no big deal. Hemangiomas are harmless and usually go away on their own, but the pediatrician thought it should be removed since it never started to resolve. There isn't anything else, just the hemangioma." She returned her attention back to the newspaper and briskly turned to the next page.

*　　　*　　　*

That evening, I began drafting requests for copies of marriage certificates addressed to the twelve health departments. Before finishing, I realized this Steven Knightly studio, if it was as famous as Mom said, must still exist. I opened a current phone book. Quickly flipping through the pages, I saw three listings in Bergen County for Steven Knightly, each in a different town. I also had a Passaic County phone book, and again, there were more studios listed. It was shocking that this particular dance studio was so popular, and yet I'd never heard the name. *It must be a chain,* I thought, copying all the phone numbers for the studios into my notebook. After a moment, I decided to call one of them. Why not? It seemed more of a long shot now that there were so many studios. She could have worked for any one of them. Even though it was highly unlikely she'd still be there today, I dialed the number of the first one on the list anyway, a studio in Goshen.

An older woman answered.

"Hello," I began. "I'm trying to locate a friend of my mother's who worked at Steven Knightly in 1966." I paused, trying to think of what to say next. "Would you happen to remember a girl by the last name of Cusack who was a teacher at the time?"

There was silence on the other end of the line. Then I heard her mutter "hmm" in the earpiece, apparently trying to remember the name.

"Sorry," she finally said. "The name doesn't ring a bell with me. Anyway, I began in the 1970s, and I never heard of anyone with that last name."

"Thank you anyway." I hung up, feeling completely discouraged.

The next studio on my list was in Livingston, but I didn't place the call. This was a waste of time. There were too many dance studios, and I was sure the instructors came and went. Besides, it was more than twenty years since she'd last worked there. It was more likely she'd stopped working after her marriage, especially if she had a couple of kids. The people working at these studios today wouldn't know her.

Returning to my original idea, I diligently finished the task of drafting the letters to the health departments, explaining that I was doing genealogy research and needed to locate a distant cousin's marriage certificate. I stated that only her maiden name was known and sent the exact same letter to all twelve towns along with a prayer to God.

*   *   *

In the meantime, there were other pressing matters—my upcoming wedding. The date was less than a year away, and Mom nagged about finding a florist and a wedding gown. I spent many weekends dropping by bridal stores until finally deciding on wearing my mother's own gown. Packed away after her wedding in 1960, her gown was preserved beautifully. The once bright white color had faded evenly to a lovely ivory. It was difficult imagining Mom wearing this size-eight dress on her wedding day; she wore an eighteen lately, always struggling with her weight. We took her wedding gown to a local seamstress who took it in four inches, in order to fit my size-four petite frame, and added extra lace to the sleeves and train, making it more modern.

Another item was removed from my wedding planning list. The next thing I wanted to tackle was the honeymoon.

"Anne, whatever you want," Matthew told me, eyeing a pile of brochures I'd picked up at the local travel agency.

"I was thinking maybe Bermuda or even Hawaii," I said sighing. "But I always dreamed of going to England." I remembered Jane Austen's, *Emma* and *Pride and Prejudice*, my current favorite books, which I'd read at least half a dozen times each. They were both set in the English countryside. "Wouldn't it be nice to see London and all those old castles?" I said dreamily. "Oh," I said flipping through the pile. "Look. Here's a charming place in Killarney, Ireland. It's an old castle converted into a hotel."

Matthew looked up at me and smiled.

"We can go there if you want—both England and Ireland."

I threw my arms around his neck and planted a big kiss on each of his cheeks before giving him a longer one on his expectant mouth.

*   *   *

The happy wedding atmosphere that persisted for months and months abruptly halted when one summer night, Thomas never returned to his apartment. Shelley waited for him all night, sitting in his living room alone. The next day, she showed up at our front door in tears. Dad looked everywhere for him: his job, which he failed to show up for; his friends' apartments; the local hospitals in case he was in an accident; and finally, the local pubs he frequented with Shelley. He was nowhere to be found. Shelley told my parents the wedding was off. There was no way she was going to marry someone so inconsiderate of her feelings. Mom was speechless; she didn't know what to say or what to do. For the second time in my life, I watched her cry. Three days later, rather nonchalantly, Thomas showed up at his apartment. He wouldn't disclose his whereabouts, not even to Shelley, and not wanting to confront him about his behavior, my parents only expressed relief that he returned.

"Maybe it's just pre-wedding jitters," Mom suggested.

Thomas swore he'd never do it again. Shelley reacted the same way as my parents, never demanding an explanation, quickly forgiving him. The wedding was back on for December as planned.

But I decided to at least try to see what was going on with him.

"I'm worried about you," I said a few weeks later. He'd stopped by the house one afternoon to borrow some tools, and already, I could smell the liquor on his breath. "Do you think maybe you should see someone about your drinking?"

"Anne, don't worry. I can handle it. I'm not an alcoholic," he said grinning. "Come on ... I can stop whenever I want to."

*   *   *

By summer's end, Thomas and Shelley were blissfully happy again. They finished arranging the last details of their wedding and made an offer on a house. They closed by late September and moved in together the following week. It was a cute little colonial with a screened-in porch on the side and a new country kitchen overlooking a pool in the backyard. They eagerly awaited their wedding day, only three months away. As for me, my wedding gown and honeymoon plans were completed, but my search for my origins had stalled. Thus far, I'd received eight replies to the letters sent requesting a marriage certificate: All were negative. They didn't have any record of a Cusack marrying in April of 1967. Rather than leaving me dispirited, each negative response only further steeled my determination. If need be, I'd redirect the search. There had to be a way to find my biological family.

Nineteen

Telephone Calls

By the time fall arrived, I'd received the responses from the remaining four health departments, and they too were negative except for the one from the City of Bayonne. The Bayonne letter simply stated that they didn't keep marriage applications on the premises. I read it over, disappointed, then didn't give it more thought—until I remembered something the registrar at my health department told me. She said records from years past were typically filed away and a nuisance to search. No doubt the registrar from Bayonne didn't want to make the effort to look, since the record was from more than twenty years ago, probably buried deep in a storage room.

So I decided to write back. This time, I sent my letter in an envelope stamped with a return address from Edgewood's health department. In an amicable yet straightforward tone, I explained the marriage application should be available and asked the registrar to look for it once more. I stressed the information was needed to complete a branch in my family genealogy. This wasn't a complete lie; the information would help to complete a part of my family tree, but it was the trunk I was seeking, not a branch.

*　　　　*　　　　*

It was a Tuesday afternoon late in October 1989. The day was unseasonably warm. I hurried out of my car and jogged up the driveway through the fallen leaves. They crunched like crackers beneath the soles of my shoes. Sliding off my jacket, I dashed to the mailbox. There was an envelope with a return address from the City of Bayonne. I didn't expect a response so quickly, thinking the registrar would be vexed at my having made a second request for the same information.

I snatched it from the pile and stuffed it inside my purse.

"Hi, Mom, I'm home," I called out, entering through the front door. I dropped the rest of the mail on the dining room table.

"How was work?" she asked. She was sitting on the recliner in the family room, still in her white nurse's uniform.

"It was all right," I answered. "No restaurants were closed down today."

"Don't forget, we're going to the store after dinner."

I'd forgotten all about our plans to go to the mall that evening. The next month, I was attending a friend's wedding and needed to buy a dress.

"Oh yeah ... can we go tomorrow night instead?"

"If you don't get a dress soon, you'll have nothing nice to wear. You can't wait till the last minute. What if it needs to be altered?"

"Okay ... we'll go."

Heart pounding, I trotted upstairs with the swiftness of a thoroughbred. In my room, door closed behind me, I tore open the envelope from Bayonne like a child on Christmas morning opening presents. Inside was a short typewritten letter:

> *Dear Ms. Willoughby: After searching for some information for you on the name of Cusack, there was a Josephine Cusack who applied for a marriage license in February of 1967. Her address was listed as 215 Washington Ave., Bayonne, N.J. Enclosed you will find your check which I am returning to you. Wishing you good luck in your research, I hope I have been a little bit of help.*

I reread the letter to make sure I wasn't dreaming. Had I actually pinpointed the town where she'd lived at the time of my birth—and was this her first name? If so, the search process was unfolding much faster than anticipated. I sat at the foot of my bed, letter in hand as my eyes returned to her name typed in bold black ink. Slowly, I traced the letters with my finger, whispering the name, trying to incorporate each syllable into my mind, *Josephine Cusack*.

Now I knew the full name of the person who'd given me life. The information received about the wedding date was wrong. She married in February, not April. The next logical step was to check the current phone book to see if someone in her family still lived at the same address. Although it was wishful thinking, I went over to my bookshelf, bulging with all the search guides, telephone books, and notebooks, and opened the most recent one.

Quickly thumbing through the pages, I saw four Cusacks listed, including a T. Cusack at the same address shown in the Bayonne letter.

"This is too good to be true!" I said out loud, grabbing the notebook containing all the collected search data. I looked at the page of names copied from the old telephone books from the Newark library. Listed first was a T. Cusack from Bayonne, also at the same address. How ironic—the information needed was listed first in my notebook. Since her family still resided at the same address, I figured there shouldn't be a problem locating her. She must see them on a regular basis.

I sat down on my bed, closed my eyes, and focused on this new revelation. A thought flashed through my mind. Perhaps I should just pick up the phone right now and call their house. This search could only proceed through her family, because only her maiden name was provided in the letter from the registrar. But what would I say? The adoption agency stated she'd kept me a secret from her family. I couldn't just call up and say, "Here I am." That would be shocking! The decision to inform them about my existence was hers, not mine.

What I needed was a pretext for calling, something that wouldn't give away my identity. I contrived a story, an honest way to deal with her family. I picked up the telephone, dialed the number, and held my breath. After several rings, no one had answered. Perhaps they were shopping or still at work. I put the letter from Bayonne in my notebook and concealed it back on my bookshelf.

After changing from my work clothes into a fresh pair of jeans and a light cotton sweater, I headed downstairs, but the last thing I was thinking about was shopping.

The clocks had been turned back an hour the weekend before, marking the end of daylight savings, and darkness was already falling by the time we arrived at the mall. We browsed through the petite section at Lord & Taylor's department store, and I quickly found a purple silk suit. Mom was looking through an adjacent rack, and I held it up for her to see.

"What do you think of this one?"

"It looks nice," she said, quickly looking the suit up and down, her face scrunched as she scrutinized my selection.

"I'll try it on," I said, heading to the dressing rooms.

It fit perfectly; no alterations were needed. Walking over to the cashier, I noticed Mom wandering off.

"Where are you going?" I asked, as my heart dropped. I knew exactly where she was going. She wanted to keep shopping and browse through everything!

She pointed towards the women's department.

"Don't rush me," she snapped. "I want to look around a bit more."

It was obvious we weren't going to be leaving soon, so after paying for the suit, I waited near a group of elegantly dressed mannequins posed in various positions. The blank expression on each face was a haunting reminder of the uncertainty waiting for me when I returned home. As eager as I was to make the call, another part of me wasn't quite sure as those same old insecurities resurfaced. Would she be happy when she realized I was searching for her?

Mom eventually made her way over to where I was sitting. Apparently, she wasn't able to find anything.

"Do you want to go over to Paramus Park Mall?" she asked.

"Noo," I practically whined, "I wanna get home and try to call Matthew at the hotel. He's in St. Louis on business for the entire week, and I need to talk with him."

"All right. We'll go home," she sighed heavily.

It was pitch dark outside as we silently drove home along Route 17. There were butterflies in my stomach as I scanned the radio stations in search of a suitable song to take my mind off of the upcoming call. Only commercials and news warning of incoming thunderstorms were currently being broadcasted. As soon as the car pulled up to the curb, I jumped out and headed for the front door. Mom called out, and I spun around and saw her waving my shopping bag. She looked puzzled as I darted back to the car, grabbed the bag, and rushed to get inside.

"Anne, you better hang it up right away or the suit will get wrinkled," she called out.

"I will. Don't worry," I said as I ran into the house.

I dashed upstairs to my bedroom, dropped the bag on the floor, and immediately dialed the Cusacks, not taking the time to call the hotel to consult Matthew first.

In my haste, I didn't even rehearse what to say, and before I'd thought of an opening line, someone answered the phone on the first ring.

"Hi, could I please speak to a Josephine Cusack?" I asked in a shaky voice.

"No, there's no Josephine living here." It was a woman with an accent.

"Would you happen to have the number where she's living?"

"No, Mrs. Cusack hasn't seen her daughter Jo in over twenty years," she answered. "I'm Mrs. Cusack's nurse aide."

Twenty years! I didn't know what to say next. If this was true, locating my birth mother would be as likely as finding a needle in a haystack.

"Umm …" I thought quickly. "Do you know where she's living? You see … my mother worked with her years ago at the dance studio, and I'm trying to locate her."

An old woman was mumbling in the background. That must be the voice of my grandmother.

"Who is it, Tammy?" she repeated several times.

"Somebody looking for your daughter."

"My name is Anne Marie Willoughby."

"Her name is Willoughby," she yelled to the old woman.

"That name doesn't sound familiar," I heard her say.

There was an overwhelming urge to blurt out my real identity, the long-lost child of her daughter, but though it pained me to lie, the words didn't escape my lips. At any rate, the prospect of contacting my birth mother didn't look too promising, given that her own family hadn't seen her in more than twenty years.

"Hold on," Tammy said. I could hear them both talking in the background but couldn't make out what they were saying. After a moment, she returned to the phone. "I think she still has a letter Jo's son sent a few years ago. I'm pretty sure it's around here somewhere. She never throws anything out." She laughed.

I laughed along nervously.

"Let me call you back. I'll go look for it now."

"Okay, great." I gave her my name again and my phone number.

I sat on my bed, bouncing my knees up and down and prayed for the return call. The telephone remained beside me, and I found myself staring at it for a full ten minutes as if it would disappear if I dared look away. It felt as though this whole evening so far had been a dream. Surely it had to be; after all, I had discovered my birth mother's full name and heard my grandmother's voice. I was numb.

Reality started to come back when I heard Mom calling for me from downstairs.

"Anne, what are you doing up there?"

I dashed to my door, flung it open, and went to the top of the stairs.

"Nothing … I'm just waiting for Matthew to call back. I haven't spoken with him yet. He was in a meeting," I answered loudly, not wanting to go downstairs in case the phone should happen to ring.

She didn't say anything else, so I quickly returned to my room, closing the door behind me. The inside of my head began swimming with worries. Tammy still hadn't called. Maybe she couldn't find the letter. Without it, how could she ever tell me the address? Before despair had a chance to creep its way in, I thought of Grandma. What would she do if she were in my shoes right now? The answer quickly came—she'd be sitting here thumbing her rosary beads and praying to Saint Jude. Too bad I wasn't as devoted to the Catholic faith as she was—not that I couldn't have used a set of rosary beads; anything would've helped. I turned and looked again at the silent telephone perched on my bed. *A watched kettle doesn't boil,* I heard Grandma say in her knowing tone. I turned my eyes away from the phone. *She'll call ... she'll call ...* I kept telling myself but still fretted as I plopped back down on the bed.

After another ten minutes, I got to my feet and swept across my bedroom over to the bookshelf where I kept all my search materials. Thumbing through the pages of the ALMA search guide, I idly looked through the list of search suggestions pondering what my next move could be, just in case. It was obvious the only recourse left was to send a request to Bayonne for the marriage certificate. The document would include her married name, a fact I still didn't know. For an entire hour, I remained there on the bed, contemplating other ways to pursue this search, and *still* no phone call from Tammy. Unable to wait any longer, I dialed the home again. Tammy answered after the first ring and didn't seem annoyed. What was the right protocol for such things? Perhaps I should've waited until the next day, giving her more time to locate the letter. But there was no way I could sleep without first hearing from Tammy.

She sounded chipper, saying she was glad to hear from me because she had already forgotten to return my call. Then she told me she couldn't find the letter.

My heart plunged.

"Don't worry," she said sensing my despair. "I remember it was postmarked from a town called Mountaindale, New Jersey."

"Mountaindale," I repeated. "Do you know where it is?"

"I think it's located out west, near Route 80."

"Oh ... okay," I said appreciatively. "Thanks so much for your help. My mom really wants to get in contact with everybody for the reunion," I added, remembering what I initially told her my purpose was for contacting Mrs. Cusack's daughter.

"Was she a good friend of Jo's?"

"Yes, my mother knew Jo from the dance studio, and she attended her wedding back in 1967. Uh ..." I hesitated. "What was the name of the man she married again?"

"Umm ... hold on. What's Jo's husband's name?" I overheard her call out to Mrs. Cusack.

"Crowley, Richard Crowley. That guy ..." I couldn't make out what else she said.

Tammy got back on the line and told me the name. I didn't press for any more information. "Thanks again for your help."

After hanging up, I scribbled "Richard Crowley" on a piece of paper. Wow! Now I knew her married name and her husband's full name. I wasn't sure which county Mountaindale was in, so without delay, I dialed 411 for directory assistance. This was all happening so fast, and my heart was pounding against my chest. When the operator answered, I asked for a listing for either a Josephine or a Richard Crowley in Mountaindale.

The operator hesitated and then said in a monotone voice, "I'm sorry but that is an unlisted number. It isn't available to the public."

I could have screamed. Just when I thought I'd finally found her, she was yanked away as quickly as she had come. My heart, having soared at the prospect of locating her tonight, plunged again. Why did she have to have an unlisted number?

"But there is a listing under the name Crowley?" I persisted.

"I'm sorry, but I can't give out that information."

I thanked her and slowly put the receiver down. Tammy was right. They were living in Mountaindale. Despondent, I dialed Matthew's hotel room, desperately needing to speak to someone, but the answering machine clicked on.

What a night, I thought as my head whirled from so much activity. It was overwhelming, and I really needed to speak with someone. But besides Matthew, who wasn't available at the moment, there wasn't anybody else. I felt so alone.

Twenty

Bridging the Gap

Suddenly I thought of Janine. *Why in God's name didn't I think of her before?* I chastised myself. She too was in the know about my search.

She answered right away.

"Hey, what's up?"

"You'll never believe it."

"What? Tell me!" she said excitedly.

"I think I may be able to find my birth mother. Can you believe it?! I know her name, the full married name she goes by today."

I told her about the call to my grandmother's house and how I found out about my birth mother's married name.

"Have you tried calling her yet?" she asked.

"I can't. She has an unlisted number."

"Hmm … Why don't you call the police department? They can find her address and phone number easily, especially with a full name."

"Would they do that for anyone?"

"Probably not," she answered. "You need to know someone who works there. Do you know anybody?"

"No." I sighed. Then it came to me. "Janine, let me go. I think there's way to actually talk to her tonight. I'll call you back," I said, hanging up before she could utter another word. Remembering a story a colleague told me at work some time ago about how an operator was allowed to call the residence of an unlisted number in cases of an emergency, I quickly dialed zero.

"May I help you?"

"Yes, I need to speak to my mother immediately, and I lost her new number. It's unlisted. Can you please make an emergency call and give her my phone number so she can call me back?" The words came out so fast I was afraid she wouldn't understand me.

"Okay," she answered. "But all I can do is leave your name and number. I can't put you through to her."

"That's fine." I gave her my name, phone number, and the name of Richard or Josephine Crowley from Mountaindale.

"Hold on ... I don't have a listing for a ... What did you say the first name was again?" she asked.

"It's Richard or Josephine."

"Yes, I have a listing for an R. Crowley. I'll call and leave the message now."

"Thank you." I slid down from my seat on the bed and hung up the phone. There on the floor, with the phone directly in front of me, I started waiting—again convinced this time the phone would ring. And indeed it did. After about five minutes—the proverbial eternity—I was jolted to my knees by the jangling noise. I snatched the receiver up, trying not to panic.

"Can I speak to an Anne Marie?" a boy's voice said.

"Yes, speaking."

"I just got a message from the operator to call you."

"Yes, I need to speak to Josephine Crowley."

"She's not home," he stated with a finality that would surely squelch any hope of my talking to her.

"I need to speak to her now. It's an emergency," I exclaimed, edging on despair. I didn't want to frighten him, but it was crucial that he not toss the message aside, because I couldn't depend on another operator being willing to connect me again.

"Is it bad?" he asked, his voice cracking.

"No ... it's not bad," I answered in a reassuring voice. "But I do need to speak to her right away."

"I can call her and have her call you right back," he offered.

"That would be great. Thank you."

I'd just spoken with my half brother. I wondered if he knew about me, his sister. Perhaps he was an only child. Well, I'd find out soon enough. For the third time, I found myself waiting. Everything was happening so quickly. It felt like going for a ride down a rushing stream with no control of the speed or the current. My throat was raw, but I didn't dare leave my room for water in fear of missing the call. Crouching down, I stared at the phone, and within a minute, it rang. A chill went down my spine. What would I say? Quickly, I snatched up the phone.

"Anne Marie Willoughby, please." A man's voice was on the other end.

"Speaking," I said slowly.

"This is Richard Crowley, her husband. Can I help you?" he asked, rather straightforwardly. He seemed a bit perturbed and in a hurry to wrap up this minor inconvenience as quickly as possible.

"Yes," I answered him. "I need to speak to Josephine Crowley."

"Can't I help you with something?"

"No," I said firmly. "I need to speak to her directly."

"What's this in reference to?"

"It's personal."

"She's busy at the moment." His voice lightened. "Can she call you back in about twenty minutes, sweetheart?"

I sighed deeply. "Yes, that's fine."

What else could I say? I wanted to shout, "No ... no! Please tell her I need to speak with her now!" This whole waiting game was torture. I hung up the phone and hugged my knees to my chest, rocking back and forth. It was hard to envision speaking with her. She was beyond reach, like an image in a 3-D show, seemingly real but can't be touched. Now I'd not only heard her mother's voice, but I also spoke with her son and her husband. Everyone in her family was easily accessible this evening, everyone but her. If only she would call!

I glanced at my watch and saw fifteen minutes had elapsed. All our years of separation came rushing back. The pit of my stomach ached to hear her voice, and especially ached to be able to get a chance to know my original mother. My dream of finding her would soon be fulfilled.

After a half hour, panic started to set in. She wasn't going to call. Maybe Richard hadn't given her the message. And if he had, perhaps my mysterious call to her coupled with the unrecognizable name was enough for her to suspect who it was—her long-lost daughter. Maybe she didn't want to talk to me. That thought brought tears to my eyes.

And then, just as I was beginning to lose all hope, the phone rang. I nearly jumped out of my skin.

"Hello?" I answered breathlessly.

"Can I speak to Anne Marie?" a woman's voice asked tentatively.

"This is she."

"I don't think I know you." Her words came out slowly.

"You did at one time," I said then paused and cleared my throat. I could hear her breathing on the other end of the line.

There was a brief hesitation, and I racked my brains trying to come up with something else to say, but my mind was blank.

And finally, she said in a soft voice, "I had a feeling it was you. What's your full name? The message I received from my son doesn't make much sense."

"It's Anne Marie Willoughby," I said slowly and then quickly added, "Are you upset that I contacted you?"

I held my breath.

"Of course not … I'm happy you contacted me." She sighed deeply. "I had a feeling it was you when I first heard your voice, because it sounds a little like mine." I could hear music playing in the background. "Where do you live?" she asked.

"In Wyckoff … It's in New Jersey."

"I know Wyckoff. Richard's brother lived there many years ago."

"I still live at home with my parents, and I'm engaged. I'll be getting married this coming June."

"Oh, you're getting married," she said in a long sigh.

"Yes, my fiancé is named Matthew. We've been together for five years."

"That's so wonderful. And your birthday is on the thirteenth next month?" she asked cautiously.

"Yes."

She sighed again. "What do you look like?"

"My eyes are blue-green and my hair is sort of brown with a lot of red highlights."

"Blue eyes! I have two babies with blue eyes," she said softly.

I was at a loss for words. She referred to me as her baby. All along I'd thought of her as my birth mother, the person who brought me into this world. I'd never considered it the other way around, that I was her baby. Luckily, she continued talking. She said I had a brother named Matthew who was sixteen, the one I'd spoken with earlier. Also, there was Sara who was nineteen and Jessica who was four and a half.

Sisters!

At last, my childhood prayer was answered, and now there wasn't just one, but two. She went on to describe them. Sara had reddish-brown hair with green eyes, and Jessica was a true redhead with blue eyes. My brother, Matthew, had strawberry-blonde hair with green eyes. Now I knew where my red highlights came from.

I sat perfectly still on my bedroom floor, trying to determine if this was a dream. It was too hard to believe that I was actually on the telephone with my mother!

She began to talk about my birth father. I hung on every word.

"His name is Sam Kohlpann, but I'm sorry, I know very little about him. We worked together at the Steven Knightly dance studio in Hoboken. We were both ballroom dance instructors, but we were only friends. We never had a relationship." She paused. "You came to be from one night we spent together. You see ... I had a bit too much to drink."

"Ooooh," was all I could manage to say.

So, I was the result of a one-night stand. The news was unnerving and didn't come close to my earlier preconceptions. They weren't a poor couple living on the streets; nor were they teenagers. Instead, they were adults about my age who hadn't bothered with the consequences of their actions. Even though my earlier presumptions were wrong, elation that I found her overrode any other emotion.

"I never told Sam I was pregnant with you," she went on. "I didn't think it was fair to drag him into this, since we had no relationship."

"So my father doesn't know about me?" I asked, quite overwhelmed at this disclosure.

"No, he has no idea."

I mustered another, "Oh."

"When you were born, he wasn't living here anymore, so I couldn't have told him anyway." She paused, perhaps waiting for me to say something. Again, it wasn't what I expected, having assumed they both made the decision to place me for adoption.

She continued, "During the summer before you were born, Sam left the studio and we lost contact. So even if I had decided to tell him about you after the birth, he wasn't around and I had no way to contact him," she said defensively as if she had just read my thoughts. "I think he went back to where he was originally from, New Mexico."

"He wasn't from New Jersey?"

"No, I remember he mentioned going to school here, but he was from another state. I have no idea where he is today."

The news was deeply disappointing. How in the world was I going to track him down in New Mexico or wherever he was? The possibility of reuniting with him seemed hopeless.

"Do you know his ethnic background?" I asked.

"To tell you the truth, we never talked about those things."

I asked her how to spell his last name, and as she told me the spelling, I jotted it down on a piece of paper. Looking at his name, I thought a moment.

"Was my father Jewish?"

"No ... no, I'm sure he wasn't."

"I'm only asking because the last name sounds Jewish, especially the first half, the Kohl."

"I always thought it was German. It sounds German to me. No, he couldn't have been Jewish. I distinctly remember one time we all ate bacon together one morning at the studio. One of the teachers, a girl about my age, was Jewish and was insulted it was present. Sam didn't say anything, and I think he would've said something if he was Jewish." Her words tumbled out quickly, one right after the other.

There was a certain amount of defensiveness on her part about my suggesting he could be Jewish, but her explanation sounded reasonable. The adoption agency did say the name could have denoted a Scandinavian background. I wasn't an expert on names and their origins, but the name could be researched.

"My family's Catholic," she said. "The last time I was in their company was the week before my wedding to Richard, more than twenty years ago. My mother found out about your birth a week after I arrived home from the hospital."

"So your mother knows about me?" Since she seemed so willing to talk, I grabbed a notepad and began scribbling down information.

"Yes. At the time, she claimed she happened upon a bill left in my room. But I had a feeling she must've known all along while I was pregnant, or at least suspected. But she never confronted me with her suspicions, not until after I was home and my baby was gone." The line crackled. "My mother was more upset about me getting married to Richard than having been pregnant. Richard proposed the same week I arrived home."

"You became engaged right after you gave birth to me?"

"Yes, uh ..." she stuttered. "Richard proposed on Thanksgiving. Immediately after I accepted, I told him we should try to get my baby back since we were getting married but Richard said we couldn't do that to the parents who adopted you. It wouldn't be fair."

She hesitated, perhaps waiting for me to agree. I didn't say a word. My mind raced with this information. The letter from the adoption agency was true. She did get married right away. How could she claim to be unable to take care of me when she was getting married?

She continued, "And Richard, well ... he wasn't your father."

Was she trying to make an excuse for him? *Yes, it's true,* I said to myself. *Richard wasn't my father but I was your baby.* I almost dropped the phone.

"My mother liked Richard before we became engaged, but ..." She sighed heavily. "Immediately afterwards, she was against the marriage. Richard is part Italian, and she's terribly prejudiced against every nationality except, of course, her own, the Irish."

"Isn't your father part Spanish? The letter I received from the adoption agency said he was Spanish."

"Yes, actually he's half Cuban. The other half is German. I never understood why my mother married him, when all she ever did was make comments against every other race. She once told me that her own parents were very suspicious of my father. She told them that he was dark Irish; otherwise, they wouldn't have allowed her to marry him."

She fell silent as I continued jotting down the facts. I wasn't saying much, just interjecting an occasional *uh-huh* or *hmmm*.

"You see," she went on, "my mother's family was all Irish. They were from Hoboken. My grandfather, Peter Keenan, worked for the Hoboken Fire Department. It was a very prestigious job at the time. The red hair came from him. His color was considered strawberry blond. My mother was also a redhead, like her father. My brother takes after this side of the family, while I resemble the other side," she explained. "My father's name was Charles, and he had black hair like mine. His father was from Cuba, and his last name was Vidal. I never met him. He died when my father was four years old."

I was still on the floor, sitting with my legs curled beneath me, beginning to feel numb. Still jotting down facts, I got up and sat on the edge of my bed.

She continued without a pause, "Apparently, my grandfather was a witness to a mob crime and was under the witness protection program. He was staying in a jail cell for his own safety. They found him one morning hung by the sheets from his cot, but they didn't think it was suicide. They were sure it was a hit, but it was never proved. The case was reported in all the newspapers at the time. After his death, my father's maternal grandmother raised him, even though his mother, Sophie, was alive. She never took responsibility to raise her own son. That's why my maiden name was Cusack instead of Vidal. I think my grandmother adopted my father, or he just went by her last name or something like that. I'm not really sure."

All of this spilled out of her mouth without hesitation. I couldn't believe she was being so candid and revealing so many intimate details about her family—really my family too. The music still played in the background, and my curiosity overcame me.

"Where are you?" I interrupted. "I hear music playing."

"Oh," she said laughing, "I'm at work at the studio. I teach ballroom dancing. The music you hear is a mixture of songs to the beat of the cha-cha. Another teacher has a group class going on now; mine ended right before I called you."

So she still teaches ballroom dancing, I thought, wanting to kick myself for not having called more studios.

"Anne ... would you like to meet me in person?" she asked cautiously.

"Yes, I'd love to," I answered right away. "I'm dying to see what you look like."

"My hair is black, and my eyes are green. I'm not tall, just over five feet."

"I'm not too tall either." I laughed. "Only five feet." I hopped off the bed and stood in front of the mirror over my dresser. I peered at my image, trying to imagine myself with black hair.

"Everyone in my family is on the small side," she explained. "Your father, Sam, wasn't tall either." She paused. "Why don't we meet this Friday? It's the only day I'll be able to get a sitter to stay with Jessica. Maybe we could meet in the afternoon for lunch."

"Friday would be fine with me," I said happily. "Where do you want to meet?"

"I'm familiar with the Garden State Plaza Mall, and I know there are some restaurants there. Does that sound okay for you?"

"Yes, that would be fine."

"I'll call you Thursday night to confirm the time and restaurant."

"Great, talk to you then."

After I hung up, all was still in the house except for my thoughts, which were racing. I'd spoken with my birth mother! At last I had found my origins, and as intricate as they were—and disappointing—they were mine, unique to me.

Feeling self-assured, I heaved a big sigh until it hit me like a brick in the face—I didn't have her phone number! She had inundated me with information about herself and her family, and in the midst of the deluge, I had forgotten to ask for it. What if she didn't call me back? I considered it for a moment. No, she had my number. She brought up the idea about us meeting in person. She'd call.

More than anything, what elated me was our upcoming meeting, just three days away. We were going to see each other in person. I was convinced we must look exactly the same, except for the color of our hair. I was deliriously happy and could hardly wait until Friday.

As I pulled my nightgown over my head, the phone rang again. It was now past midnight, and everyone was in bed except for me and my dog Shannon, who had wandered into my room and was lying loyally at my feet. It was Matthew. In a whisper, I frantically told him my news.

"Who is this?" he interrupted.

"Matthew! It's me," I said, trying to curb my excitement so I didn't wake up the entire house. "I'm whispering because everyone else is sleeping. I'm serious. I found her."

"Come on," he said incredulously. "There's no way you could have found her already."

"Believe me, I'm not making this up." I described the conversation with my birth mother from start to finish while he remained silent. "What do you think?" I asked eagerly.

"I don't know," he said slowly. I could almost hear his mind tallying the information. "I never imagined you'd find her this quickly."

"I know," I said proudly. "It took less than six months."

Adoptees normally take years to dig up information, and many are never able to locate their birth parents, even after years of searching.

"Isn't it great?" I asked, still feeling giddy.

"I guess so."

I guess so? I repeated to myself. I expected more from him, at least a little excitement. Where was my Matthew?

"You don't sound too thrilled," I said disappointed.

"I'm sorry. I'm tired. I can't think straight right now. I'll call you tomorrow night."

I was tired too, mentally exhausted, but I'd still find some enthusiasm if he'd just told *me* similar news. My elation was slowly being chipped away by his jaded reaction. Why did he have to be so negative? I felt blood fill my face, and I wanted to shout at him to at least be happy—for my sake.

After hanging up the phone, I crawled under my bedcovers. Already I was calming down and wasn't as mad at Matthew. *He probably was just very tired from being overworked and from being out of town,* I assured myself. I closed my eyes but couldn't sleep. Suddenly, I felt wide awake and my heart swelled with apprehension: How was I going to tell my parents about all of this?

The thought had never crossed my mind the entire evening. I sat up in bed and stared out the window into the darkness. There was a waning moon hanging low in the sky partially covered in a misty haze. Mom wouldn't be too happy with the news—that fact alone was certain. I still remembered how she'd reacted ten years earlier when Sharon and I read the letter from the adoption agency. She'd been livid and didn't even want to discuss any possibility of ever finding my birth mother. All I could do was picture her sullen face and cool attitude over the years whenever this topic was mentioned. Maybe I should wait awhile before telling them. Maybe I shouldn't tell them at all. But that was ridiculous. There was nothing to be ashamed of, to feel guilty about. I was an adopted child with a burning desire to discover her origins. What was wrong with that? I'd tell them in the morning. Honesty was always the best approach.

Twenty-One

Uncharted Waters

The next morning, I woke up early to a cool breeze coming through the window. The air carried the dry, bracing smell of autumn, and outside, the trees, already bare of their leaves, swayed stiffly back and forth.

The previous evening had taken a toll on me. Weary and anxious over how all this would work out, I got into the shower and let the hot water run down my back. My birth mother's voice echoed in my head. She sounded so happy, almost relieved, to talk with me. But I had a hunch that her reaction wasn't all that positive. I couldn't quite put my finger on it.

I couldn't eat breakfast—My stomach was tied in knots. Lunch evaded me as well. Later that day, when I returned from work, Mom was watching television in the family room.

"Anne?" she called out, hearing me enter through the front door.

Deep down, I knew what had to be done, Mom needed to be told. I breathed in a long, deep breath and slowly let it out as I walked towards the family room.

"Yeah, it's me," I answered, setting down my purse on the dining room table.

Mom was sprawled out on the couch and had already changed into her favorite light blue housecoat. Her feet were resting comfortably on the coffee table. She looked up at me.

"Make yourself a TV dinner," she said. "I'm not cooking tonight."

"Actually, I'm not hungry," I said, drifting over by the couch. *Oprah* was featuring an adoptee/birth parent reunion; both parties were elated. How convenient, I thought as I plopped onto the couch next to her. There must be a God—with a sense of humor. We both sat and watched it together in silence while I peeked at her expression from time to time trying to get an idea of her reaction to the various reunions being showcased.

So far, Mom sat and watched with a level expression. It was hard to gauge what she was feeling. I, on the other hand, was completely mesmerized as one mother and daughter and another mother and son cried like babies as they hugged and hugged each other. Oprah beamed from the side.

At one time, I didn't think something like this could ever happen to me. Being reunited with a birth parent! It was a topic only read about in magazines or watched on talk shows or an afternoon soap opera.

Now, it was my turn.

The elation built up inside, and I wondered if I too would be crying and hugging my birth mother for dear life when we met. Tears started to swell from just the thought of it. My life was beginning to play out like one of those soap operas, a drama destined to build in intensity, with no possibility of turning back. I was so happy and felt like twirling around on the top of a grassy hill like Maria, singing "The Sound of Music."

I noticed a lit candle was placed precariously at the edge of the table near the couch. Mom loved candles and placed them in every corner of the kitchen and family room. I slid the candle over, out of harm's way, and breathed in the warm vanilla scent. The smell had a calming effect and the knot in my stomach loosened.

Oprah went to a commercial break, and I decided to seize the opportunity. There was no reason to put this off any longer.

"Mom," I said cautiously. "I found my birth mother." The words escaped my mouth so effortlessly, but the easy part quickly ended when I saw her face completely devoid of expression as if I'd told her something trivial about my day. Her attention remained with the television.

I got up from the couch, paced the floor a few times, and then sat in the chair across from her. She still wouldn't acknowledge me.

"I actually talked with her on the phone last night," I added. "Her name is Jo Crowley. Isn't that funny?" I said with a half laugh. "She has the same last name as Aunt Lorraine." I tried getting some reaction from her, bringing up the last name, the same as her sister's married name.

Finally, she fixed her eyes on me. Her expression remained impassive.

"How did you manage to find her so quickly?" she asked in a dull voice.

"Oh ..." I said keenly, meeting her eye. "It all really rested with the location of her marriage certificate."

She looked at me inquisitively, raising her eyebrows.

"A marriage certificate?"

In detail, I explained the tricky way I'd obtained her full name by tracing her marriage certificate after sending requests out to a dozen health departments.

"Isn't it ironic that I happen to work in a health department?"

Mom didn't say anything so I went on. When I got to the part about how I talked to my biological grandmother and her nurse aide and how they helped me, her eyes narrowed.

"And how long have you been doing this searching?" she asked, a hint of derision in her tone.

The bliss in my expression quickly dissolved.

"A couple months," I said cautiously, taking the exhilaration out of my voice. She obviously wasn't sharing in my happiness, and there was no doubt she wasn't pleased. Hesitant now, almost regretting I'd said anything in the first place, I wrapped up the story by briefly mentioning the telephone call shared.

When I finished, we both sat there for the longest time not saying a word. *Oprah* returned from commercial break, but neither of us bothered to tune in again.

"You seem so satisfied with yourself."

Her words hurt. Mom never gave me credit for anything. When I finally brought home straight A's in college, she paid no attention. Only Dad seemed thrilled at the time. The fact that I was able to conduct this search on my own in such a short amount of time was remarkable. It would've been nice if she had at least applauded my efforts, even though the end result of finding my birth mother was the very thing she wanted to avoid at all costs. I looked into her indifferent eyes.

"I am satisfied. I should've been a detective. Most people search for years on end, and it only took me a couple of months." I got up from my chair. "I consider myself very lucky."

"Are you going to meet her?"

"Yes, this Friday afternoon."

She shot me a dirty look, and her lips pursed together.

"I'll go with you."

I didn't know how to respond. From the expression on her face, I didn't think it was wise if she went along. Maybe her offer to accompany me was an attempt to emulate other adoptive parents portrayed on television, the ones who fully supported their child's search. We'd just seen this only a moment ago, two adoptees reuniting with their birth mothers. Both adoptive mothers sat lovingly beside their children and beamed with admiration, along with

Oprah, when their children embraced their birth mothers for the first time live on television.

"That's okay," I said, observing the sulky expression on her face. Why did she have to look so upset? Finding Jo wasn't about replacing her. "This is something I have to do by myself."

I had looked forward to a reunion ever since it dawned on me as a child that there was another mother floating somewhere out there in the world. By the look on Mom's face, I'm certain she had dreaded it for just as long.

"Fine." She waved her hand as if to dismiss me.

*　　*　　*

Later in the evening, while I was getting ready for bed, Dad came to my room to say good night. From the way he was lingering in the doorway, it was obvious he wanted to talk.

I looked at him with curious eyes.

"Dad ..." His eyes met mine. "Is something wrong?"

"No ... no ... I just wanted to say good night," he said shuffling his feet. He was nervous about something. I had a feeling Mom had already told him.

"I have something to tell you," I said taking a deep breath.

"Yes?" he asked. His eyebrows rose.

"I found her ... my birth mother."

"That was quick," he said, a confused look on his face. "How in God's name did you ever locate her so quickly?"

I quickly recounted my tale, and instead of looking annoyed, he appeared pleased, like it was no big deal. Then he stepped into my room and closed the door.

"Do me a favor, don't tell your mother any more about this," he whispered, looking over his shoulder. I looked too, but there was nobody in the hallway.

"I already told her," I said evenly.

"I know ... Shh," he said, glancing over his shoulder again. "Keep your voice down."

"Mom's in the family room."

"I thought I heard her coming upstairs," he said, looking a bit nervous. "I don't think you should've told her."

"Why?"

"Because you know how she is—exactly like her own mother," he said with disgust. "She wants to be the queen bee, and she won't like the idea of another mother in the picture."

"But Dad, this woman's not going to be my mother. All I did was talk with her. I have no idea what's going to happen."

"Do me a favor—don't tell her anything more about your bionic mother." It sounded more like a demand than a favor.

"*Birth* mother," I corrected him. "I'm sorry, but I have to. There's no reason why I should keep this from her. This is something I needed to do for me, and I don't want to keep secrets."

I was so sick of secrets! That was everybody's answer to any problem: Keep it quiet. Don't tell anyone, and maybe it will just go away on its own. Didn't they know that nothing can be erased?

Dad's shoulders slumped down, and he gave me a pitiful look. I knew that expression. He used it when he knew he was losing an argument; he was trying to win me over another way.

"Can't you do me this favor?" he pleaded.

"No," I said firmly. "We're all adults here, and I'm not going to play games by keeping things from each other. It's not healthy. Keeping secrets will only cause problems further down the road." I tried to explain, but Dad didn't seem to be agreeing by the way he just stood there, his eyes looming over me. "Secrets always have a way of coming out," I added.

"I don't want to see your mother get hurt," he said in a cold voice.

"Dad, I don't want to see her hurt either," I said calmly. "I didn't do this in order to hurt Mom—or you. To tell you the truth," I said taking a step backwards. "It hurts when you want me to ignore this whole issue. There were many questions I needed answered, things I needed to know in order for me to feel complete."

"I know … I know. But please do me this one favor." His voice softened again. "Even though your mother and I fight a lot and there are times when I want to leave the marriage … I don't." He leaned closer. "Your mother comes first with me. She always has …" His voice rose. "… and *always will.*"

Was his comment meant as a warning that he wasn't going to support me? His eyes narrowed sending a chill down my spine.

"I know … you've told me this before," I reminded him.

It always made me uneasy when he talked liked that, making it a point that I knew exactly where I stood in the pecking order. I personally thought it was tacky for him to even bring up such a subject.

"I want to avoid any arguments between your mother and me concerning this. There's no winning with her," he continued, still whispering. "We already discussed this, and she's very angry. Can't you forget about meeting your birth mother—for my sake?"

I shook my head.

"Can't you do this, for me?" he pleaded.

He was up to his old games, playing me like a violin. This time, I wasn't about to let him finish his song.

"No, I can't," I said firmly, jutting my chin out. "I plan to meet her this Friday."

"You'd be doing me a big favor ... Please?"

Dad, as usual, was looking after his own welfare. He wanted a quick fix to this crisis, anything so that he didn't have to argue with Mom. He knew how she yearned to maintain an illusion of peace in the household, how she wanted problems to be ignored in the hopes of them eventually disappearing. But this was too important and couldn't be brushed under the carpet.

No, I was going to face this with or without their support.

"My interest in finding her is about me. It means so much to know the circumstances surrounding my birth. After we meet, I have no idea what will happen. We may never see each other again. For right now, I'm going through with the meeting."

"You won't do this for me?" he asked, looking heartbroken.

Since he could no longer make me afraid, he tried to make me feel guilty. He was good at this, and always had been, and though I almost felt sorry for him, this time I wasn't about to budge.

I stood erect, hands on hips, and shook my head.

"All right," he finally said, looking defeated. "Would you like me to go along?"

"Thanks for offering," I said. "But I want to do this on my own."

Why were my parents only concerned with their own feelings? What about mine? Finding my birth mother was one of the most important steps I'd ever taken in my life. It promised to fill a void within, to give me a sense of completeness. Didn't they care about that?

*   *   *

Before I got into bed, Matthew called from St. Louis, sounding a lot more enthused.

"You were so lucky. Honestly, Anne, I didn't think you were ever going to find her."

"That goes to show you're not always right," I said with a small laugh.

"I'm usually right," he said quickly. "So tell me again, how did you manage to find her?"

After explaining, I told him the other things my birth mother and I talked about.

"Wow. You mean she hasn't spoken with her own parents for more than twenty years?"

"Not since she left home shortly after I was born. She said it was because they didn't approve of her marriage. Don't you think cutting your parents out of your life is a bit extreme?" Somehow, that scenario in my life didn't seem possible. Family was family, and you don't walk out on anyone.

"Yeah ... very extreme."

"I'm going to meet her this Friday," I said happily.

"This Friday," he repeated.

"Um-hum," I answered, sipping a glass of water.

"Anne ... I wish you'd wait until I return home." There was an air of uneasiness in his voice. "That way, I can go along with you."

I had a feeling he was going to try to postpone the meeting.

"No," I said firmly. "I'm meeting her this Friday. I don't want to put this off—not after waiting my whole life for this moment. Another day or two would be torture."

"At least take someone with you."

"Mom and Dad offered to go along," I said, thinking about Mom's angry countenance and Dad's feeble attempt at manipulation.

"They did?"

"Yeah ... But I'm doing this on my own."

"Anne, I don't want you to be by yourself. What if she's some crazy person? ... She may try to hurt you."

"Don't be silly. She didn't sound crazy." *Matthew is just being overly protective,* I told myself. "Anyway, I'm the one who called."

He let out a long breath and didn't argue further, knowing in the end, I'd be meeting her this Friday—by myself, no ifs, ands, or buts.

*	*	*

The next day, I tried to take my mind off the upcoming meeting and welcomed the opportunity to work. Though I was busy with inspections, my mind could barely focus. I should have been deliriously happy, but for some unknown reason, my eyes kept welling with tears.

At dinner, I managed to swallow only a few spoonfuls of instant mashed potatoes then drifted off to my room. Later that evening, I called Janine and told her the news. She offered to accompany me but then remembered she had an important meeting she couldn't miss that afternoon.

"Remember to call me after you meet," she reminded. "I'm dying to know how it goes."

Matthew called an hour later, appealing once more to postpone the meeting.

"Anne, everything has happened so fast. Let's slow it down a bit and think this out before proceeding ... Okay?"

But I wouldn't budge. "No. You know I don't like to put things off. I've waited forever for this, and I won't put it off another day."

"I don't see why you can't wait until the weekend," he argued.

"Matthew, I'm sorry, but I feel I should meet her by myself anyway."

"I disagree," he said flatly, a definite amount of discontentment was in his voice. "I'm afraid she may try to hurt you."

Maybe he was right, I thought. Not that she'd try to hurt me physically, but she might not want to see me again. Still, I wouldn't allow fear to keep me hostage. I needed to take chances in order to satisfy my curiosity, to fulfill this inner drive. Matthew saw my impulsive nature as a handicap; I saw it as a virtue.

Remembering that she was calling on Thursday to confirm a place and time, I spent the remainder of the evening in my bedroom, going through and arranging in chronological order a stack of copied childhood photos. It was silly, but I felt like a schoolgirl waiting for a boy to call. When it was almost ten, my stomach turned over. She wasn't going to call. Maybe she changed her mind and decided the meeting wasn't such a good idea. Before there was more time to despair, the phone rang.

"Hello ... Anne Marie?"

What would I call her? It felt odd to call her "Mom," so I avoided the issue.

"Yes, it's me."

"Sorry I'm calling so late, but I just got home from teaching a dance class at the studio. I have another idea about a place to meet. Do you know where the Casa Maria restaurant is in Ramsey?"

"Yes, I go there a lot."

"Good." She sighed. "I know how to get there. I believe it's on Route 17."

"Yes, it's right off the highway. Not too far from where I live."

"We can meet there." She paused for a second. "How about two in the afternoon?"

"Two is fine."

"I'll call you if something comes up or if I'm going to be late."

I hesitated. "Could I have your number in case something comes up with me as well?"

"You don't know my phone number?" she asked, sounding a bit dumbfounded.

"No, no, I don't ... Your number is unlisted."

"Oh, yeah ... it is."

I'd forgotten that I never explained how I managed to find her.

"You made it very difficult for me to locate you." I laughed. We got onto the subject of the multitude of calls made that evening. "Lucky for me, your mother's aide was helpful."

"It doesn't surprise me she's sick and needs someone to take care of her. My mother never ate right or took care of her health."

"So you never saw her again?"

"No," she said unyieldingly. "I made the decision to never look back when I left. That was the winter of 1967, and I never did."

I wasn't quite sure how to respond so I didn't say anything.

"Let me tell you my phone number," she said on a brighter note. "Do you have a pencil?" I wrote down her number. "About our meeting, you should be able to recognize me because I'm sure I look similar to you, except my hair is jet black, chin length, and cut in a bob. It's also crimped."

"I'm sure I'll recognize you," I said assuredly.

"I'll be wearing a pink and white dress," she quickly added. "Oh ... and let's meet in the foyer." She sighed deeply. "I guess I'll see you tomorrow?"

"Okay, see you then."

*   *   *

That night, I dreamt of a young girl about twenty years old and nine months pregnant. She was in an old tenement building standing by the window, caressing her swollen belly as she solemnly considered her plight.

The scene quickly dissolved into a dull gray tiled operating room where the same young girl was lying on a stretcher under a large bright round light. In her arms, swaddled in a pink blanket, was a newborn baby. The baby screamed and screamed while the girl cried softly along.

A nun, dressed all in dark gray, entered and ordered the girl to hastily sign a piece of paper. The young girl signed and reluctantly handed the baby over. The girl was left alone, her face full of despair. She would never see her baby again. Crying hysterically, she wailed out loud, "My baby—my baby!"

I tossed and turned then sat bolt upright in the darkness. It was only a dream. This entire week I had slept through dreamless nights, my body too tired and weary to conjure up any nighttime fantasies. It was a relief to start dreaming again, but there was something different about this one. It was too real, and it wasn't even midnight yet. I had only been asleep for about ten minutes, and yet that dream seemed to go on for hours. I returned to my favorite sleeping position on my side with my knees curled up close to my chest. But I couldn't get back to sleep. My eyes were wide open, and the scene from the dream wouldn't go away. It was my birth mother. She was devastated, and her pain came rushing in like a fast-moving flame and burned from the inside out, devouring me.

* * *

On my way to work the next day, tears welled in my eyes. I was a bundle of nerves. Every time an old song played on the radio, any song, scenes of Jo pregnant and alone with me came alive in my head, intensifying my melancholy. Only the week before, my life had seemed so average, so uneventful. Now I was going to be meeting the person who gave me life. Every time the thought struck me anew, it seemed extraordinary.

The ladies who worked in the office at the health department were chatting over coffee. After receiving my schedule of inspections for the morning, I made myself a cup of tea and joined them. Suddenly, the conversation stopped, and three pairs of eyes were staring at me.

"Anne, are you still planning to meet with your mother this afternoon?" one of the newer secretaries, Jane, asked. Over the summer when I was looking up addresses for health departments, I'd been up front with them about what was going on.

"Yes, this afternoon at two. I'm leaving work around noon so I can go home and change my clothes."

"Does your mother know about her?" Mary, the main secretary, asked, a hint of apprehension in her voice.

I nodded.

She looked sideways at the other two secretaries.

"Is your mom upset?" Mary asked.

"Well … she certainly isn't exhilarated. She's more upset that I was able to find anything out; she feels the information should've been locked away forever."

"I'd imagine she must be terribly upset," Mary piped in.

I didn't answer. There wasn't enough vigor left in me to argue my reasoning for searching. I'd barely eaten in three days, and the thought of finally facing Jo this afternoon had me almost faint with fright.

"Make sure you bring in pictures of her on Monday and tell us all about it," Jane said with a shaky smile. She looked at Mary, then back at me again.

I smiled. "I will."

* * *

After arriving home from work, I reapplied my makeup, combed my hair, and slipped on a pair of burgundy pants and a crème-colored blouse. Looking at myself in the mirror, I saw a sad, exhausted face staring back. I applied a bit more blush to my cheeks, hoping it would perk up my appearance, but my complexion was still as pale as a ghost. *It'll have to do,* I thought hastily, grabbing my purse and rushing out of the house.

At ten minutes before two, I arrived at the Casa Maria restaurant and sat in the parking lot, craning my neck to see a woman with short black hair and a pink dress. There were some businessmen standing near the entrance, and a few others, but no one resembled the description she'd given me. I sat in the car, frozen, knowing eventually I'd have to go inside, where she might already be waiting.

Finally, after finding some courage, I left my car and made my way across the parking lot. Low clouds blew in and covered the sun, turning the sky gray. I hugged myself, shivering in the cool wind. At the entrance, I hesitated, then the wind seemed to push me from behind through the door.

Two was a dead time for restaurants, and the foyer was empty. The door was made of a heavy, dark-stained wood with beveled glass. I peered through it, my eyes fixed on the parking lot entrance. She hadn't mentioned the type of car she would be driving. I expected to see her pull up in a family car like a wagon or a four-door sedan.

A few people came in the restaurant and glanced my way. I shifted my weight and checked my watch. Time appeared to be moving more slowly with each passing minute. When my watch read twenty-five minutes past two, I thought my worst fears had been realized; she had changed her mind and wasn't coming. The thought of her losing her way or perhaps being stuck in traffic didn't seem possible, and as I mulled over the possible scenarios, a red Jeep Cherokee pulled into a parking space and a thin-figured woman with black hair emerged from the car. She wore a pink and white dress and her hair was in a chin-length bob.

Twenty-Two

First Encounter

I stood stock still, peering out the window as she briskly made her way across the parking lot. An attractive woman, she walked with determination, her head held high, full of confidence, the very thing I lacked.

As the distance between us lessened, my pulse quickened and I backed away from the door in a panic. I was getting more nervous by the second. What would I say? How should I greet her? How many times I'd longed for this moment, being reunited with the person who had been an illusion throughout most of my life! Twenty-two years might not seem long to an adult, but to a child, it's an eternity.

And now the moment was here. It was happening, and there was no time to pull myself together because the door opened, and she entered like a breath of fresh air.

The figure standing in front of me was my mother. I wasn't able to bring myself to look at her. My eyes filled with tears, so I glanced at the floor. My body turned, and I motioned with my hand for her to follow me. It was an unnatural invitation, one made without a smile or a handshake. She accepted it anyway and walked behind me into the restaurant.

I was mortified at my reaction and wished I'd given her a hug or at least looked into her eyes and said hello. Instead, I concentrated solely on trying to stop the trembling that washed over me.

She must think I'm cold and calculating, I thought. *She must think I hate her.* She remained behind me, and I yearned to turn around and see her face.

The hostess greeted us and led us to the back of the restaurant. My birth mother trailed behind, out of my sight. I heard the clickety-clack of her shoes on the ceramic floor. A spicy odor lingered in the air and clung to my nose as I inhaled. The room was dimly lit, and I saw the familiar sombreros hanging on the wall and the brightly colored Tiffany-style lamps hanging in each booth. A few patrons chatted over frothy margaritas. Finally, as we slid into a booth, I was forced to face her.

I quickly took in her eyes, her nose, her cheeks, all her features at once. *She doesn't look anything like me,* I thought with gut-wrenching disappointment. Her hair was jet black, smooth, and styled in a chin-length bob. It was slightly crimped and pulled back in a barrette on one side. Her eyes, dark green, were shaped differently and much smaller than mine. She had a soft, flawless complexion and appeared younger than her forty-three years. Her skin was slightly darker than mine, and her features were clearly Spanish.

As we sat there in momentary silence, studying each other, I fought back my tears and wondered what to say.

"You look like your father," she whispered, gazing at me with amazement and smiling.

"We don't look anything like each other," I heard myself murmur. I bit down on my lip. Why did I say such a dumb thing? But she didn't appear affected by my awkwardness. She continued to stare at me with a broad smile.

"I think there are a few similarities, like your lips and your nose." She leaned forward, trying to get a better view. "They're shaped very much like mine," she pointed out.

"I guess so," I responded, not convinced. I was beginning to doubt she was my mother at all. Maybe the adoption agency somehow mixed up my file.

She reached into her purse and took out an envelope.

"I have pictures of my family," she said, opening the envelope and taking out about a dozen pictures. She handed me the photos.

"Thank you. I also brought some," I said taking out my pictures and pushing them across the table.

She sighed deeply, appearing relieved.

"I'm so glad you brought these. On the phone last night, I forgot to ask you to bring pictures of yourself growing up."

She began slowly looking at them, tilting her head from side to side as she looked at each one. Her eyes were intense and focused as she came upon a photo of me at fifteen months old. It was a professional black-and-white photograph taken in my home by a photographer. She browsed through the other photos, but kept going back to the one of me at fifteen months.

Hands still trembling, I began to shuffle through a dozen or so pictures, hoping to find a family member who looked like me. They were mostly of her three children. Hesitating briefly while holding a photo of Jessica, the four-year-old, who had beautiful long red hair and big blue eyes, I sought desperately for a similar feature. It was taken at school, and she was sitting at a table with books in front of her. Perhaps in the eyes, there was a resemblance. Her other two children, Sara and Matthew, looked like each other, and there was no denying they were siblings. Their faces and noses were similar in shape. I put the photos back in the envelope and handed them back to her.

"Anne, those are for you to keep."

"Thank you." I placed them on the table in front of me. "You can keep mine too."

Smiling, she handed me a faded white folder marked "West Point Hotel" in large letters. When I opened it, I saw a picture of a group of people sitting around a table.

"See if you can pick out your father."

I noticed she was in the forefront of the photo and a man sat alongside. *He couldn't possibly be my father,* I quickly thought, *not with his large, pointed nose and his rather large head.*

"He's not sitting with me," she added with a playful laugh.

I glanced at the others in the picture, and then my eyes focused on a man sitting on the opposite side of the table. It was my father.

I looked exactly like him.

And what astounded me the most was the way his eyes stared up at me from the photo. They were haunting, telling me I'd seen those same eyes every time I looked in a mirror. They were my eyes. There were no words to express my astonishment at finally seeing someone I resembled. My mouth practically hung open, while I marveled at the striking similarities. Any uncertainty about our being related was put to rest. He was my father, and she was my mother.

"I haven't been in contact with him since 1966," she reminded me as I studied his features in the photo. "We were dance partners at the studio where we worked together. We were at a competition in this picture," she said, pointing to the front of the photo holder. "It was at the West Point Hotel in Upstate New York."

She reached into her purse and pulled out a folded paper.

"This is the program from that evening. See my name printed here." Her finger scrolled a list of names until it reached her name, Josephine Wood. "This was my professional name," she explained and then laughed. "In those days, teachers had different names so that male students wouldn't be able to call and ask for dates." She sighed deeply. "Sam was very nice, and I guess I did have a small crush on him."

I concentrated on the photo of my father.

"You're right," I said, suddenly finding words. "He does look like me. I can especially see it in the eyes. He has large, sleepy eyes with gray bags under them. I can remember as a child, my parents commenting about how I looked so tired all the time, with the bags under my eyes. I'd run to a mirror to see what they were talking about, but I never saw any *bags* under them."

She laughed.

"His eyes were green like mine."

"Yes, I read that in the letter from the adoption agency."

"Do you have that letter with you?" she asked, suddenly losing her smile. "I'd like to read it, if you don't mind."

"Yes. I'm not sure why I even brought it with me, but I stuck it alongside the photos." I reached into my purse.

"I'm just curious what they told you about me."

She took it from me almost reluctantly, and as her eyes scanned each sentence, her face became sullen. I was sure she was going to cry, but she didn't.

"They didn't make me look too good." Her voice broke.

"They were just providing the basic facts," I said, taking care to sound reassuring even though I'd thought the exact same thing upon first reading it. It was a cold, impersonal letter, making her sound like a selfish mother, and I wished I hadn't brought it along.

"I know." Her eyes remained on the paper. "But still, it sounds as if I didn't care." Her voice trailed away. She folded the letter and handed it back across the table.

"I didn't think that," I said warmly. "Thank you for bringing this along." I indicated the photo. "I was hoping you'd have a picture of him."

"You can keep it."

"Thank you." I put it on top of the other photos in front of me.

She forced a weak smile.

"Do you have any questions for me?" Before I could answer, the waiter came over to take our order. We asked for two Diet Cokes, and he suggested we try the nacho appetizer.

I tried to formulate a question, but nothing came to mind. Finally, slightly embarrassed, I said, "I have so many questions I want to ask you, but right now, I'm drawing a blank."

Again, the tears were welling in my eyes, and there was a lump in my throat. Jo, however, seemed completely relaxed and was smiling easily. This wasn't the way I'd imagined myself at our first meeting. Where was all the excitement and joy? All I could think of was the many years we were apart, never knowing each other's names. That thought gripped me.

"Maybe we should've written down the questions beforehand," she suggested with a small laugh.

"Yes."

"I have so many questions I want to ask you, but I'm also drawing a blank. When I'm home, I'm going to write them down so I don't forget."

I nodded my head again, trying to read the expression in her face. Was she upset too? Did she too feel the intense sadness? It was hard to tell as I searched her eyes for an answer. She seemed cheerful as she gazed at me, her expression frozen in a fixed smile. It made me uncomfortable.

I excused myself to go to the ladies' room and tried desperately to pull myself together by splashing water on my face, but all that was accomplished was the removal of some of my makeup. Now my skin looked pale and blotchy. I could only imagine what she was thinking of me.

After calming down, I returned to the table, more relaxed and ready to face her again. Sliding into my seat, I eyed the nacho appetizer, sitting tantalizingly in the center of our table. Normally, I would've polished off at least half of it, but my stomach was still in knots. Neither of us touched the nachos.

There was an uncomfortable silence, until she said, "I do have something else to give you." She reached into her purse, retrieved a folded piece of notebook paper, and handed it to me. "It's something I scribbled down a few years ago." It looked as if it was hastily torn out of a spiral notebook. "Read it later on, not now. I almost decided to throw it away and not give it to you," she said, her voice cracking. "But I think you should have it."

"Okay." I placed the paper underneath my pile of photos.

"I wrote it a few years ago," she repeated. "I never thought I'd be giving it to you someday." Her cheerfulness vanished, and she began fumbling with her pile of photos, trying to arrange them in some order. Finally, she looked me straight in the eye. "What are your intentions regarding me?" She stiffened in her seat, waiting for a reply.

Her question took me by surprise. What did she want me to say? It was hard to tell; her expression was blank, her eyes wide with anticipation. I paused, trying to think of an answer as close to the truth as possible.

"I'd like to get to know you better," I said slowly. Deep down, my intentions were to have her become a part of my life. I couldn't admit this yet in fear of being disappointed. "Would you mind?" I added uneasily.

Relief seemed to wash over her.

"Oh yes, I want to see you again too." She seemed livelier and smiled. I smiled back. "I suppose I'll have to tell my children."

"They don't know?"

"No, I never told them, since I thought it would make them worry and want to find you."

"But your husband knows?"

"Yes, he knew me when I was pregnant," she began. "You see, we started dating when I was about five months into the pregnancy, during the summertime. He was teaching at Steven Knightly too, and he began to get suspicious. I didn't tell him I was pregnant until it was time to go to the maternity home." She stopped and took a small sip from her soda, followed by a deep breath. "You see, before I met Richard, a friend of mine told me about a women's shelter. I was hoping to find help there, but when my friend Cindy and I arrived, the shelter was closed. We were both standing outside the entrance when I noticed a priest nearby. I guess we looked pretty desperate, because he came over to talk to us. After telling him about my pregnancy, he said I should contact a Catholic agency that helped unwed girls. They'd be able to help me with my problem."

I listened intently.

"I remember thinking much later, he was probably sent by God to guide me to that place, because I had no idea what to do next. I contacted the sisters there, and they explained the policy about providing a place for pregnant girls. It was a maternity home located in an old Victorian house in Newark. The nuns thought up an elaborate scheme for each girl whose family didn't know about the pregnancy. They needed a cover story to explain the need to be away for a couple of months. Since my parents didn't know I was pregnant, the nuns decided to have me tell my parents I was going to learn new dancing techniques with a dance studio in Maryland."

"You mean the nuns told you to lie?" I asked.

"Yes."

I was stunned and thought about the nuns at Saint Matthew's and again at Saint Bartholomew's.

"I knew lots of nuns when I went to Catholic elementary school, and they reacted strongly whenever someone was caught in a lie. Lying earned you a smack on the knuckles with a ruler or worse. If it was a big lie, they'd paddle you in front of the whole class."

"But the nuns didn't see it as lying. To them, it was a small price to pay, a white lie that would nullify the larger one," she said, raising her eyebrows.

"You mean the pregnancy?"

"Yes."

"But who were they to compare sins?" I asked, more to myself.

"The nuns were in control," she said simply. "I was uncertain but didn't dare question their authority. In fact, at the time, I felt grateful to them for wanting to keep my pregnancy a secret. They told me adoption was the only route to solving my problem and wiping the slate clean. The nuns gave me a phony address in Maryland to give to my parents so they could write me. The letters mailed to Maryland were forwarded to the maternity home. When I wrote back, I sent the letter to Maryland in order to have it postmarked there."

"Didn't your parents try to call you?"

"The nuns covered that aspect also." She laughed, running her fingers through her black hair. "They told me to tell my parents that there was only a pay phone in the hallway, and it was impossible for them to call me. Instead, I called my parents when I knew they'd be home. The entire time I was in Newark, my parents thought I was in Maryland." She stopped to take another sip from her glass.

I sat at the edge of my seat, half enthralled at her story and half at her being here right in front of my eyes!

"This is all so amazing. So your parents never realized you were pregnant?"

"No, not during the pregnancy … Richard was supportive of my decision. He visited me every weekend while I was at the home. He often took me out on Sundays to get hot dogs, and we'd eat them near the cliffs in Paterson." She smiled briefly, then grew serious and leaned forward. "He had nothing to do with my decision," she insisted. "It was made before I ever met him. When I told him about my pregnancy, we had been together for several months and things were quite serious between us. We started to discuss the possibility of marrying, but he said he couldn't promise me anything if I decided to keep the baby. He made it clear he'd probably not stick around. You see, we were both very young and there was nobody for me to rely on." She leaned back in her seat, looking fragile, as if she were about to blow away in a breeze. "Richard was with me when I went into labor with you. He took me to the hospital. It was Saint Michael's Hospital, and they had several rooms reserved for us girls from the maternity home. After I had you, I shared a room in the hospital with another girl. Her name was Julie. She had a baby girl too … like me." Her voice cracked again. "Richard came to visit me every day for the five days I was there. He did try to see you in the nursery, but the nurses wouldn't let him. Because I wasn't seeing the baby, the nurses wouldn't let anyone else see the baby. So they kept you far back, away from the nursery window. Richard told me he could only see your black hair sticking out from under the blanket," she said sadly.

"You never saw me?" I asked, clutching my hand to my chest.

She glanced around the room nervously, almost as if looking to be rescued from the answer.

"No ... no, I didn't," she answered slowly, wiping her eyes. "While you were being born, they knocked me out with gas, and when I woke up, you were in the nursery."

"They wouldn't let you come to the nursery?" I asked, shifting in my seat, unable to believe that a baby would be kept from its mother.

She was quiet for a moment.

"Yes, they would, but I thought if I saw you, I wouldn't be able to give you up." Her words came out slowly, deliberately. I was sure she was going to cry.

I was speechless, fighting back tears again.

She continued, "Julie saw her baby each day and cried hysterically. I only cried when no one was around." She stopped for a minute and glanced at the ceiling as if trying to recall another memory. "I constantly used to hear a baby screaming from my hospital room."

"That must have been me," I said with a half laugh. "My parents told me I cried all the time. I was colicky for about two months."

She looked down.

"I knew it was you, but the nurses kept telling me it wasn't. I almost went in to see you at one point, but then I didn't go through with it."

She continued staring down at the table. Then she mumbled something about needing to call her husband and went off to find a phone.

While she was gone, the scene she'd described in the hospital swelled in my head, squeezing out all other thoughts—I saw her filled with anguish, wanting to see her baby, knowing she shouldn't, knowing it would prevent her from going through with the adoption. I sat back in my seat, bracing myself for what she might divulge upon her return.

When she came back, the conversation turned to her children. She told me about the schools they attended and what activities they were involved in. We sat together chatting for another half hour until the waiter placed the bill on the table.

"Are you through?" he asked, surveying the untouched appetizer.

We nodded, and as she picked up the check, I savored the last few minutes of our meeting, sitting in the company of my birth mother—It was almost unbelievable, and I wondered if the dream would ever end.

We discussed when we should meet again.

"My schedule revolves around Jessica. I usually need to get a sitter because Richard works every day of the week except Sundays. He doesn't get home until eleven. Those are typical dance studio hours, during the evening."

"How often do you go to work?"

"One or two evenings a week, depending on the number of students. Lately, I'm too busy with Jessica and I want to be home for her as much as possible ... Anne," she said leaning forward. "I'm going to tell my children about you this weekend."

"Oh ... okay," I said nervously, leaning back in my seat. I wasn't quite sure what their reaction would be. Would they welcome me with open arms or would they resent there being another sibling, an older sister who was technically their mother's firstborn? "Could you call me afterwards and let me know how it went?" I asked tentatively.

She smiled. "Of course. And I'm sure they'll be delighted to hear about you," she added as if she sensed my uneasiness. "I'll call you next week, and then we can arrange another day to be together again."

She looked at me long and hard and smiled again, though her eyes looked sad. We got up, gathered our things, and hesitated. How should we end our first meeting? I didn't want it to end on the same awkward note it began on.

"Well, good-bye, then," she said, taking a few steps away. Then she turned back toward me and held out her arms. We embraced. She clutched me so tightly it hurt.

Twenty-Three

The Letter

It was dusk when we left the restaurant. We waved good-bye, smiling once more to each other as we parted and returned to our cars. From my window, I watched her car exit the parking lot and enter the highway.

When she was out of sight, I sat for a good ten minutes and cried, then drove away with blurry eyes. I'm not even sure how I found my way back home through the tears, but when I returned, the house was completely quiet except for the faint sound of the television coming from the family room. Assuming Mom was there, I lingered by the front door, needing to pull myself together. I took several deep breaths and wiped away the remaining tears.

"Back so soon?" she called out.

I glanced at my watch and saw it was ten past five. "I was there for about two hours," I said quietly, entering the family room.

She was sitting alone on the couch, eating her dinner and watching the evening news.

"So tell me. How did it go?" Mom asked. She appeared both sulky and annoyed.

I sat on the couch next to her and briefly described the meeting. Mom stared straight ahead listening with an impassive face, and when I finished, we both didn't speak. The photos my birth mother gave me were clutched in my hands, and she eyed them suspiciously. "What are those?"

"She gave me some pictures," I answered happily, eager to hear that I looked like so-and-so in the family, a simple thing most people experience throughout their lives. However, adoptees never hear that their eyes look like an Uncle Tom's or their hair color comes from the grandmother. "Would you like to see them?" I asked slipping the photos out of the envelope.

"Sure." Her face was expressionless.

As she looked through the pictures, I pointed out who was who and when we happened upon a photo of my birth mother, Mom hesitated, staring at it. I wondered if she was taking in the fact that we didn't look anything alike or that my birth mother was exceedingly thin. My mother tilted her head.

"She looks Jewish."

"Jewish?" I asked astonished. Even though I had briefly considered the possibility that my birth father may have been Jewish, never did the thought cross my mind that she was Jewish. I shook my head. "She looks Spanish. Look at her eyes and her black hair," I said leaning over and pointing at one of the photos.

Mom didn't bother looking again at the photo. Her eyes met mine.

"To me, she looks Jewish." There was a satisfied look on her face as if she squelched any possibility of my having an Irish birth mother.

"Actually, she's half Irish," I said matter-of-factly. "But I don't think she looks Irish at all. I think she looks Spanish."

Hearing me mention the word *Irish*, she quickly returned her eyes to the photos still in her hands. She switched back to a picture showing all three of my half-siblings together.

"They must look like their father. I don't see a resemblance to you."

I nodded my head and silently agreed. My hope of having a relative look like me vanished into thin air—except for my father from New Mexico, and who knew if I'd ever see him.

Mom's expression remained impassive as she handed me the photos and continued to watch the news. I didn't break the silence that stretched between us, but slowly got up from the couch and headed upstairs.

On my way, I saw Brian in his room watching television. He looked up as I passed by.

"What's up?" he asked, rather apprehensively. "Are you okay?"

Turning and entering his room, I heaved a big sigh.

"Yeah, I'm fine. Did you know I was meeting my birth mother today?" I asked trying to remember if I told him about her or not. The week had been a blur, and I wasn't sure if I was coming or going anymore.

"Yeah," he said letting out a long breath, returning his eyes to mine. "How'd it go?"

"It was wonderful," I said simply, not sure what kind of detail he was willing to hear. I hesitated. "Would you like to see a picture of her?"

"Sure," he answered halfheartedly. I handed him the pictures, and he quickly flipped through them. "They look like nice people," he said blankly, as though the people in the photographs were of no concern.

Hastily, I took back the photos and stuffed them in my purse, seeing the letter my birth mother gave me earlier. I was dying to read it.

"Are you okay with this?" I asked before leaving.

He shrugged his shoulders.

"Of course … I'm happy you were able to find her."

A wave of relief pulsed through my veins. Even though Brian sat there looking completely blasé and it was impossible to tell what he was thinking, I knew his statement was sincere, and somehow, it ever so slightly made me feel a little bit better.

"I know Mom isn't." He hesitated and took a swig of his soda. "But I can understand why you needed to do it," he said on a brighter note.

I didn't dare press him for more, though I was busting at the seams to discuss this further. I think Brian noticed my wide eyes, but he made no response except to return, almost absentmindedly, to his dinner on his tray and to his usual subdued self.

I excused myself and retreated into my own shell, my bedroom which was quickly becoming my new haven. Closing the door, I sat on the bed, heart pounding against my chest as I unfolded her full-page letter, written in large cursive handwriting in blue ink. I leaned back against my pillow and silently read.

9/12/87

Dearest Little Girl, I never knew you—but I love you. You were my firstborn. I miss you. I never saw you with my eyes, but I know you with my heart. I don't even know your name. I was told you had dark hair and fair skin. May I guess? The hair turned light maybe reddish. The skin is very light, the eyes green or hazel (bluish). You are probably a wonderful person, loving, kind, caring, and wondering about your roots. I don't blame you. I would be too. Not one year, or week, or day has gone without your being in my heart and thoughts. How is she doing? Is she happy? Are they being good to her? Do they love her as much as I do? To love a child and give that child up is the worst thing to happen to a mother. But maybe it's not the worst thing to happen to a newborn baby. On Nov. 13, 1966, a beautiful little girl was born to an immature twenty-year-old person (me). This person loved the baby, but couldn't provide her the proper life. Believe it or not, a baby needs more than love. She needs a crib, food, a roof overhead, clothes, a Mom and Dad (very important), and a stable home. These I tried to give to you. I hope I didn't go wrong. The adoption agency promised they'd screen the parents to match the baby. How could they miss with such a beautiful little girl? Maybe someday soon I'll be lucky enough to get up the nerve to contact you through the adoption agency. Maybe I'll never find you, my first little girl. But if I do, I hope you will forgive me for doing what I thought was the best for you, I love you always. Love, Your Mom

I was unable to move. Her words tore through my flesh and sunk deep within to the very core of my body where they mingled with the essence of my being, and for a split second—where time seemed to stand still—every emotion she had felt during the unplanned pregnancy, the birth, and the twenty-three-year void rippled through my body. She'd been completely heartbroken, and I ached from the pain she had suffered. None of it was fair. Why wasn't anybody willing to help her at the time? The nuns were only concerned with wiping away the evidence. Did they stop to think about the effect this might have on the mother or on the child? Everyone wanted me to believe that she felt nothing at the time of the birth—that she had been the numb bionic woman. If that were true, how could she have written such a letter?

It was clear why she couldn't keep me, and I felt no animosity. If anything, I felt compassion and could see why she viewed her only alternative at the time as being adoption. Not even her fiancé offered to help. My sympathies rested solely with her.

Rolling over on my stomach with the letter clutched in my hands, I burst into fresh sobs, burying my head in my arms. I was so swamped with sorrow that it was difficult to breathe. Finally, I hauled myself out of bed and went and peered out the window.

A haze covered the moon, and it appeared ethereal, dreamlike. I replayed her story in my head. Clearly, the decision she made hadn't been easy. She not only went through the torment of giving away her newborn baby but continued day after day without any knowledge of my welfare. She had no information as to where I was or which family had adopted me. This was punishment too cruel for any mother to endure. Yet her only mistake was becoming pregnant before marrying.

Carefully folding the letter, I rose from my bed and tucked it beneath an address book in my nightstand drawer. All my important documents were kept there; I dreaded ever losing it. This letter was tangible evidence that my birth mother loved me. Still, the knowledge didn't make me feel any better, only sadder. I'd been robbed of knowing about her love. There was no reason why we had to be kept apart—Why couldn't I have at least seen her picture and maybe from time to time received a letter as well? What a difference that would've made for her benefit and for mine!

Matthew was just getting home from his trip, and needing him desperately, I flew out of the house with her pictures clutched in my hands. And as I drove along, every song playing on the radio propelled me back to the 1960s, the time when she was pregnant and alone. First, it was Simon and Garfunkel's 1966 hit "The Sounds of Silence," then after switching to another station, *Dirty Dancing's* hit song, "Time of My Life." It was all too much to bear; each song tormented me further, and eventually, I clicked off the radio altogether.

Things didn't get any better when I reached Matthew's house, it was like facing the Spanish Inquisition. My mild-mannered fiancé was boiling.

"You should've waited until I got home before meeting with her," he shot out.

I was too shocked to respond and instead followed Matthew into the living room, where his parents sat like two stone pillars on the couch, apparently waiting to add more insult to injury. Mr. Bauer flashed angry eyes my way.

"How could you do that to your folks?" he yelled.

I stopped dead in my tracks, momentarily stunned by his outburst. I'd grown accustomed to his gruff manner but never expected him to look this angry. Mrs. Bauer sat alongside him on the couch, glaring my way, without so much as a nod to welcome me into the house. I looked at Matthew, but he wouldn't meet my eyes. Letting out a long breath, I steadied myself and then faced Mr. Bauer.

"All I did was find my birth mother."

"As far as I'm concerned," he said pointing his finger directly at me, "your mother and father are in your house in Wyckoff!" His head nodded as he said each word.

Mrs. Bauer continued to look at me disapprovingly, a somber frown plastered on her face.

Is anyone on my side? I wondered, following Matthew into the dining room.

"You're lucky she didn't try to hurt you," he said, pulling out a chair.

"How was the flight?" I asked, plopping down on the chair.

He must've sensed my fragile state, because his rigid stance loosened. He leaned over and kissed me on my cheek.

"It was fine," he answered.

"Matthew," I said frowning. "I spoke to her on the phone twice. Plus, we met in a public place." My head pounded, weary of explaining myself over and over.

"Still … I could have gone with you this weekend."

"I was fine by myself. She's not some crazy woman."

His expression showed me he thought differently.

"What about your parents?" he asked taking the seat next to me. "How are they taking this?"

I looked down. It hurt that he didn't even ask how I was doing or how the meeting went.

"Mom is angry," I said miserably. "But what can I do? It's not my fault I'm adopted." The tears suddenly came rushing into my eyes, and I quickly brushed them away with the back of my hand.

Matthew shook his head and reached for a napkin on the table.

"You didn't have to go and find her," he said handing me the napkin. "Here, wipe your eyes."

I took the napkin and dabbed at my eyes. When was he going to understand my need to know about my origins? When was anybody?

I sat there for the longest time not saying anything. Matthew was quiet too with a distant look on his face. I wasn't sure if he was thinking about my predicament or about one of his accounting entries. Either way, I'd never felt lonelier.

Finally, he looked my way.

"You know, this is only going to cause problems."

The tears let loose again and this time streamed down my face.

"It may cause problems," I agreed. "But I can see the problems being solved over time."

"I just don't understand."

"You have no idea how it feels to be told you came from another set of parents without any information about them. I wasn't even given a photo of the woman who gave birth to me. There was no image in my mind of what she looked like. Always, there were nagging questions about why we weren't able to know each other. Throughout my whole life, these questions remained unanswered," I explained, feeling his eyes watching closely as if he was truly trying to understand. "You mean to tell me you wouldn't even have one pressing question to ask if you were adopted?"

He reached over and put his hand on mine. His expression softened.

"I just don't know. It's hard to understand something like that, especially because I'm not adopted."

After a long silence, I asked him if he wanted to see the pictures. He nodded, and I opened my purse to retrieve them. He pulled his chair closer and looked through the photos.

"They look like a very nice family."

"Yes, they do. And isn't the little one, Jessica, adorable? I've always wanted a sister, and maybe we'll eventually have a daughter … Oh, and I brought along a photo of my birth father." I took out the faded folder and opened it up. "They were dance partners and often competed together. See if you can point him out."

Matthew quickly glanced at the photo and then winked.

"Is he the waiter?"

"No, he's not the waiter!" I laughed.

He looked again, this time scanning each face.

"There he is," he said pointing. "That must be your father."

"Yes," I said beaming. "There's no way he could ever deny that I was his daughter, could he?"

"No, he looks a lot like you. Where's he living?"

"I have no idea. He never knew about the pregnancy, and a few months before I was born, he moved away somewhere. She hasn't been in contact with him since."

"So he doesn't know about you?"

"No," I said, pausing as I realized for the first time the ramifications of this fact. If I found him now, what would he say? How would he react? It would be different if he knew all along that he had a daughter somewhere out there in the world. He probably would've wondered about me too. But how do you explain such a revelation to someone who was kept completely in the dark? "He had no idea she was ever pregnant," I said slowly.

Matthew shook his head, a smug look on his face.

"I don't buy that. Come on. He slept with her. How could he not know she was pregnant, especially since they worked together?"

I considered his comment.

"She said she hid the pregnancy. Nobody could tell."

"All right, so she hid the pregnancy ... but why didn't she tell him she was pregnant?"

"She claimed they weren't dating. It was a one-night stand, and she didn't want to burden him with the news."

"*That's* no reason for not telling someone they fathered a baby," Matthew said shaking his head in disbelief.

"I know," I said, nodding my head. "The same thought ran through my mind."

"And still ... he had to suspect something was going on. He *slept* with her. I just don't buy that story," he said placing his hands behind his head and leaning back in his chair.

"It's what she told me. Anyway, I also want to try to find him. But she has no idea where he lives now. She only said she thought he was from New Mexico."

"New Mexico?"

"That's what she said. I only know his first and last name, well, definitely his last. His first name is Sam so I'm guessing his given name is Samuel. He was twenty-two when I was born," I hesitated a minute. "I'm concerned about finding him because he doesn't know about me. Do you think something like this could be terribly upsetting?"

Matthew raised his eyebrows and let out a long breath.

"Let's wait until this passes over before searching for him. One birth parent at a time."

Twenty-Four

Her story

Nearly a week had passed since that fateful night when we first talked on the phone, and my stomach remained in turmoil, barely tolerating food. First thing on Monday morning, I weighed myself on the bathroom scale and saw that I had dropped fifteen pounds. There was no doubt I'd lost some weight—my pants were looser—but never did I guess it was this much in such a short amount of time.

My birth mother called me the next day to arrange another date. Breathlessly, she explained she was on her way to the studio to teach a dance class. She sounded in high spirits.

"How about meeting this Friday night?"

"Yes … sure," I answered, trying to return her enthusiasm, even though it was hard adjusting to this new reality of knowing her.

"I know a nice little restaurant called the Fireplace. I think it's in Paramus."

"It's located right on the highway. I go there a lot."

"I ate there years ago and remember they have the best hamburgers."

"Yes, they do."

"Okay, we'll meet there," she said happily, then in a more serious tone, "I want you to know I told my children about you."

"You did?" I was surprised she'd told them about me so quickly. "What were their reactions?" My stomach fluttered in anticipation.

"Matthew didn't say much, and Jessica doesn't really understand. I showed her your pictures, and she thinks you're a baby. She's only four, and

I don't think she can understand the situation. I told Sara earlier because she was going away for the weekend." She sighed deeply. "I had to explain it in detail to her because a friend of hers became pregnant last year and kept the baby. She couldn't understand why I decided to give you up for adoption. I explained about times being better now and how the public's attitude was different back in the 1960s." She cleared her throat. "You see, when I was a child, there was a woman who wasn't married and had a baby, a little girl who was a few years younger than me. Well, they stigmatized her. Whenever anybody from the neighborhood referred to her it was, *that child*. Even though this happened in the 1950s, it was still the same outlook ten years later. No unmarried girl kept her out-of-wedlock baby. If anyone did get pregnant, no one knew. It was hidden and taken care of."

"Can I ask you something?" I said hesitantly, not sure if this was a good idea or the right time to ask such a question.

"Yes ..."

I sensed she knew what was coming.

"If abortion had been legal back in 1966, would I be here today?" I sucked in my breath, afraid of the truth.

"Honestly, Anne Marie, you'd be here. I don't believe in abortion, and I never even considered it when I was pregnant with you."

Then she began expanding on the story she'd told me earlier. "I never was completely sure I was even pregnant until my fifth month. The first three months, I was sick all the time. My mother noticed the change in my nature. My usual bubbly self was gone, and instead, I moped around due to the nausea. She picked up that something was amiss and thought I had a bad case of the flu. She made me drink this eggnog mixture every day, and I think that stuff kept me going. By about the fifth month, I realized something was going on. You see, I was a very naïve nineteen-year-old and didn't actually turn twenty until August. Finally, after visiting a doctor, I was told I was pregnant. My belly was still flat, and that's why up until that point, I never believed it myself. Actually, the night I was with Sam, we never really got that close."

"What do you mean?" I asked, swinging the telephone cord around and plopping myself on the bed. It didn't appear this was going to be a short telephone conversation.

"We were together," she answered slowly. "But ... I never thought we were that close ... I didn't think he even got inside of me."

I was speechless. What was she trying to tell me, that he wasn't my father after all? The photo of him was completely convincing; he was my father. The resemblance between us was uncanny.

"That night, we were drinking tequila, and I remember us kissing on the couch ... but that's it. We got close, but I have no memory of us actually doing it. I originally thought you were a virgin birth, an immaculate conception. It wasn't until years later that I guessed he must have gotten close enough on the outside, and those things are able to swim, you see ... Cindy and I planned to sleep over; later, I must have passed out. We were all drunk, and I'm a very heavy sleeper, especially if I drink too much."

Again, I was speechless. There were a multitude of questions waiting to burst forth from my mouth, but I did not ask the question that was foremost in my mind: *Why are you telling me this?* Instead, I asked if she was absolutely certain there was no other man.

"Oh no," she said vehemently. "I hadn't been with anyone else for many months before that night and not until after I gave birth to you. No, he's the only one. He's your father. I even put his name on the birth certificate."

"You did?" I asked, shifting my attention to this topic. Original birth certificates were a delicate subject in the adoptee community. It was the one piece of information we were not ever allowed to view, even as an adult. "I wish I could get a copy of my original birth certificate," I sighed, feeling the burning desire to be able to obtain my own vital documents. Even though the information contained on my original birth certificate was now known, due to the fact that I had found my birth mother, I still wanted the right to have access to something that ultimately belonged to me. "But it's practically impossible for any adoptee because the records are sealed," I explained.

"Oh, I thought you had the birth certificate," she said, confused. "Then how did you find out my name?"

"My father had the final adoption papers, the ones from the lawyer," I explained. "According to those, my name was Female Cusack. No other names were on the document, not even yours."

Jo interrupted. "I never named you because when I filled out the birth certificate, they told me if I gave you a first name, it would eventually be changed by the new parents. I thought it would be confusing for you to have one name and then have it changed." Her words came out fast, as if she were apologizing.

I didn't respond, thinking about Sharon and Thomas, who were both named at birth. I wasn't sure if being renamed after adoption had any effect on them.

"So, you're sure Sam is my father?" I asked.

"Oh yes, without a doubt. But he never knew. I hid the pregnancy from everyone."

"How did you hide it, especially from your family?"

"I never looked pregnant until the last month when I was at the maternity home. While I was still living at home, I wore my regular clothes and didn't gain much weight. I was still dancing at the studio, and by the end of the summer, I just wore looser shirts. Nobody could tell since there was really not much to see. You were very small." Her voice began to lose some of its enthusiasm. "I left for the maternity home at the end of September, in the beginning of my eighth month, and still I didn't look pregnant."

"Really?"

"Yes, it wasn't until I was at the maternity home that I gained weight. Those nuns fed me well and made sure I ate. I think by the end, I gained around nine pounds, total."

Her tale amazed me. Recently, I'd heard of a teenage girl who went into her ninth month of pregnancy claiming ignorance of her condition until the birth. Her own family didn't even realize she was pregnant. It was astounding, and now I was hearing that my own birth mother's family never realized it either. I'd been one of those unbelievable babies, hidden from the world.

"Only my close friend, Cindy, knew. We worked together at the dance studio. She used to swear she thought Sam, your father, knew about the pregnancy."

"But I thought you said he didn't know," I interrupted.

"One time, Cindy and I were talking at work. She said Sam was watching us from across the room and she got a feeling he knew something was up. But I kept denying it."

"So you're not sure if my father knew about me or not?" I asked again.

"I didn't think so, because I remained so thin and there was no belly to see. He probably thought I was sick or something because I looked so pale. It took many months for the nausea to go away."

On my bookshelf were the photos Jo gave me. My hand shook as I picked up the photo of my birth parents sitting at the table at the dance competition. My eyes gazed at his picture.

"Cindy was the one who went with me to see the doctor and then to look for a maternity home. She also visited me in the hospital, along with Richard."

While she talked, my eyes remained fixed on his image. It was hard to believe I was the tiny baby that nobody realized existed, not even my real father.

"Once I arrived at the maternity home, you finally made your presence known. You were just a tiny little swell, and then about a week before you were born, you were finally visible."

"What was it like living in a maternity home?" I asked.

"It wasn't bad. Actually, it was one of the most peaceful and relaxing times in my life. It was located in Newark."

"Oh, that's the location of the adoption agency's office, where I sent my request for background information."

"Yes, the home where I stayed was right across the street," she said, then lapsed into silence. When she spoke again, it was in a dreamy whisper. "We would sit by the window and watch new parents take the babies home. Sometimes, we were able to figure out which girl's baby it was."

"That must have been so sad."

"Each of us realized it would eventually be our baby, and we figured it was a way to help us prepare for the inevitable. I can remember to this day sitting around a piano, singing songs from *The Sound of Music* as one of the nuns played. Those times were happy. But I haven't been able to listen to that music since then."

"Ohh," I breathed, nearly falling over. I thought about those songs, always making me feel as if anything and everything were possible. "Have you ever seen the movie?"

"No," she said sadly. There was a definite longing in her voice.

"I watch it faithfully each year when it appears on television around the holidays."

"I haven't seen it to this day." She sighed. "I know listening to those songs again will make me cry, and when I get started, the crying can go on for days. Every year around this time, I get depressed. My husband can tell when those sad times are coming. It starts in October and lasts through November, the last months when I lived at the maternity home. Now I won't have to be sad at this time of year anymore," she exclaimed, sounding hopeful, as if waiting for me to confirm her statement.

I felt the need to say something in response, but I was temporarily lost in thought. Perhaps it was just coincidence, but maybe, just maybe, I'd heard the music in utero and remembered it.

"So, this Friday night would be a good time for you?" she asked, after a short pause.

"Yes, Friday night would be great."

"I'll meet you at the entrance around seven."

*   *   *

I didn't mention the Friday meeting to my parents. Clearly, Mom wasn't happy. Each time we met in the house, the air was thick with tension. Our relationship, never strong, seemed to be weakening. The unspoken house rule still prevailed: Don't bring up a subject, and it will cease to exist. Several times, I caught Mom speaking in hushed tones on the phone, quickly hanging up when I got near. I knew she was talking to Aunt Lorraine and that I was the topic of conversation.

Dad seemed crankier with me than usual but didn't mention my birth mother again. I think they were both hoping she'd just disappear. We had our one visit, and that would be it.

The good news was Matthew didn't object when he learned of the next meeting. We were watching TV together upstairs in my house on Thursday evening, and he seemed confident enough about my birth mother. He no longer feared she'd try to hurt me.

"Just try not to mention it to your folks," he warned. "At least for now."

He was right. Mom and Dad needed a cooling down period; we all did. It was especially nice to have Matthew finally acknowledge my feelings, and from that moment on, I was actually hungry again. It was slightly more than a week since we'd first met, and I hadn't regained an ounce. I was skinnier than ever, though oddly, nobody seemed to notice.

Unfortunately, I didn't take Matthew's advice. Just as I was leaving the next evening, Mom came down from upstairs.

"Where are you going?" she asked, pursing her lips.

From her expression, I had a feeling she knew exactly where I was headed, but it was impossible because I'd been careful not to mention anything.

I was just about to lie and say I was meeting Janine for a movie when the words wouldn't escape my lips. I wasn't a liar. My nature was to be straight and upfront.

I took a deep breath.

"I'm meeting my birth mother at the Fireplace."

"Again?" she practically growled.

I nodded.

She didn't say another word, but the expression on her face couldn't be missed: She was angry.

*   *   *

We met outside the restaurant as planned. My stomach tightened when I saw her—not because I was nervous again, but because I knew my actions were hurting Mom. There was really no turning back at this point—not that I ever could; this was my life path, a road I had to follow. I'd always known someday I'd find my original mother, and I did. Now I needed to make sure I didn't destroy my relationship with Mom. There had to be a way for both mothers to remain in my life.

The air had turned sharply colder, and I wore a denim jacket lined with flannel. She was wearing a black jacket with "Steven Knightly" stitched on the back. As we entered the restaurant, she saw me eyeing her jacket.

"I got this from Richard's dance studio. He owns one in Livingston."

"Livingston?"

"Yes. It's located close to Trenton State University."

"Oh," I said, stopping in my tracks. "Did you know I was going to call that studio months ago when I started searching for you?"

She looked at me in disbelief.

"If you'd called there, you definitely would have found me right away."

"I called the studio in Goshen first," I explained. "But nobody'd heard of your maiden name. I assumed you didn't work as a dance teacher anymore and figured it would be a waste of time to call the other studios."

"It worked out anyway," she said, stepping up to the restaurant counter and glancing at the menu displayed on the back wall. "You were definitely meant to find me."

Our food came quickly, and we carried our trays to a table next to the window. The face-to-face meeting was a lot easier the second time around. The anxiety hadn't completely vanished, but I was a lot more comfortable now. Little by little, the circumstances surrounding my birth and adoption were falling into place.

I poured Italian dressing over my salad and began eating.

"I want to tell you something," she began. "About a year ago, I visited a psychic." She looked up at me waiting to see my expression at the mention of the word *psychic*. When I didn't respond, she went on. "She told me many things that eventually happened. For one, she predicted Richard would be flat out on his back ... and you know what?"

I looked at her expectantly.

"A couple of months later, Richard pulled something in his back and was out, literally on his back for months. He needed physical therapy, and he's fine now, but this psychic was very good. She also told me that a red-haired woman was going to come into my life again. She said she was going to change my life forever. And I immediately thought, *Oh my God, not my mother!* She had red hair—I was convinced it was going to be my mother, but ... it was you, eventually you came."

I didn't know what to say.

"I should set up an appointment with you to see her. She's very good. Have you ever been to a psychic before?"

I told her I hadn't. For some reason, the idea of visiting a psychic never entered my mind. Throughout my life, there was a broader awareness that I was in tune with, being able to perceive people's feelings and attitudes simply by being in their company. I had my own sense of knowing—sort of a sixth sense. However, psychics intrigued me, and I figured that someday, I'd eventually go and see one, more out of curiosity than needing to know what was going to happen in my future.

"Did you think of any questions to ask me?" she asked, bringing me back to the moment.

"Yes, I wrote them down."

But before I could reach for my purse on the table, she took a deep breath and smiled.

"I seem to be the one who does most of the talking. There are some things I want to ask you. I was wondering if you ever took dance classes while you were growing up."

"Yes, I did," I said gulping a mouthful of root beer. "When I was about three years old through the first grade, I took tap and ballet. But the lessons stopped when we moved to Florida."

"You lived in Florida?"

I explained that my family had lived in Lantana for five years.

"We hated Florida. It was hot and muggy all the time, and there were bugs everywhere." I grimaced. "Flying palmetto bugs! Every month, the exterminator would come. We missed the seasons, especially the fall and winter. There were no changing autumn leaves, and I went through most of my school years without snow. I think I missed that the most."

She listened intently. It was the first time I'd actually spoken at any length, and she took in my every word and gesture. When I paused to take another bite of my salad, she broke in.

"Anne, do you like to ski?"

I quickly swallowed and nodded my head. "Matthew and I go skiing at Vernon Valley a lot, and sometimes we go to places in Pennsylvania."

"We like to go to Utah for skiing. We try to go at least once a season, usually in March or April, when the weather is warmer."

"I've never skied west of Pennsylvania."

"If you like to ski, you and Matthew should try Utah sometime. One of the pictures I gave you was taken there."

I talked a little bit about the Florida town where my family lived and my current residence in Wyckoff. I mentioned my large family and how I saw my grandparents, cousins, aunts, and uncles on a regular basis.

"That's so nice. I always imagined you were an only child."

"My two brothers are also adopted."

Out of the blue, she leaned toward me, a serious expression on her face. "I think you should call me Jo."

I nodded in agreement. Now the question was settled. I'd called her Jo.

Jo smiled and continued talking about her life. It had been full of hardships, especially after her marriage to Richard.

"We waited a couple of years before having children. Sara came first, and then I became pregnant with Matt two years later. While pregnant, I discovered Richard was cheating on me and I kicked him out. I wasn't going to put up with that. He went to live with the other woman, and there I was, six months pregnant. We separated, but never went through with an official divorce. I pretty much raised my older children on my own."

"Did you ever try to get in contact with your family at that point, to help out?"

"No, I didn't want their help," she said, lowering her eyes. "I never had contact with them again. They didn't even know I had children. I went to work and survived on my own. For a while, I dated, and there was even a steady boyfriend who lived with us for a short time. He was Hungarian, but it wasn't serious."

"Was it difficult raising two children on your own?"

"Yes." She sighed deeply. "Richard helped out and gave me money. But I needed to pay rent, so eventually, I got a job working as an exotic dancer in Newark." She lowered her eyes again.

"Oh," was all I could manage to say. What, exactly, did exotic dancing entail? I didn't dare ask.

Jo picked up her fork and pushed the remaining salad around on her plate. Then she looked up and forced a smile.

"It paid well, and you do what you need to do."

I shifted uneasily in my seat while Jo sat up straight, regaining her confidence.

"The hours work out wonderfully when you have small children. The babysitter used to come in the evenings at seven, and Sara and Matt were already bathed and in their pajamas. All she needed to do was get them into bed a half hour later. Richard was good, though. He made sure they had new coats for the winter and new clothes for school and stuff like that," she added, almost defensively. "After ten years, Richard and I decided to get back together. I wanted to have another baby and told Richard we should do it right this time. Within a year, I became pregnant with Jessica. I was thirty-seven when I had her." Quickly, I did the calculation: I was seventeen when she gave birth.

"It was very hard not to have a father for Sara and Matt. Matt really needed a man in his life while growing up, like all boys do. Life has been very hard …" She paused again, her mind far away. "But recently, things have been working out better. I did consider trying to find you a few years ago, after you turned eighteen. But Richard thought that Sara needed me more at the time. You see, we had some trouble with her while she was in high school. So I didn't bother trying at that point. Actually, we're having problems with Matt now. He's been cutting school too much, and we're considering sending him away to a military school where they should be able to whip him into shape," she said with a small laugh. "I'm so happy you were able to have such a good childhood, with two parents, siblings, and a happy home," she said, waiting for a response.

I sat back in my chair. She must have sensed my uneasiness because the color nearly drained out of her face. I couldn't validate her comment. How could I explain my upbringing wasn't what she hoped for? It was true there was a roof over my head, food to eat, and clothes to wear, the things she wrote about in the letter. They were necessary, but they were just an outer shell of family life.

I thought about the many nights when I cried myself to sleep after being berated by my father, the many days I sat in school, exhausted and unable to concentrate on my studies. There was no way to describe the fear present in a house where a father, who was charming one moment, could unpredictably swing into a dark, menacing mood, and where the mother never intervened on the children's behalf.

Jo was waiting for a reply, a hint of apprehension in her eyes. It appeared as though she didn't want to hear anything negative, only a fairy tale about how the daughter she gave up for adoption was taken into a wealthy family, lavished with love, and given everything she needed. Listening to the hardships in her life made me think twice about whether or not she should know about my childhood—all the intricate details. I wanted her to know, but she looked so positively afraid, so ready to break. I would have given the world to be able to take away the look on her face as she sat there waiting for me to calm her worst fears. Her life was difficult indeed, and I didn't have the heart to tell her about what it was like growing up with my family.

Nodding, I forced a weak smile, and her tension vanished in the blink of an eye.

I thought about the nuns and how they hid the pregnant girls. Was I any better than they were, covering up the mistakes of others with lies? Maybe their actions were right, protecting the girls and their babies, trying to cover up the shame of having a baby out of wedlock. Wasn't it the motive behind each action that mattered?

Jo smiled again, and a rush of warmth engulfed me. Surely, I'd done the right thing.

*　　*　　*

As I drove home, the what-ifs danced in my mind. I hated thinking this way. The what-ifs shouldn't matter. How could they? The past was over, never to be recaptured. What-ifs never came true.

But the question didn't go away. What if she had kept me? Squeezing my eyes tight, I saw exactly the burden I'd have been. Her family wouldn't have supported her, and even if Richard had agreed to marry, he still cheated years later. In the end, my presence would be blamed for the failed marriage. I couldn't see my life being any better if Jo had raised me instead. In fact, it was more likely it'd be worse.

The more I thought about it, the more at peace I was that the what-ifs never occurred. Jo had my best interest at heart on that surrender day in 1966. Although my adopted family was nowhere near perfection, my parents tried their best. Nothing was deliberate. They were still my family, and I couldn't imagine living the rest of my life without them.

*   *   *

Later that night after arriving home, I talked with Matthew on the phone. I told him about Jo's difficult life.

"You know what I think?" he said smugly.

"What?" I asked, bracing myself, even though it was obvious what was coming, one of his snide remarks.

"Life is a series of choices—you have to live with whatever decisions you make," he said simply.

"I see your point, but things aren't always so cut and dry."

"I think they are."

"There were influences in her life that shaped the decisions she made. We all come from different backgrounds, and some of us have better support systems in place than others."

"Regardless of her family life, she made a bad choice jumping from one guy's bed into another's. After giving birth to you, she quickly married. She could've kept you. She had choices; she made them."

There was no point arguing with him further. Where I saw light, he saw darkness. If I showed him one of my father's shiny gold coins, Matthew would turn it over, looking for the tarnish.

"Ah, this isn't worth that much money," he'd say.

But he was right—people made choices and reaped what they sowed. Unfortunately, children weren't in the position to make choices. They had to live with the conditions created by their parents.

Part Three

"However long the day, night must fall." —Irish Proverb

Twenty-Five

Repercussions

The last two weeks had been the longest in my life. So much had happened. Assimilating all the information about my origins was extremely difficult, but slowly, the emotional fog was lifting. Almost everybody in the family knew about Jo—Mom, Dad, Brian—all but Thomas. He'd been away on a training seminar in Dallas and had arrived home the day before.

When I awoke the following morning, I discerned the voices of Mom and Thomas coming from downstairs. Sound traveled well through the heating ducts in my house. They were arguing about something. I rolled onto my stomach and pulled the pillow over my head, hoping to sleep late and willing their voices away.

But their voices grew louder, and my name was mentioned several times. Suddenly, there was pounding on my door.

"Wake up!" Thomas yelled.

"What do you want?" I asked wearily, even though I knew perfectly well what was on his mind. Mom had told him about Jo. I sensed a burning rage from him, a rage I wouldn't be able to ignore.

"How could you do that to my mother?" he shrieked, flinging open the door.

"Do what?" I replied, yawning. I tried to feign ignorance, hoping he'd give up and go away.

But I wasn't that lucky because he stood towering over my bed, his green eyes piercing through me.

"You know what you did," he said through gritted teeth. "You hurt my mother!"

Mom, hovering in the hallway, began pleading with him to stop. "Thomas … You're getting too excited."

"No! Anne's wrong! She had no right to find her!" he shrieked.

"This has nothing to do with you," I stated calmly, returning Thomas's glare.

"He's only concerned about me!" Mom screamed.

"I know … but he has no right coming in here like a maniac," I pointed out, sitting up and pulling the covers around me. Two pairs of eyes were glaring at me, as if I were the family traitor. "You both knew that someday I'd look and eventually find her. I mentioned it many times over the years."

"But we never thought you'd actually go through with it," Mom hissed.

"I'm not trying to replace or hurt any of you," I said pausing. I looked from one face to the other, but their angry expressions didn't change. "I needed to find answers …"

"It was wrong!" Thomas cut me off. In his fury, he looked slightly mad. Just then, he turned and started to cry.

"I know you're only feeling bad for me," Mom crooned to Thomas, glaring my way. She went over and put her arm around his shoulders and led him out of my room. Thomas turned, about to say something else, but she pulled him along, and they went downstairs together, leaving me in bed, exasperated.

Why was Thomas attacking me in this way? Never before had the three of us treated each other in this manner—we all got enough of it from Dad. I knew his accusation about hurting Mom wasn't the real reason be barged through my bedroom door. There was something deeper gnawing at him, driving him to another incident shortly before this business trip when he'd stayed out all night. Shelley told us he was stone drunk when he returned home early the next morning. He was in no shape to go to work that day. Like Mom, Shelley didn't think he had a serious problem, just needed to get his pre-wedding jitters out. But I thought he drank way too much and wondered if it had anything to do with the fact that he was in the dark regarding his origins. If only he'd consider learning the details surrounding his own birth, there was a good likelihood this would provide him with closure. Being kept in the dark and wondering is far worse than learning the truth, no matter how horrible the truth may be. For me, now that I knew, the questions were gone and my life had a clearer road ahead. Thomas was in limbo.

I quickly took a shower, allowing the hot water to pound my shoulders and back. The weight of the world seemed to rest there, and the heat, although soothing, didn't seem to be helping much this morning. I toweled dry, put my hair up in a ponytail, and then pulled on jeans and an old black sweatshirt, heading straight for the front door. Matthew was coming to pick me up, but I never made it outside; instead, Dad cut me off at the bottom of the stairs and motioned me into the family room.

"Sit down," he said sternly, his eyebrows drawn. "We want to talk to you."

Reluctantly, I took a seat on the couch across from Mom, who was still in her bathrobe, a wrinkled tissue clutched in her hands. She stared at me with icy eyes. I could feel the coldness pierce through me, twisting and turning. I braced myself for the onslaught.

"We want to tell you how disappointed we are," he began. "You deeply upset your mother and me. We don't appreciate what you've done to us … after all we've done for you."

His accusations made me pause. After all, he was the one who provided me with the information to start my search. Without his help, I may never have located Jo.

"There was never any intention of hurting either one of you," I slowly responded. I looked at Dad and then over at Mom.

Dad's eyes glowed darker, darker than I'd ever seen before.

"We're your parents, not her," he lashed out. "She left you after you were born, and we raised you."

"Dad, that isn't the point—" I interrupted, but before I could say more, he glared viciously down at me and I shrank backwards.

"I can't understand how you could want to know someone who did that to you!" His voice grew even stronger. "Why would you want to even bother with someone like that?"

My voice came out barely above a whisper.

"I needed to know about my background and the reasons why I was placed for adoption."

"There's no excuse for what she did!" he boomed.

It dawned on me that his anger was directed more at Jo than at me.

"I don't see why you're mad at her for giving me up. I'm glad she did; otherwise, I wouldn't have lived with you and you wouldn't be my parents."

"I'm mad at what she did to you!" he shouted. He ignored my reasoning. Apparently, blaming Jo was a welcome excuse to unleash his inner turmoil.

But I hadn't seen Dad this mad in such a long time. A sense of dread washed over me; he appeared to be going out of control, and his comment about Jo not wanting me was enough to stir a fiery argument, but I knew it wouldn't help the situation.

"She did nothing wrong," I said anyway in Jo's defense. Knowing her story made her action, however horrible it appeared to my family, perfectly sensible. She was a young girl in trouble with no one willing to help. If anything, I thought, her decision displayed courage.

"I think she actually did the right thing. She made sure I was adopted into a family. I'm thankful to her for that."

"You're right," he agreed with sarcasm, walking directly in front of me so that he stood towering over where I sat. "I should thank her for giving you away. If she didn't, then we wouldn't have you. If I ever meet her, I'm going to tell her exactly that."

His tone was mocking, and I knew he was trying to tempt me into a fight. He craved any opportunity to throw his weight around, and today, I was his sacrificial lamb. I knew he was watching for signs of weakness, an opportunity to deepen his attack, but I wasn't going to make it easy for him.

Instead, I stared directly into his eyes and said in a low, calm voice, "Jo isn't ever going to replace the two of you." I hesitated, then added, "I guess only time will prove it. You'll see that you're both still my parents."

Glancing first at Mom and then at Dad, I looked for a glimmer of softness in their expressions. Perhaps it was foolish for me to expect some understanding, but lately, it was what I really needed. Instead, I only received more of the same.

"We think you're acting ungrateful for all that we've done for you," Mom snapped.

"That's right," he echoed. "We were the ones who fed, clothed, and took care of you."

"We took you into this family when she wouldn't," Mom added. "Is this how you repay us?"

Their words cut through me like a knife. I tried to tell myself it didn't matter, that nothing they said mattered. But deep down, I knew it did.

Dad kept on.

"You especially hurt your mother." He pointed her way. She began to wipe her eyes, nodding vigorously. I saw no point in trying to reason with them. They may have heard my words, but they weren't listening. "You were wrong, goddamn it!" He turned and almost punched the wall. But instead of hitting the wall, he caught himself and slammed his fist into his other hand.

"Son of a bitch!" he said, shaking his hand and wincing. Rather than trying to calm him, Mom seemed almost glad he was angry with me. "What the hell is the matter with you? Did you think she'd like this?"

"I didn't mean to hurt either of you, and I'm sorry if I did." I began to feel a lump in the back of my throat as I fought back tears.

He was unmoved by my apology.

"You were fucking wrong!"

I didn't flinch at his profanity, as most people did, and instead held my ground, determined as ever.

"I always knew about being adopted, and it's very hard to know and not wonder," I said, my voice cracking. "Why did you even tell us anyway?"

"We had to tell you," Mom answered.

"Why? I'd never have guessed I was adopted. I look more like this family than my natural one," I explained. "Didn't you think someday there was a possibility one of us might search for our birth parents?"

"No," she said coolly. "We never thought any of you would do it."

"Many times I said I was going to try and find her. I know I mentioned it."

"I guess I didn't think the records would be accessible; they're supposed to be sealed."

Yes, they were supposed to be sealed, but how long can you keep such a secret hidden? There are always ways to uncover the truth. I thought about the ALMA guidebook and the suggestions they recommended for dealing with adoption agencies and government record keepers. It was all such a big game. A lot of problems would be easily avoided if the truth was revealed right from the beginning. Tell us who our birth parents were, why they couldn't raise us, and let us see some pictures. And for those families who may want to venture a little further, maybe periodic letters and perhaps a visit once or twice a year could be arranged.

I looked at them curiously and wondered if my solution would've sat well back when they adopted the three of us. By the way they were currently reacting, it was highly doubtful. They both teemed with anger.

"I still can't believe you were able to find her," Mom said, shaking her head.

"I was able to find Jo because I knew about being adopted," I started to explain. "There's always a trail left behind every secret. Why bother telling us we're adopted if you can't accept that someday the birth parent may be found?"

I'd never understand how they could consciously expect us to know about having other family and in the same breath, expect us to simply ignore that fact.

"Well, we did tell you," she said flatly. "And you should be grateful to us for raising you."

"I am grateful, but it should make no difference whether or not I'm adopted. All children should be grateful to their parents." I shifted in my seat and then looked directly into Mom's eyes. "You wanted me to know that I'm adopted … but then you wanted me to forget about it?"

"Yes."

"I thought the whole purpose of adoption was to give a child a home and parents who will treat the child as their own. Parents are supposed to put their children first, to sacrifice for them. Children should not have to sacrifice for their parents. How can you expect me to be able to ignore the fact that I have other family somewhere in the world?"

Mom didn't answer. She wiped her nose with her tissue and looked away.

I jumped up from my seat.

"We have feelings just like you do!" I added with a bit of desperation. I walked toward the doorway where my father was now standing, but he didn't budge.

"Well, our feelings are hurt!" Mom exploded.

"So are mine!" I shot back. "The way you're treating me is making me sick. Haven't you even noticed that I've lost so much weight?" I cried, pointing towards my middle.

Mom turned her head to the side. She didn't want to even look at me.

"Do you think I deliberately wanted to hurt you? My finding Jo had nothing to do with hurting you and Dad."

"You're the one who is causing all the grief," she responded, her head still turned to the side.

"Sit down!" Dad bellowed. He was rocking back and forth on his feet, his eyes wild and furious.

Quickly, I plopped onto the couch, resigned to the fact that the conversation was far from closed. I didn't want to be there—none of us did. But we were tangled in this ugly web, unable to escape—Dad the accuser, Mom the victim, and me the accused and accursed. Yet our parts were interchangeable; we all had a bit of each role within us.

I chanced a quick peek out of the window behind me. A silver car was circling the cul-de-sac, but it was a Subaru, the neighbor's car, not Matthew's Camaro.

"Look at me! I'm not done talking!" Dad screamed. "We buy you everything you need."

"That's right." Mom turned and looked at me again. "You always had a new outfit for Easter and Christmas."

They went on and on about all the material things given to me over the course of my life. I pretended to listen, but my thoughts were lost to them, and instead focused on Matthew. I needed him so desperately and wondered why he hadn't arrived yet. Eventually, Dad lowered his voice. His dark eyes penetrated mine.

"I hope you still want to live in this house with us."

"Yes, of course I do," I answered immediately.

"We thought you might want to go and live with your real mother now."

"I never said I wanted to do that. I'm going to stay here until I get married."

"That's what your mother and I want, you're staying here." Dad's eyebrows scrunched together. His request was more like a demand.

"I'm not moving out. Like I said earlier, you'll see I'm not trying to replace you."

Finally, I heard Matthew's car pulling up in front of the house. Mom's expression remained mournful and angry.

"Are you going to continue seeing her?" she asked.

I nodded, not wanting to lie.

"Umm ..." I hesitated, not sure if this was the right time to bring this up. "Would you like to meet her?"

"Yes," Dad replied, glancing at Mom. "Erin, what do you think?"

She didn't answer right away; she was looking down at her feet. After a moment, she looked up at Dad.

"I don't know right now," she said sharply, giving him an annoyed look.

There was a short pause, and I sprang from my seat and bolted out of the family room, sweeping past Dad. I knew that I had to run and get far away immediately. No sooner had the front door shut behind me when their voices rose in argument. Mom was yelling about Thomas's wedding rehearsal dinner, only a couple of weeks away. This was the only preparation Mom was asked to do. Shelley's mother decided on everything else. Mom didn't mind. Mrs. Carter was paying, after all.

"You were supposed to make the reservation. I called the restaurant today, and they don't have our name and now they are solid booked for that night!" Mom screamed.

"Oh ... it's my fault, huh?" Dad started.

But I was already outside before I could hear more. My lungs filled with fresh air, and my body began to relax; the heavy burden of guilt weighing heavily upon my shoulders lightened. Although it was late fall, it felt like Indian summer. The weather, like my life, was unsettled, trying to decide what season it was supposed to be. I removed my shoes and strolled across the lawn. The dew was heavy in the grass. My feet, now wet, felt like running as fast as they could to any place without yelling, fighting, or constant barrages. I turned my face up toward the sun, allowing the heat to penetrate my skin.

As it worked its way through my body, hope spread that the family chill might eventually warm.

From here on out, I'd have to proceed with extra caution. Walking through the minefield of the future, I didn't really know what to do—how to react anymore.

Perspiration formed around my hairline and began to trickle down my cheeks. Flushed, I waited as Matthew maneuvered his car along the curb, an inquisitive look on his face. I bent down to slip my shoes back on. As he got out of his car, tears filled my eyes. When we reached each other, I broke down.

"What's wrong?" he asked, noticing the tears that were now streaming down my cheeks.

I wiped them away with the back of my hand. I was trembling and tried to steady myself.

"I feel as if everyone has ganged up on me," I said miserably. "You seem to be part of the gang as well … I thought I could have you to turn to."

Matthew breathed in deeply. He hated to see anybody cry, but I couldn't turn off my tears.

"I'm not taking their side. You know I'm always there for you," he said, moving closer.

"This isn't about taking sides. This shouldn't be a battle. My parents feel I should hate Jo because she gave me away, but I don't. I can't turn my back on her. It seems nobody can understand this except—me."

Matthew let out a long sigh.

"You can count on me to be there for you. I'm sorry for the way I acted." He put his arms around my waist.

"You mean you won't yell at me anymore?" I asked, brushing away my tears.

"I'm sorry," he said hugging me. "I can't understand what you did because I've never been in your shoes. I always knew my background … I guess I can see how you needed to know those things."

I buried my head in his chest.

"I did need to know."

"But all you've done is cry." He stepped back and gently lifted my chin. "And you look so upset. I don't see the benefit of knowing her if it's going to cause you so much misery."

"I'm not miserable because I found Jo," I said looking up. "I'm miserable because everyone is making me feel so guilty—even your parents. I'm being made out like some criminal on a quest to replace my Mom and Dad."

"That's what your parents fear," he whispered.

"That they'll lose me?"

"Yeah ... and ... they're jealous."

"So far, they've seen I haven't left them to go and live with Jo. The jealousy is something they need to handle. You know I'd never allow Jo to replace them."

"I know."

"They're my parents, the ones who raised me. Still, I can't help but feel for Jo. She's my mother too. I know she didn't raise me, but there's some sort of connection, and she seems so happy. I'm sure she wants to be a part of my life." My stomach ached. I wanted to be a part of her life too. How could I walk away now?

"And you know what?" I asked on a brighter note. "I'm happy when we're together. Why should we be forced to stay apart? Nobody should ever be excluded ... I think we have suffered enough."

He took my hand and led me to his car. The warmth of his touch stirred a craving inside to be a little girl again, sitting on my grandmother's lap. Those times were so peaceful, so innocent—they took precedence over the unhappier ones. Matthew was aware of the way my father carried on over the years, but lately, Dad hadn't flown off the handle—until today. Maybe it was Thomas's wedding, only three weeks away. It seemed all their accumulated stress released on me today.

We pulled away from my house, heading toward the highway. Where we were going didn't matter. At that moment, I felt safe and secure.

We didn't say a word for the longest time until Matthew broke the silence. "You look so sad," he said glancing my way.

"It's better to feel sad than to feel nothing at all." My eyes met his. "At least the empty space inside is filled ... I know this is hard to understand but I have two mothers, one who raised me and one who carried me for nine months. I won't ignore either one; I consider both very important and want them to be a part of my life."

"I think I'm beginning to understand a little better."

"And Jo, she's been so easy to talk to. That's something I never had with my mom."

"I don't get it. Your parents went out of their way to adopt you and your brothers. It should've been a happy home."

"It wasn't bad all the time."

He looked at me sideways.

"It wasn't ... My father can be very nice—at times. Even though he was nasty and blamed us for everything, I don't think he ever realized how much he terrorized us."

"What about your mother? Why did she allow it?"

"She's so distant and unemotional. Who knows what's running through her mind? I can remember a couple of times she confronted Dad about his behavior, but then again, it was mainly because he was so loud and she was afraid the neighbors would hear." I sighed. "It's so hard to explain … Mom needed to work through my childhood. She was sleeping all the time. When she wasn't sleeping, she cooked dinner, read books, and drove us to sports practices—and that's it. I have no memories of her ever talking or playing a game with my brothers or me."

We spent the evening at Matthew's house by ourselves. His parents weren't home, and I fully savored this quiet time, cuddled up close. Already, I was feeling a whole lot better; the encounter earlier at my house now seemed a distant memory, one that I wanted to forget. I didn't think it would be easy to shake off such a bad scene so quickly. Maybe it was the way Matthew held me in his arms the entire evening or maybe it was the fact that he was starting to come around—he was actually listening to my explanations without jumping down my throat—but I didn't care what the cause was for my current state of calm, I was just glad there was at least one person standing beside me.

*   *   *

The next day, before leaving for work in the morning, Dad confronted me again. *Apparently, he got such a high from yesterday's argument that he wants a replay,* I thought to myself as he rehashed yesterday's argument ending with an exaggerated, "I can't believe you're doing this to your mother and me." I didn't respond and instead stood perfectly still, waiting till he was finished and then left for work, crying the whole way there. It continued every evening that week; Dad and Mom telling me how ungrateful I was. By Friday, I bypassed going home after work and instead drove straight to Matthew's.

By the look on his face when he opened the front door and saw me standing there, trembling, I knew Matthew sensed that I was at my wits' end. He tried everything to cheer me up, first bringing me for Häagen-Dazs ice cream and then going to the Palisades Cliffs to take in the magnificent view of New York City, but nothing could shake the chill that coursed through me. Even hearing him whistle or sing his silly cartoon theme songs couldn't lighten up my mood, and by the time Matthew drove me home, he was just as melancholy as I was.

We slowly got out of the car and walked up to my front door. The air had finally turned cooler, and the sky was a clear cobalt blue, the moon glowing in the background. All was quiet except for the sound of a dog barking in the distance. As we stood together, I looked up at him; his eyes were warm and caring. *This is what I live for,* I reminded myself. Soon, we'd be married, and things would get better. Matthew always told me that someday it would be just the two of us, but I didn't think he meant it literally. Now that was a possibility. There had to be a way to reach my parents without first destroying what little bit we had left between us.

I broke the silence.

"What should I do?"

He shook his head.

"I know …" I said suddenly. "Let's go find an apartment, and we'll move in together."

"That wouldn't go over so well with my mom," he said chuckling.

Mrs. Bauer still forced everyone to attend mass every Sunday, even though her sons were in their twenties. I went along with it for Matthew's sake, though my beliefs were far from the Catholic doctrine whose main purpose seemed to be fear and manipulation of the masses.

"It couldn't be worse than what she thinks of me now. Anyway, I'm not going to live my life based on someone else's beliefs. There's nothing wrong with living together before you're married."

The smile vanished from his face.

"I know … I know … but there's enough trouble with your folks, why add mine to the mix?"

"We're both adults and work full-time! We're not dependent on our parents anymore, and we shouldn't have to live our lives dictated by what our parents want—this isn't the dark ages, for Christ's sake! If we want to live together now, we'll live together, whether or not my parents or your parents approve." I was getting annoyed. He always wanted to take the easy road, even if it meant giving in to avoid confrontations. I lived my life one confrontation after the other in the shadow of my father. It would take a lot more than our parents' sour faces to get to me. "And furthermore," I continued, "I'm not going to remain living in such horrid conditions, with everyone badgering me left and right just because you want to make your mother feel better by upholding her religious convictions." It felt good to get some of my spunk back; the last few weeks had been so draining. It was so unusual for me to be down all the time. "If things don't improve at home, I'm leaving and getting my own place. You can join me if you'd like."

"Anne, calm down … You're right. If it gets any worse, you can leave. Come and live with me at my parents' house until we find something of our own."

My eyes widened. "Let's do it."

Matthew shook his head.

"No. First go and try again and ignore the yelling. Our wedding will be here sooner than you think … Let me see … only seven more months. In the meantime, this should pass."

"Do you really think so?"

"I don't know." He squeezed me tightly then looked into my eyes with a serious expression. "I just don't know."

Twenty-Six

The Crowleys

Things did lighten up at home. Instead of my family barraging me all the time about Jo, they simply didn't talk to me. However cold it may seem, I welcomed the peace and took advantage of the tranquility. The following weekend, I visited Grandma. She hadn't changed much. Her face shone like porcelain, and her spirit, the little bit she had left, seemed to elevate when she saw me come through her door.

"Anne ..." She smiled. Her eyes lit up. "Come ... give me ... a kiss." She sat in her wheelchair, stationed next to the navy blue velvet couch, dressed in a pale pink housecoat with white slippers on her feet. A documentary about wild bees was on the television.

I kissed her cheek and gently hugged her.

"Hi, Grandma. It's so good to see you." I looked around. "Where's Grandpa?"

"Out ... food ... shopping."

"Ahh," I said settling onto the couch.

Grandpa shopped every weekend for their groceries, tobacco for his pipes, and different odds and ends for the house.

"I wonder what he'll bring home today," I mused.

Grandma smiled, shrugging one shoulder. Last month, he'd bought new wallpaper for the bathroom and hung it himself that very same evening.

After telling her how my job was, the easy stuff, I told her about Jo and about Thomas, and then hesitantly told her how Mom and Dad were reacting.

"I know ... Your Aunt Lorraine ... keeps me ... informed."

"What do you think?" I asked. "Am I such a monster?"

Her eyes filled with tears, and I regretted bringing the subject up at all. This was the last thing she needed. She still had Grandpa coming home drunk from time to time. She couldn't walk anymore and depended on an aide to clean her every day. I looked into her tear-filled eyes, and what I saw surprised me. There, beneath the tears, was a determined look.

"You ... did ... the ... right ... thing. Don't ... let ... anyone ... tell ... you ... otherwise."

We both smiled, and a warm feeling spread through my body. It was just what I needed to hear. And it was so nice being with Grandma; I only wished I could spend more time at her house. I took her advice and ignored any further comments. Over the course of the next two weeks, I busied myself with my daily routine: getting up each morning, going to work, and then spending time with Matthew.

*   *   *

The weekend before Christmas, Jo invited Matthew and me to dinner to meet her family for the first time. My stomach turned over in anticipation of seeing my half siblings.

Her house was in a small neighborhood on top of a mountain, Cooley Mountain, as Jo called it. I liked her house the moment I saw it. It was a lovely brick colonial on a large lot, surrounded by an abundance of oak and pine trees. As we were pulling into her driveway, my stomach did another flip-flop as a realization came over me: This was the place where I possibly would've been raised, if Jo and Richard had decided to keep me.

The wind had whipped the remainder of the golden and crimson leaves, leaving the branches bare. Jo was standing outside her front door. She was wearing a pair of slim black slacks and a silver and gold sequin top that accentuated her slender figure. Her jet-black hair blew in the wind around her flawless complexion. I was again reminded of how young Jo appeared.

"Ready?" Matthew asked, pulling behind Jo's red Jeep.

"I don't know," I said nervously. Then I grinned. "Of course, I'm so excited!"

Matthew laughed and took my hand, and together, we made our way to the front door.

"Hello!" Jo greeted us.

We quickly embraced, and I introduced Matthew. Richard was standing just inside the front door waiting for us. He stared directly into my eyes then looked suddenly away.

"This is Anne Marie and her fiancé Matthew," Jo said proudly, a smile plastered over her face. "Doesn't she look like her father?" she said turning to Richard.

He was still standing there with a dumbfounded look on his face until he finally snapped out of it and exclaimed rather loudly, "Wow! You're right, Jo," he said, scratching his square jaw. "She does look exactly like him."

He came over and kissed me on the cheek. He was a man of average height with a long Roman nose, a ruddy complexion, and a balding head with light brown hair. He flashed me a wide smile showing his perfect gleaming teeth. He stepped back, studying me further, shaking his head in disbelief.

"Richard remembers Sam," Jo explained, seeing the confused expression on my face. "When Richard started at the studio in Hoboken, Sam was still working there." Jo turned toward her husband.

We stepped further inside, and Richard hurriedly took our coats and disappeared into another room with them. The house was bright and large, with an oversized entrance hall. To the right was the living room, adjoined to a formal dining room, and to the left was a family room, adjoined to a kitchen and dinette area. The furniture was modern with a combination of black and beige leather chairs and a mahogany dining room set that was formally set with fine white china, long-stemmed wine glasses, and crimson dinner napkins.

Once in the living room, I looked up to see a tall, long-faced boy sitting on the arm of the couch. His auburn hair, exactly the same shade as mine, was pulled back into a ponytail. *This must be Matt.* Slumped into the couch next to him was Sara. She looked about my age, and like me, she too wore black jeans and a turtleneck sweater. Her hair was a much darker auburn, almost brown, and there was an abundance of freckles on her face. In person, it was even clearer they resembled their father. A *Simpsons* episode played on the television, and they both turned their eyes from the screen to look at me when I entered.

"Kids," Jo's voice broke the short silence. She motioned for them to rise. "This," she said, turning her eyes towards me, "is Anne Marie."

Suddenly, there was stomping coming from the stairs leading down into the foyer.

"Is she here?! Is she here?!" a little voice cried. Then, like a bolt of lightning, she sped into the living room and stopped short when she saw me standing next to Matthew and her mother. *This must be Jessica,* I thought smiling. She had gorgeous dark red hair, the shade of a copper penny.

"Don't you look pretty," I said to her.

A smile spread across her beautiful pale face. She was wearing a red velvet dress with a green sash and shiny red patent leather shoes.

Jessica squeezed onto the couch next to Sara, peeking at me and giggling. Richard brought in some chairs from the dining room, and we sat next to a bare eight-foot evergreen tree. It stood directly in front of the bay window, overlooking the front yard.

"We're going to decorate it tomorrow," Jo explained. "We just cut it down yesterday."

"I'm sure it'll be beautiful," I said, looking up at the top. "It's so tall. We always have an artificial tree every year. We didn't get ours up either. We're all crazy with my brother's upcoming wedding. It's next weekend."

We made small talk for a half hour, discussing Matt's passion for fixing cars, Jessica's preschool activities, and Sara's former glory years when she was much younger and played the trumpet in the school band. Richard stayed mostly in the kitchen, cooking.

"Richard owned his own restaurant a few years back when he needed a break from the dance business," Jo explained. "He loves to cook."

I felt so comfortable and right at home in her living room, surrounded by my half siblings—that is, until I saw it hanging over the couch. On the wall was a very recent family portrait, the five of them, gold framed and matted in ivory.

Jo saw me eyeing the photograph.

"Oh, we just had that portrait taken two weeks ago. Richard was in such a hurry to get it up that I settled for the gold-trimmed frame instead of the black one."

"You all look great," I said softly. My own voice startled me. There was a hint of envy laced in my tone when I realized I wasn't a part of their family portrait. Their smiles in the photograph, frozen in time, taunted me as if saying I'd lost my chance. It was too late to be a part of their family.

Richard returned from the kitchen, balancing a silver tray in his hands that contained goblets of red wine.

"Please take one." He offered one to me and Matthew.

"Thank you," we both replied, taking a glass. I sipped the wine slowly to be polite. I rarely drank alcohol, never having developed a taste for it.

There was a grand mahogany piano located in the far corner. Jo commented that Jessica took lessons once a week, and Sara and Matt played when they were younger. We talked more about Jessica.

"She isn't going to play sports," Jo said, shaking her head as if the very idea gave her the chills. "She's too talented in dancing. She started tap, ballet, and jazz classes when she was three. It's such a shame that Sara didn't want to continue with dancing when she was younger."

"Sara took dance lessons too?" I asked.

"Yes, but only for a few years. When she got older, she was more interested in playing soccer. And where did that get her?" she asked, glancing over to where Sara sat with a sour look on her face.

"We even gave them both lessons at Richard's studio. They both know the basics for ballroom dancing. But … they'd rather waste their talent on other things. Their grades were never too good in school, you know, so going into the dance business is a very good idea for them, especially Sara."

"Ma, I can't stand being at the studio," Matt said, standing up. He sauntered out of the room toward the kitchen.

Sara just rolled her eyes as she took a sip from a Pepsi can she was holding.

Matthew looked at me. We held each other's gaze for a second and then looked again at Jo. We both knew what the other was thinking: Mr. Bauer was the same way when he talked about his favorite subjects, food and fishing.

Soon, Richard announced that dinner was ready and led us into the dining room where we were met with a serving of salad waiting for each of us on our plates. Two bone-china candleholders held burning red candles, and Richard dimmed the lights as Matthew and I slid into our seats next to each other.

"I hope you like Italian food," Richard said, taking a covered bowl from the side hutch and placing it in the center of the table. It was full of steaming rolls.

It was apparent that Richard loved to entertain. He had prepared the Caesar salad we were already eating, followed by pasta, then the main course, chicken franchise, filet mignon, and sautéed broccoli with roasted garlic. Afterwards, he went back to the kitchen and started preparing hot fudge sundaes with fresh raspberries. Even Matthew, who was accustomed to eating large meals with his family, sighed deeply when he saw there was another course. I'd been a guest for dinner at other homes many times but had never sat down to such an elaborate and delicious meal. We were stuffed, but obligingly, Matthew and I ate everything placed before us.

We all lingered a bit longer at the table. Jo continued to chat about Jessica, who happily bounced in her seat, her eyes gleefully following the conversation. Across the table were Matt and Sara who didn't say much all evening. I glanced at my three half siblings, again remarking to myself how they all looked like their father. Jo seemed to stand apart from us all. She didn't resemble anyone. All I could think of was that this was the family I would've been a part of ... if only ... yes, if only ... They appeared sitting before me like fruit on the forbidden tree in the garden of paradise. I wasn't supposed to take a bite. But did I really want a bite? I couldn't be sure. Would I have been happy growing up with them? The more I entertained this possibility, the further I was from an answer. I looked across the table at Jo. She was sitting quietly, her hands clasped together on the table, a broad smile on her face, and her attention focused on me. There was only one certainty in my mind: It was thrilling to finally be with my other mother—and my other family.

Twenty-Seven

A Wedding And A Funeral

Despite the upcoming wedding competing with last-minute shopping, Christmas and all its preparations were made, and suddenly, the day was upon us. Like I did every year, I spent Christmas Eve at Aunt Lorraine's house with the entire crew smoking, drinking, telling stories, and singing old songs. On Christmas morning, my family opened presents around the Christmas tree. Later, Mom and Dad drove back up to Aunt Lorraine's during the afternoon to see Grandma and Grandpa again, giving Thomas and me the opportunity to go to our future in-laws' houses for dinner.

The minute I breezed through the Bauers front door, presents overflowing in my arms, I knew something was wrong. For one thing, Pop wasn't in his usual spot, rocking by the Christmas tree. Secondly, everyone spoke in hushed tones.

Mrs. Bauer, who was wearing a pair of wrinkled black slacks and a dull blue cardigan, came over and helped me with the packages. She looked at me with sad, tired eyes.

"Last night while you and Matthew were up at your aunt's house, Pop developed a fever and was having trouble breathing," she explained. "We took him to the hospital in the middle of the night."

I looked over at Matthew. His eyes looked red, like he'd been crying.

"Why didn't you call me this morning?" I asked, sitting next to him.

"I didn't want to upset your morning. I knew this would be the last time you'd wake up at home on Christmas."

193

My heart skipped a beat. That was my Matthew, caring to the core.

"They think he may have pneumonia," he whispered in a strained voice.

"I'm sure he's going to be all right," I said, putting my arms around him.

Like Grandma, Pop didn't walk too well after the stroke and relied on a walker at all times. But his speech was fine, and besides a weak heart from a case of rheumatic fever as a child, his health had been good. Mrs. Bauer, who looked exhausted beyond belief, welcomed cooking. She made a turkey with all the trimmings and said it kept her mind off of her father. After dinner, we all stopped by the hospital, bringing presents and trying to cheer Pop up as best we could.

"He looks bad," Matthew whispered to me as we were leaving. "I have a very bad feeling."

His skin was sallow and sunken, and he barely opened his eyes when we were present.

"He'll be all right," I said, looking back. Even though Matthew was right, I wanted to think positively, but his appearance scared me as much as it seemed to scare the rest of the family.

"Thank you for coming," Mrs. Bauer said, reaching out and holding my hands. Tears filled her eyes. "We're going to stay a bit longer."

I nodded, trying not to cry myself. Mrs. Bauer looked completely wiped out.

"Make sure you try and get some rest," I told her.

She nodded.

"Please tell your parents we're not going to be able to make the wedding on Saturday," she said sadly. "I'm sorry, but we need to be here."

*   *   *

We were all surprised when, a few days later, Thomas's wedding went off without a hitch. To begin with, the rehearsal dinner, the evening before, was a success. Mom and Dad were able to find another suitable restaurant, calming their nerves, and they both felt relieved to fulfill their one duty related to the wedding.

Snow softly fell just as the newlyweds exited the church at the end of the ceremony.

"What a beautiful effect for a December wedding," I exclaimed, standing outside the church in my black velvet and taffeta bridesmaid's gown.

"If you ask me, I think it's an ominous sign—worse than rain," Matthew said in a hushed tone.

Thomas looked dashing in his pin-striped tux, and Shelley wore a gown bought in New York at Valentine's studio. A tiara of white sparkling stones and baby roses completed the look, and the new Mr. and Mrs. Willoughby appeared like something out of a fairy tale. Rice was flying through the air as they ducked into their limo. The driver slowly cruised the circular drive in front of the church, two times for effect, before they pulled out onto the street.

The reception was held in the formal dining room at the Carters' country club. Last month, Mom finally lost the last ten pounds on her diet and looked fabulous in her emerald green evening gown. She claimed that for once in her life, she felt glamorous. I helped her with her makeup and hair and was in awe at her appearance. She swore she'd never gain the weight back again.

It was a fabulous reception with lots of food, a fantastic band, and even Brian came out of his shell and boogied the night away on the dance floor. He brought along one of his recent girlfriends, Claire, a nice, quiet, shy girl with flawless skin and shoulder-length flaxen blond hair. Mom hoped they'd get serious, but Brian only shook his head whenever he overheard the comments about his need to settle down. I didn't think Brian had any intentions of marrying anytime soon.

Mom was in her glory the entire day. Her father was at her side along with Dad, and her favorite sister and brother, Lorraine and Jimmy, sat at their table for dinner. The only thing missing was Grandma. She wouldn't attend, claiming it was too embarrassing to be in a wheelchair. Nobody could convince her otherwise. When Grandma made up her mind, it was pointless to even try.

Thomas and Shelley left the next morning for their honeymoon in Palm Beach, Florida. They were staying at Shelley's uncle's private villa right on the beach for a week. Two days later, weighted down with both Jo's and Thomas's wedding photos, I met Sharon, my fellow adoptee, and Janine for lunch.

Sharon wasn't living in the area anymore, having moved to North Carolina along with her family after graduating high school. The change in location did wonders for Sharon. She attended beauty school and currently worked as a hair stylist, whipping up trendy styles at an exclusive salon in the city of Raleigh. Her dyed platinum blond hair, which she presently had curled down to her shoulders, was a testament to her new occupation. She and her family were back for a week visiting relatives.

"You gotta be kidding me?" she said when I first told her about Jo on the phone.

"No, it's true." I briefly recapped Jo's story and promised to bring the photos when we met for lunch.

It felt so good to be in Sharon and Janine's company, they were both loyal in their affirmations that I'd done the right thing by seeking my birth mother.

"See if you can pick them out." I opened up the photo from the West Point Hotel competition. I showed it to anyone who expressed an interest and playfully made the person try to identify my parents.

Sharon's eyes scanned all the people in the photo.

"That's her." She pointed to the girl sitting across from Jo.

"No," I said. "That's not her. Look again, they're not sitting together."

"Oh, that's your father," Sharon said next, pointing directly at Sam.

"Can't you tell?" Janine giggled, having already gone through this guessing game. "They look like clones."

"Yes, it's him," I said giving Janine a sideways glance. She was always the jokester. I honestly enjoyed the lighter atmosphere. Everything was so serious lately, and I wished she was around more often.

"And can you tell who my mother is?" I asked Sharon.

Her eyes scanned the photo again. Janine pointed to the girl with the big blond hair and grinned. Sharon looked up at me. I shook my head. Then Sharon pointed to Jo.

"Yes, that's her. Can't you tell?"

"Your father looks like you, but she doesn't look anything like you," Sharon said. She studied her image more closely.

"Not even a little bit in the nose or maybe the lips?"

She shook her head. "I can definitely see a resemblance to your father. So tell me, what happened between them?"

By now, the story was well rehearsed. It was only two months since I'd found Jo, but it felt as if I'd known her for an eternity. Clearly, the story behind my adoption was intriguing. Janine sat wide-eyed, even though she'd heard it already, but Sharon stared straight ahead with a blank expression.

"Sharon, did you ever go and visit your birth mother?"

"No," she answered frowning. "My mom keeps bugging me to go."

"Then why don't you?" I asked incredulously. If only Mom was more like Mrs. Compton, things would be so much easier.

She shrugged.

"Sharon, she's been dying to meet you. Your own mom even wants to take you. What's the matter?"

"It's a long trip to San Francisco … and I'm not sure if I want to meet her."

I thought about what I'd read concerning adoptees and how many were torn between feeling guilty for wanting to search and the innate need to know their own origins. It was also common for adoptees to feel abandoned, especially when the reason behind their adoption was unknown, and this usually led to anger. It was obvious that Sharon, like my two brothers, was angry.

"Why not?" I asked. "Are you mad at her for giving you away?"

There was a short pause.

"I don't know," she said finally. There was a faraway expression on her face. "She gave me away, and that's that."

*   *   *

Three days into the New Year, Pop took a turn for the worse and needed a ventilator to breathe. We all stood outside his hospital room, waiting it out, Mrs. Bauer never left his side. He only hung on a few hours and peacefully died shortly before midnight.

His death took a toll on everyone, especially Matthew's mother. She sat directly in front of his coffin throughout the wake, dressed in a black wool skirt and sweater; a single string of pearls dangled around her neck. Her eyes were red and swollen, and she held up a white handkerchief to her face and stared at her father, dressed in his Sunday best, from her seat.

I knelt in front of the coffin, said a prayer, and proceeded to console the Bauers and other family members who lined up alongside to receive visitors. Then I stood next to Matthew the entire time, holding his hand, and telling him that Pop was in a better place along with his wife.

"I know ... I know." He squeezed my hand. "But I'm going to miss him."

The funeral had all the typical ingredients of a traditional Catholic funeral: two days of viewing at a funeral parlor, followed by a morning mass, and burial in the family plot at Windmere Cemetery. Afterwards, friends and family gathered for food and further condolences at the Bauers' house.

*   *   *

It was a long holiday season, and by the time January got into full swing, things had quieted down and settled into place. Thomas and Shelley returned from Florida, all smiles and deeply suntanned. They were deliriously happy and started redecorating their new house. They talked about starting a family right away, pacifying Mom's earlier worries. And Mom no longer verbalized any disapproval about Jo. If she harbored any resentment still, it didn't show. The subject simply wasn't brought up—for now.

Twenty-Eight

Dance Class

In the meantime, Jo and I continued to see each other. We went skiing in Pennsylvania and shopping at outlet stores and spent many Sunday dinners together at her house. Jo enjoyed telling old stories about her estranged family, the dance studio, and raising her children. I considered telling her something about my family life if she asked again, but she never did.

Jo's and Richard's lives were dominated by ballroom dancing. Jo offered to teach Matthew and me how to waltz so we could do something special at our wedding. We happily accepted and the next week began lessons at their Steven Knightly dance studio in Livingston.

We arrived a few minutes early for our first lesson and were immediately overtaken by the glamorous atmosphere. All the people in the studio, clients and teachers, were dressed as if they were going to a wedding. Jo told me to wear a dress and heels, but I hadn't expected such formality for dance lessons. It was a different world.

While Jo was finishing up with another couple, Matthew and I watched in awe. She had an easy, graceful style that was a pleasure to behold. When it was our turn, she came over and took my hand, pulling me to my feet. Matthew followed, and we were led into an adjoining room where mirrors adorned the walls from floor to ceiling. There were four brilliantly lit chandeliers hanging low, giving off light that bounced from mirror to mirror. Tucked away in the corner was a stereo. Jo put on Frank Sinatra and began to demonstrate the first steps of the fox-trot.

"Watch closely, Anne, these steps are for the female. You need to walk backwards while Matthew goes forward. Back, back, quick, quick," she chanted as she demonstrated the first step.

I tried to concentrate on what her legs were doing, but I was too caught up with her demeanor. She was full of animation, and her face glowed, alive with excitement.

"Come, let's do the first steps," she said, holding out her hand. I took her hand, and she led me to the center of the whitewashed hardwood floor. "Now I'll do the male step while you do the step I just showed you."

We danced the first step of the fox-trot over and over while Frank Sinatra bellowed "It Had to Be You." When we finished, it was Matthew's turn. Jo demonstrated the male steps, then switched to the female role while Matthew joined her.

Every time Jo and I were together, it was an unforgettable experience. Every night in bed, before falling asleep, I marveled at the fact that I knew Jo and looked forward to Tuesday evenings when we had our dance class. We learned not only the fox-trot but also the waltz, the cha-cha, and the rumba. A few times, I casually mentioned it to Mom and told her we planned to waltz at our wedding.

"Your father and I know how to dance too."

"You do? Maybe you can show me and Matthew some steps." I looked at her expectantly.

But no sooner were the words out of my mouth than her sulky expression clearly told me that she was in no way interested in teaching us anything. Although we weren't actively arguing, the atmosphere remained thick.

She shrugged, not seeming interested in my suggestion.

"Everybody knew how to dance when I was in high school. We didn't need to take lessons. We all learned from each other."

"It's a lot different today. Nobody knows how to dance anymore."

She nodded her head and returned to the evening news.

"Did you think about meeting Jo and her husband?"

"No," she answered quickly. "I haven't thought about it."

*   *   *

Eventually, Mom agreed to meet Jo, after much prompting from Dad. Despite his ranting after I first found Jo, he was getting used to the idea of her and was looking forward to finally meeting the "bionic" mother.

The visit was planned in February, a clear and chilly Saturday. About an hour before they were due to arrive, Dad, not able to ignore his impulse to control every detail, decided to build a fire. Mom told him not to bother. She didn't care one way or the other. As long as food and coffee were served, she was happy.

Matthew fetched the wood from the side of the house, and together, we crumpled some newspaper for the kindling and then joined Mom in the family room.

After a few minutes, we heard Dad from the other room. "Goddamn it … Anne," he yelled. "Go and get me some more newspaper. This damn fire won't start."

After several attempts, the fire ignited, giving a magnificent orange-red glow to the room. They were due to arrive soon, so I strode up and down the living room, glancing out the window looking for their car. Five minutes later, they arrived. I stepped outside and waited as they made their way up the driveway. Jessica skipped along, her blue eyes shining with delight. She was wearing a red-and-white striped skirt and red sweater. Her hair was pulled back and tied with a matching red ribbon.

"Hi, Jessica," I said happily. "I love your little outfit."

Jessica was grinning from ear to ear.

"Hello," Jo said, reaching over and kissing me on the cheek. She was wearing beige leggings and a red cashmere sweater. Richard was at her side, wearing a dark blue suit and tie. "Matt couldn't come, and you know Sara left last week to live in Florida with Armando." Jo glanced at Richard. "We're not too thrilled about this … but she is nineteen."

A sense of disappointment washed over me. I was hoping to get a chance to know Sara better, especially since she was so close to my age.

Dad must have heard them pull up and was already at the front door waiting. Dad, who held no grudge against Richard, immediately reached for his hand, shook it firmly, and patted him on the shoulder. He then half bowed to Jo and smiled at Jessica.

Mom came in from the family room and looked at Jo long and hard. Time almost stopped.

After an awkward pause, I said, "Mom, this is Jo." I forced a smile. "Jo, this is my mom."

Mom stood a little apart from the rest of us, her eyes fixed on Jo—sizing her up. Finally, her gaze shifted to Jessica.

"Isn't she adorable?" I said, following her eyes. There was no denying Jessica was adorable. Mom loved little red-headed girls. Everybody who was Irish loved red-headed girls.

But Mom just nodded her head and briskly turned away. Couldn't she at least be happy that I had a sister?! After all, she had three.

The room fell silent as we hovered near the doorway.

"So, what can I get you to drink?" Dad asked, cutting the tension. He took their coats and handed them to me.

"A soda will be fine," Richard answered.

"Oh, but I have Scotch, vodka, beer—name your drink," Dad persisted. "How about a martini?"

Richard smiled. "A martini sounds good."

"None for me, a seltzer will do," Jo said. There was a tense smile on her face.

No one knew quite what else to say, and after what seemed like an eternity, Shannon, our Irish setter, rambled in and began licking Jessica's hands.

Jessica giggled and hid behind Jo.

"Mommy, they have a dog!"

"Shannon, come here." I bent over, and my dog trotted over. "This is my most favorite dog, Shannon," I said, turning to Jessica. "Do you want to pet her? She doesn't bite, just licks, as you already know."

Leave it to a dog to lighten up the atmosphere! Everyone appeared more relaxed while Jessica petted Shannon, and afterwards, I gave Jo and Jessica a tour of the house while Mom, Dad, Richard, and Matthew retreated to the family room.

"Would you like to see more photos of me when I was younger?" I asked coming down the stairs. Dad's voice drifted by, followed by Richard's laughter. All was going favorably until we joined everyone else and found Mom glaring our way as if she wanted to snap the cord of life that still pulsed between us.

Quickly, I grabbed a photo album from the cabinet and sat on the couch alongside Mom.

"This is a picture of my dog from Florida, Patsy." I held up the photo for Jo to see. "She ran away a year before we moved back to New Jersey. She was my favorite dog, up until the time I got Shannon."

In an attempt to draw Mom into the conversation, a few times, I asked her about some of the people in the photos, but it was like trying to squeeze water from a stone.

Instead of answering my inquiries, Mom looked the other way. Matthew and I traded looks while her eyes remained narrowed, telling me she'd rather be anywhere else.

Meanwhile, Dad and Richard got along wonderfully, talking and laughing like old buddies who'd known each other for years. Later, we sat around the dining room table eating pastries Dad had bought for the occasion. By then, Mom had loosened up a bit and started talking to Jo.

"Anne was extremely active when she was younger. She never sat still."

"That was only when I was really young," I pointed out, taking a bite of a cannoli.

"At one point, I even took her to the doctor to see if they could prescribe something to calm her down, but because I'm a nurse, the doctor said I should know how to handle her. But you have no idea what it was like trying to keep her occupied. When she was barely a toddler, she used to escape from her playpen even though I'd fill it with all sorts of toys. Instead of playing with them, she always managed to find a way out. One time, she even got out of the house and was crawling down the sidewalk."

Jo leaned back in her seat.

I laughed. "Oh, I didn't get hurt. A neighbor saw me and brought me home."

Another hour passed as we all ate, drank coffee, and chatted about my younger years. The evening ended on a happy note with the usual farewell pleasantries. Once back inside, after having walked them to their car, I found Dad, who never wavered in his obsession of keeping a clean and tidy house, already clearing the dining room table. Mom retired to her bedroom. I didn't dare ask him his impressions about Jo and Richard as he was muttering curses under his breath about what a pigsty Mom left on the counter. Coffee was spilled and was running down the cabinets to the floor. Jo was the furthest thing from his mind when there was a mess to behold. I helped him clean up the mess and put the kitchen in order and said good night. I went and found Matthew flipping through the channels on the television in the family room, waiting for me.

"Well ..." I said, sinking into the couch next to him. "How'd it go?"

"It went better than I expected. Your mom didn't look too happy in the beginning, but then she came around."

I heaved a big sigh. Somehow, the events that evening left me with a good feeling. Things just had to get better.

The next day, Mom, who was in no hurry to comment either way, stretched out on the couch after dinner and said in a boorish voice, "I wasn't too impressed with her."

"Why not?" I asked exasperated. "Jo and Richard were nice, and we all got along well—at least I thought so."

Mom hesitated.

"Yes ... they were nice," she said, a bit flustered. "But I still didn't care for them much ... And I didn't like the way they dressed."

*   *   *

The date drew nearer to my wedding, and the preparations took precedence over everything else. The flowers, photographer, and menu selection for the reception, all planned months earlier, were confirmed. Maggie and I shopped for bridesmaids' dresses and decided on a beautiful brushed cotton tea-length dress from Laura Ashley in pale pink. Janine and Shelley were fitted along with Maggie. And the invitations, ordered the previous month, were at the printer, due to arrive any day. I set to the task of drawing up the final guest list.

It was certain that Grandma wouldn't be attending. Her embarrassment over the wheelchair issue, same as during Thomas's wedding, still persisted. It was disappointing not to have her present especially now that Pop was gone and wouldn't be there either. I started thinking about Jo and decided somehow she had to be included.

Tentatively, the subject of Jo attending the wedding was brought up with Matthew on the way to another dance lesson.

"You know, I was thinking exactly the same thing," he confessed. "She's been going out of her way each week to give us these dance lessons. It would be nice if she could watch our first dance … And she's family. She should be there like everyone else."

If he weren't driving the car, I would've hopped in his lap and given him the biggest hug and kiss possible. Instead, a smile spread across my face.

"I feel the same way. But I have a feeling Mom won't want her invited."

"Probably not," he agreed grinning.

"Jo already commented that she was looking forward to seeing us dance at the reception. It's obvious she wants to be there, and I want her to be there. I don't think Dad would mind. Ever since their visit, he's only said good things. He even asks when we're going to get together again. I'd love to be able to introduce her to everyone at the wedding," I said sighing deeply again.

Matthew's eyes widened.

"I know … right now, it's too soon for my mom, and I don't want to upset her. We could have Jo sit with people from your side of the family," I suggested.

"I think that's a good idea."

"Besides, she missed my entire life. Why should she miss my wedding?" I said more to myself. "What do you think we should do?"

"We still have some time. Let's just wait and see what happens. In the meantime, maybe your mom will come around."

Every evening, Matthew and I practiced our waltz in my driveway. At our next lesson, we were eager to show Jo how quickly we had mastered the last two steps shown to us the previous week. One included a double step that ended in a twirl, and Matthew was having difficulty keeping his feet off of mine. Richard greeted us at the entrance.

"Sorry, but Jo couldn't make the lesson this evening. She couldn't get a babysitter."

There was a moment's pause in which Matthew and I exchanged looks while Richard seemed to be looking past us at something in the parking lot.

I looked at Matthew and then at Richard again.

"Oh, we can do it another time."

"No, Jo wanted me to give you the lesson instead. She said you only have a few more weeks before the wedding."

"Are you sure?" I felt a bit uneasy.

He nodded and led us to the front dance room. Richard was a fabulous teacher and gave us many pointers on style. We thanked him when it was over and told him we'd see him next week on Tuesday, our usual lesson time with Jo. From the expression on his face, it seemed as though he could wait forever for that moment.

"So what did you think of that?" Matthew asked once we were in the car. "Richard didn't seem too pleased, giving us the lesson."

"Why do you think that?" I asked, hiding my own reaction. "He took the time to explain the different steps. He seemed okay with it."

"I know, but don't you realize? He doesn't like the idea of you being around, especially at his studio. He's uncomfortable."

I didn't say anything.

"I get the same feeling every time we go to dinner at their house."

"You do?" I asked wearily. I did not really want to admit it, but there was something amiss, a certain edge in Richard's demeanor the numerous times we'd all been to dinner at their house and on the occasions when we'd also gone out to eat after a dance lesson.

"I just get that impression," Matthew said shrugging a shoulder. "He must feel bad about when Jo when was pregnant with you."

Matthew's words about Richard disturbed me. I didn't want to believe it, and yet deep down, I knew he was right.

Twenty-Nine

Dr. Vitelli

The wedding was just around the corner, and the topic of inviting Jo was unavoidable. Mom and I were at the dining room table shuffling through the invitations. They were all addressed, stamped, and ready to be mailed. Every so often, I'd glance her way trying to gauge whether this would be a good time or not to broach the topic. Sensing my awkward glances, Mom, ten minutes later, said in a firm voice, "What do you want?"

There was a fair amount of annoyance spread evenly over her face as if she knew what was going through my head.

"I ... uh ... just wanted to talk to you about—" My voice broke off. *Maybe tomorrow would be better,* I thought, flipping aimlessly through the envelopes.

Mom looked away, a satisfied look on her face.

"It seems we have it all done," she said, getting up from her seat and walking over towards the coffeemaker. "When did you say the flowers would be delivered to the church?"

"They should arrive no later than ten that morning," I answered, sucking in my breath. It was now or never. I needed to ask before the invitations went out. "Mom, I need to ask you something."

She poured out a cup of coffee and stirred in some milk.

"What is it?" she answered nonchalantly, as if she didn't have a care in the world.

"Matthew and I want to invite Jo."

Mom stopped dead in her tracks and began to shake so violently that half of the coffee in her cup spilled onto the floor.

"Son of a bitch," she muttered, turning around and grabbing the dish towel on the counter. "Why are you bringing this up?" she asked angrily throwing the towel on the floor and mopping up the spill with her foot. She gave me a defiant stare and put her hands on her hips. "I knew you were going to start with this."

"Start with what?"

She only appeared angrier.

"You know what I'm talking about—wanting her to be present at the wedding." She bent over and picked up the soiled dish towel.

"Well, we do. I think it would be a nice gesture."

She started taking deep breaths as if trying to constrain her irritation, but it wasn't helping; her face remained tightly clenched. She picked up the cup of coffee, topped it off with some more, and turned to face me.

"I don't want her there!" She started for the stairs, then stopped, and spun around. "I don't want to discuss it anymore."

"I think we should. This is my wedding day we're planning, and I want everyone present."

Mom closed her eyes and shook her head.

"She's not going to be there as my mother—but as a guest." I picked up the sheet of paper we'd been working on. "Matthew and I discussed this. We considered your feelings and thought we could seat her with people from his side of the family."

"If you invite Jo—I'm not coming."

"Do you really mean that?"

"Yes," she said and stomped up the stairs.

*   *   *

The only thought that gave me any comfort lately was my impending departure from home. Nobody in the house was content. My parents were back to bickering constantly over the guest list, and we learned Thomas had disappeared again, this time for two whole nights. Shelley didn't tell us until he returned and was back at work. And she only mentioned it to my father. I sensed Shelley somehow blamed Dad for Thomas's behavior.

"I just want to let you know that your son is up to his old games again. He was gone for two days without calling," she told him.

Dad didn't really know what to say to her.

And when Mom heard the news from Dad, they started screaming at each other. It wasn't just about Thomas, who sparked the arguments. As usual, Mom hated that Dad cleaned the house all the time, and he hated that she never bothered to clean. Their fighting wasn't new, and normally, I just ignored it, but for some reason, it was getting to me now.

Surprisingly, when the topic of my wedding entered their arguments, Dad wanted Jo and Richard invited. Remembering the nice evening we shared together, he saw no harm in having them present that day. Now he considered them to be like old friends.

"They're just regular people," he told me, apparently realizing Jo hadn't taken me away after all.

And because Dad now agreed with me, Mom was doubly infuriated.

*   *   *

By the time the wedding was less than two months away, there was no other choice but to bring up the subject every night at dinnertime. The answer was the same every evening. "No, I don't want her there."

Even the weather was turning as dismal as this situation; all it did was rain, and every evening, there was a chilly mist hovering low in the sky. We went on for two solid weeks like this until one night, Dad piped in on my behalf.

"Come on, Erin, it's a wedding. Everybody should be there."

For a brief moment, I fancied the possibility that Mom would concede; she'd listen to Dad. However, my brief fleeting moment of bliss was instantly obliterated because, instead, she gave him a hard look.

"I'll make sure nobody knows who she is—I won't even introduce her to Matthew's family."

Dad nodded his head in agreement, expectantly waiting for an answer.

"Do whatever you want," she said, throwing her napkin onto her plate, which was still full of food. "I'm not going to attend." She stood up and turned to leave.

"Oh, Erin," Dad said, grabbing her arm before she could take a step. "Of course you're going to attend our daughter's wedding."

She started sniffling. "No ... no, I'm not ... You can all go without me."

Dad got up from his seat, went over, and put his arms around her.

"Okay, you win," he said softly. "I wouldn't want to do anything to hurt you. Anne will come up with something else, but you have to promise me that you're going to be there when our daughter gets married."

I sat straight up in my chair, dumbfounded. How quickly the winds changed course; just as his temperaments were unpredictable, so were his loyalties. It was clear I'd lost an ally—if he was *ever* on my side.

The next week, Mom surprised me when she approached my bedroom door as I was getting ready for bed.

"I'd like it if we could go to a psychiatrist," she said matter-of-factly, as if this was typical conversation in our household.

I looked up at her in confusion. "A psychiatrist?"

"Yes … there's somebody I know personally at the hospital."

Psychiatrist! I couldn't believe my ears. She wanted *me* to see a psychiatrist. I looked hopelessly into her eyes and saw that she was serious.

"Dr. Vitelli sometimes comes to my floor to visit patients," she started to explain. "I told him about our problem." She paused, waiting for me to respond, and when I didn't, she went on. "I explained how we're arguing about Jo attending the wedding." She let out a deep sigh. "Anne, he's a good psychiatrist and very respected at the hospital," she said with an air of authority. "I asked for his advice, and he feels we should come in and talk."

Mom stood with her hands on her hips, waiting for an answer.

Visiting a psychiatrist was by common consent the sort of thing not usually broadcasted to others. I was surprised Mom even dared to confide her problems to a colleague at the hospital. She was so accustomed to hiding and denying that anything in her family was amiss.

"Umm, can I think about it?" I asked tentatively. I wasn't sure what this was all leading to. She may have asked this Dr. Vitelli to tell me that I was being unreasonable.

"I need to know right now," she said firmly. "I already have an appointment for next Wednesday at five o'clock."

The idea seemed to be planted quite firmly in her head, and not wanting to disagree on yet again another issue, I curtly nodded. The moment I agreed to the visit, I wished I hadn't. There was an uncomfortable feeling that quickly rose as she sauntered away with a smug look on her face. Something didn't sit quite right. Why on earth was Mom setting up appointments with a psychiatrist?

I was dying to tell Matthew, and the next evening, it was immediately apparent upon entering his house that he was at his wits' end with the deadline for a quarterly filing at work. There were piles of papers spread haphazardly across his mother's dining room table, as well as a row on the floor against the wall.

"You brought this all home with you today?" I asked incredulously, looking at the vast amounts of paper. There was at least an acre's worth of trees sacrificed.

Matthew nodded, keeping his attention on his work.

"I need to talk with you," I said, flopping into a chair next to him. "You'll never guess what my mom wants me to do."

"What?" he asked, glancing up at me for a half second.

"She set up an appointment with a psychiatrist!" I said with a short laugh. "Can you believe that? She wants us both to sit with him in order to sort out inviting Jo to the wedding."

"Did you tell her you're not going?" he asked, lifting his eyes to mine.

I hesitated.

"No ... I told her first I wanted to think about it ... but then she insisted ... so I agreed."

Matthew shook his head. "You shouldn't have agreed to anything."

"I know ... but if I go, then maybe I can explain myself better, and she'll have to listen because the doctor will be present. Having a psychiatrist mediate certainly can't hurt." My last statement was more of a question than a fact.

"If I were you, I'd prepare exactly what you're going to say in your defense," he warned.

I thought a lot about Matthew's suggestion and rehearsed my defense against Mom and her Dr. Vitelli. I ran through my reasoning about my innate need to find and know the woman who birthed me and how having her become a part of my life was a natural progression in this seemingly uncharted territory of an adoptee. Never on the reunion shows on *Oprah* did they venture further than the initial meeting.

"Oh ... remember tomorrow night we're going furniture shopping again," I reminded him.

Matthew nodded his head without looking up. He hated shopping, whether it was for clothes, food, or furniture. The only time he liked shopping was when we bought our first television. Even when we looked around for an apartment, he didn't have any preferences. We signed a one-year lease on a garden apartment located in Saddle Brook, the next town over from his parents. It was a cute one-bedroom unit with an oversized living room, small dining area, and an updated kitchen with oak cabinets and new laminate flooring. We were moving some of our things the coming weekend, mostly gifts I had received at a small wedding shower held at Aunt Lorraine's house last weekend. Maggie let it slip when we were dress shopping so the surprise element wasn't there, but still I got loads of pots, pans, sheets, towels, and other odds and ends to help us get on our feet in our new home.

*   *   *

Wednesday came quick enough; Mom had already changed from her nurse's uniform and was ready to go to our appointment when I arrived home from work. She was wearing a pair of khaki slacks and a yellow button-down cotton shirt and had applied some blush and lipstick.

There was a certain amount of apprehension felt as we drove together to the appointment. After all, this visit was arranged by Mom with one of her colleagues from work, someone who she was sure was going to take her side; otherwise, she never would have pushed for this.

Dr. Vitelli's office was in a converted Victorian house in Ridgewood. It closely resembled the picture in my mind of what a shrink's office should look like. It was a small, cramped room with overflowing bookshelves, a couch, some chairs, a large desk, and a plush swivel chair.

When we entered, he rose from his seat and extended his hand toward Mom.

"Hello, Erin, nice to see you again." He was a man of average height, slender with a full head of black, wavy hair, which he wore parted on the side. A pair of wire glasses sat on his prominent nose. "This must be your daughter," he said, peering at me. "Nice to meet you," he said shaking my hand very briefly and gesturing toward the two chairs in front of the desk.

I nodded and slid into the chair closest to the door.

He sat down, slapping his hands on his lap.

"So, what brings you both here today?"

As if he didn't already know. I glanced over at Mom; she spoke first.

"You're aware about the situation with my daughter," she began. "Anne is an adopted child."

He nodded and adjusted his glasses then placed his elbows on the top of the desk, hands clasped together.

"Several months ago," Mom continued, "she conducted a search on her own and was able to find her real mother."

"Birth mother," I corrected. "That's the term used now."

Mom shook her head in agreement at my statement as if to tell me she didn't mean the word literally.

"Um-hmm," Dr. Vitelli said, adjusting his glasses, which looked as if they might fall off his face. He looked at me curiously and then turned his attention on Mom again.

"Anne's getting married next month, and she wants to invite Jo," she hesitated and then added sourly, "her *birth mother* to the wedding."

Dr. Vitelli nodded his head. "Go on."

Mom sighed deeply, glanced at me for a second, and returned her eyes to Dr. Vitelli.

"I feel she doesn't belong at the wedding."

"Why do you feel that way?" he asked.

"This is an event for the family. I don't believe she belongs there." She paused, bringing her hand to her chest. "This is my day and not hers. We raised Anne Marie—she didn't."

"Okay, now, Anne," he said, turning towards me, "tell me about this."

I sighed deeply, already feeling as if I'd lost the battle.

"I want Jo to come to my wedding. Even though we only met six months ago, I still would like her to be there."

"Why?" he asked.

I thought for a minute, trying to come up with a reason that wouldn't hurt Mom's feelings. Deep down, I wanted Jo at my wedding because I couldn't bear the thought of not sharing another special moment of my life with her. She missed so much: my ballet recitals, kindergarten graduation, first Communion, Confirmation, high school and college graduations. There was only one major event left in a girl's life and that was her wedding day. I couldn't see the point of deliberately leaving her out.

"One reason is because she's giving me dance lessons. For the past four months, I've been going to her studio with my fiancé; we're preparing a waltz as our first dance. It would be nice if she could see it."

"And," he prompted, leaning forward.

"Matthew and I want her at our wedding."

"That's all?" he said, raising his eyebrows.

I felt a trap. I knew he was trying to get me to say that I wanted Jo to play the role of my mother. And after it was admitted, his lecture would follow about how ungrateful I was and didn't my parents take me in, and so on. The arguments with my parents haunted me, and I wasn't in the mood for a repeat performance with a new torturous inquisitor. My words needed to be chosen carefully.

"More importantly, over the past six months, we've slowly begun to know each other, and I'd like her to share in this special day."

There! That wasn't so bad, I thought, looking first at Mom and then at Dr. Vitelli.

"Having her present at the wedding will hurt me," Mom put in, an abhorrent look on her face. "I think that's what Anne *really* wants to do here."

"No." I shook my head. "I'm not trying to hurt you. We just want her at the wedding," I assured her. Everything was always so personal. Thomas's recent disappearances were taken as a personal vendetta. I opened my mouth then closed it again, not sure what to say next.

"Go ahead," he encouraged, motioning with his hands. "You were going to say?"

"I feel very bad that she missed all the events in my life. I see no reason why she needs to miss this one."

"She was the one who made the decision to give you away," Mom responded coldly.

"I know she made that decision, but she had reasons at the time. I don't see why she needs to be punished."

The doctor's chin was resting in his palms as he followed our responses back and forth.

"Erin," he interjected, "let me ask you something. What are your feelings toward Jo?"

My mother shrugged and didn't answer.

"They did meet one time," I interrupted.

"How did it go?" he asked, looking at Mom.

"It went fine," she answered, her eyes averted. "I thought they were nice people."

He turned to me. "Anne, tell me about the meeting?"

"We all talked and got along with each other."

"Okay, Erin, what are your feelings toward Jo?" he asked again. Obviously, he wasn't going to let her ignore this question.

"All I know is that I feel she doesn't belong there. A daughter's wedding is a big event, and I'm her mother," she said, glancing at me. "My wishes should be considered when it comes to guest invitations."

"Do you think having Jo attend would detract from you that day?" he asked.

"It might ... I guess ... I feel this is also my day."

"Because of my mom's feelings," I explained, "I have no intention of telling anyone at the wedding who Jo is." Mom's mouth was twisted as if she'd just tasted something horrible. "Anyway, Jo doesn't resemble me in the least. Nobody at the wedding would recognize her."

Dr. Vitelli nodded.

"I'm not trying to hurt anybody. Like I told you before, Jo can sit with people on Matthew's side of the family. She'll blend right in."

I almost felt as if I were begging for him to please see my side of the situation. My heart pounded inside my chest as he considered us both. I tried reading his expression, but he kept a level look on his face as if he were judging a contest and was decisively comparing contestants.

"How does this sound to you, Erin?" he finally asked.

Mom looked up at him and shook her head.

"Even if Anne is willing to meet you halfway and only have her play the role as a guest?"

"Even if nobody knows who she is, *I* still will."

Dr. Vitelli leaned back in his seat and looked at her with a puzzled look on his face.

Mom started to look a bit nervous, almost as if things were suddenly not going her way.

"Mom told me that if Jo attends the wedding, she won't come."

Dr. Vitelli's eyes quickly darted to Mom, whose color drained from her face.

"Yes, I said that," she admitted before he had a chance to ask.

"Did you mean it?"

"Yes, that's why we're here." She fidgeted in her seat, wearing an anxious expression. "I was hoping you'd make Anne see she's wrong for wanting Jo at the wedding."

"My place is not to tell anyone whether they're right or wrong. I can help you understand how the other is feeling and guide you to some sort of an agreement," he explained.

"Yes, yes," she said impatiently.

"And, Anne, tell me how you think your mom will feel if Jo attends?"

"Right now, it looks as if she'll be pretty mad." I sighed deeply. "I'm trying to make everyone happy. My fiancé and I don't want to leave anyone out. And Jo is now in my life, but she isn't like a mother. She never could be because she didn't raise me. She did," I said, motioning to Mom. "So I consider her my real mother and Jo as the birth mother."

As the words left my mouth, I realized I had just given the nicest compliment anyone could give their adoptive mother. And I meant every word of it. Even though we were never that close during my childhood, she was still my mother.

The sun slowly sank beneath the skyline outside as Mom hung her head. My words didn't seem to reach her. Anguish spread evenly over her face, filling me with a considerable amount of empathy. I almost regretted having brought this all upon her. I could hear the echo of the words the social workers probably told Mom. "Everything will be held in the strictest confidentiality. The records will be sealed. A new birth certificate will make it appear as if you gave birth."

Such promises. How did these social workers expect confidentiality when they insisted the child be told about their adoption status? Didn't they realize that most of us would ask questions? Demand answers? Or was it taken for granted that all adoptees would obey the unspoken debt of silence?

"Erin," Dr. Vitelli said gently. "Do you have a response to what Anne just said?"

She considered the question.

"I guess Anne's right. You're taking her side."

"No, I don't take sides," he said. "But I do see the picture a lot more clearly now. Anne is not asking you to step down in your role as her mother.

It seems she's trying to bend a little bit concerning the wedding, out of respect for your feelings."

"I see," Mom said, her lips pressed together.

"She's willing to make a compromise. Meanwhile, you're making threats to her about not attending the wedding. Do you think that's reasonable?"

She shook her head.

"You're acting out of jealousy," he said gently. "I see you resenting this woman for being in touch with Anne and for Anne wanting to be in touch with her."

At that very moment, I felt the world shift. To my utter surprise, Dr. Vitelli agreed with *me*. But there was no rejoicing because Mom looked devastated.

"Remember, Erin," he said, "you did ask me to state my opinion after I heard both sides of the story."

"Yes, of course," she said, rubbing her eyes wearily. It seemed that the turn of events was beginning to take a toll on her. Perhaps the mention of being jealous affected her particularly badly; she hung her head as if she'd like nothing better than to bury it in a pile of sand.

My stomach began to hurt.

"Maybe Jo doesn't have to be at the wedding," I offered. "Not if it's going to upset her so much."

"No, Anne," Dr. Vitelli said firmly, "giving in is not the answer. This can be resolved in an appropriate manner. Erin, did you hear what your daughter just offered?"

"Yes," she said weakly.

"Can you do the same thing?"

The shock of his question made her sit upright in her chair. She sniffed and wiped her eyes again.

"All right. So I was wrong," Mom moped.

"Erin, look at me," he said gently.

She looked up, but by the way her bottom lip was quivering, it was obvious she was trying her hardest not to cry.

"You were not wrong; nobody is wrong. Your actions are based on insecurities that are buried deep inside. When Anne found her birth mother, you must have felt very threatened."

"Yes, I did."

"This is not an easy thing to deal with, Erin. However, you're being rigid, and you're making demands on your daughter that aren't fair. You both need to go home and try to come to some sort of a compromise. If you can't, by all means, we can meet again."

When we arrived home, I couldn't wait to get into bed and crawl under the covers. Even though Dr. Vitelli took my side, the whole ordeal of hashing out our grievances against each other was exhausting. Mom went straight up to her bedroom, and I didn't see her until I got home from work the next day.

While we sat at the kitchen table eating eggs and toast for dinner, she casually mentioned that I could invite Jo to the wedding. At first, I wasn't sure how to respond, and I momentarily stared at her with a mouthful of eggs. She only sipped her coffee and nonchalantly opened up the newspaper to the living section.

A few days later, we were sitting at the dining room table counting positive RSVPs that had arrived in the mail.

"Have you spoken to Jo about coming to the wedding?" she asked.

"Not yet," I answered. "Tomorrow … when we go for the lesson." I turned my attention back to counting the replies, but out of the corner of my eye, I could see a serene expression on her face, and I couldn't help but smile as a little flame of hope ignited.

Thirty

My Wedding

At our next dance lesson, we mentioned how eager we were for Jo to watch us finally waltz during our first dance. She grew quiet, which was odd for such a gregarious person.

"I'm so happy the wedding planning is almost over," I went on. "The details were exhausting!"

Jo looked down. "I don't think I'm going to attend."

"Why not?" I quickly asked, taken aback. She didn't know about the recent squabbles over the guest list or the whole psychiatrist affair. "I thought you said you were dying to see our first dance?"

"Richard and I talked, and he feels that we'd be uncomfortable there—with your family."

What's with everybody? I thought as Matthew leaned into me, squeezing my hand. He knew exactly how my heart was breaking.

Up until eight months ago, I'd been overshadowed by the mystery of my beginnings, which was only to be replaced now by indifference. Everybody was only concerned about my parents' feelings. How were they handling what Anne had *done*? Not once did anybody consider what might be best for me. I was the bride. It was supposed to be my day. As for the whole adoption drama, I was at the heart of it—but no one seemed to recognize that.

*   *   *

The Tuesday before the wedding, Jo gave us our final dance lesson. We devoted the entire hour solely to practicing the waltz.

"I can watch your first dance on videotape," she said toward the end of the lesson. "You're having it videotaped?" There was a definite longing in her voice.

"Yes," I replied, trying to sound cheerful. "Last week, very last minute, I called the photographer and asked if he had someone to videotape as well. His best friend was available. You should have seen Mom's face," I said turning to Matthew. "You know her and last-minute preparations. She couldn't believe that I pulled it off two weeks before the wedding day."

"I can see you dance after all," Jo said smiling. "I talked it over again with Richard, and we've decided to attend the ceremony at the church. We should feel comfortable there; it's a public place."

"Oh! I'd love to have you attend the ceremony," I said with delight. "You know you're also welcome at the reception."

Her face crumpled. "No, I think the church will be enough."

It was difficult to determine who looked more disappointed—me or Jo. Both of us, it seemed, were doomed to settle for second best.

*   *   *

Finally, June 2, 1990, arrived. The usual aroma of coffee that wafted into my bedroom each morning wasn't present, so I knew Dad wasn't up yet. The only sound heard apart from the beat of my heart thumping against my chest was the distant sound of birds chirping. I lay perfectly still in bed soaking up the feeling that this would be the last time I'd wake under my parents' roof. I knew the rantings and the constant bickering between everyone wouldn't be missed, and a part of me wanted to jump out of bed and dance a jig, but there was still a small part that was a bit melancholy knowing I'd miss living with my family.

I strolled downstairs, still in my nightgown, and put on the kettle for tea. Dad must've heard me stirring because a few minutes later, he strode into the kitchen still in his boxers. What little bit of hair he had left was sticking up on the sides of his head.

"Good morning," he said cheerfully, a wide smile on his face. "Would you like a bagel this morning?" He went over and picked up a brown paper bag on the counter. "I have poppy, raisin, sesame, and plain."

Dad's mood was especially bright this morning. The evening before at the rehearsal dinner, he had had a few too many martinis; however, the martinis didn't seem to have had the usual effect on his countenance, and he cheerfully began humming along with an old fifties song playing on the radio.

"I'll take a poppy," I said tuning in to the radio. The song ended, and I was hoping they'd give a weather report.

Dad filled the glass kettle with water from the tap and placed it on the coffeemaker.

"It's going to be a scorcher today," he warned. "Mom said so last night. It's supposed to be around ninety-two degrees."

"Ugh," I said shaking my head. "We're all going to be sweating!"

"Hey, it's better than rain," he said grabbing a sesame bagel for himself.

Later that morning, Maggie and I were dressing in my bedroom while Janine and Shelley sat with Mom and Dad downstairs waiting for the photographer to arrive. A sense of jittery anticipation formed as I stood in front of my bureau mirror and considered my reflection. Everything looked perfect; the dress was fastened securely in the back with thirty small satin buttons, the embroidered silk lace on the front accented my slim hips like the seamstress promised. The headpiece, handmade the previous summer, consisted of tiny silk ivory roses and a simple veil and was attached securely in the back to my hair, which was swept up in a bun. Everything seemed to be in order, but still there was something missing.

Sensing my uneasiness, Maggie came over and stood beside me.

"Is your real mother coming?" she warily asked. There was a funny look on her face as if she dreaded hearing the answer.

I turned, surprised. I hadn't really discussed Jo too much with Maggie. The few times we'd been together recently, we were absorbed in planning wedding details. But then I remembered.

"I guess our mothers have been talking."

"I overheard them on the phone several times. My mom is furious with you." She hesitated, an offended look on her face.

"And?" I said defensively, almost knowing exactly what was coming next.

"Anne … I …" she faltered, looking less angry. "I just don't want to see Aunt Erin get hurt."

I sighed deeply.

"Maggie, neither do I … but you have to understand how hard it is to pretend that I don't have more family out there. I've always known about being adopted, and there's always been a part of me that needed to know who this other family was, what they looked like, and why they couldn't raise me."

"But Aunt Erin and Uncle Bob raised you."

"Yes, they did … but now I know my birth mother's story and why she couldn't keep me. It's just so sad, Maggie; she had nowhere to go, and no one would help her. She wanted to keep me, but she couldn't ..." I broke off, my eyes fixed on Maggie's puzzled face. I knew my explanation was only words to her.

Maggie reached for her makeup bag and began fumbling inside until she pulled out a tube of pink lipstick. She applied a second layer while my mind searched for the right words that would reach her—make her understand.

"You know what?" I said, suddenly smiling.

"What?"

"Someday, I'm going to write a book about all of this. This way, I don't have to keep explaining over and over how an adopted person feels their entire life living with secrets and no information about where they came from."

Maggie must've thought I was joking by the amused look on her face; still, the idea of writing a book about my search for Jo was very enticing. Ever since I'd read the Little House books, I wanted to write my story too, but my life up until now never seemed as interesting as living on the prairie back in the last century.

Maggie smiled as she shook her head seeing the faraway look on my face.

"Okay, but for now, let's make sure you have everything you need to get married. Something blue?" she asked, bringing me back to the present.

"Got it," I said pulling up my gown, exposing the blue lace garter on my left leg.

"Something old?"

"The dress."

"Oh yeah," Maggie said laughing. "I forgot. It was Aunt Erin's."

I pointed to the pearl necklace around my neck. "Something borrowed. I'm giving it back to Mom after the wedding, and I have new shoes."

My concerns, from which I was temporarily sidetracked by my conversation with Maggie, returned as my heart turned over. It wasn't how my dress looked or the old wedding superstitions that held me in a state of suspension, but my doubts rising about Jo coming to the church. She said she was going to attend the ceremony, but there was something in the way she promised that wasn't very convincing.

I smoothed my hands down the front of my ivory silk dress. The small rhinestones the seamstress had sewn down the front in a circular pattern sparkled. The long train fanned out behind me.

"I think that's everything I need ... The headpiece," I said, half turning to the side. "Is it straight?"

"It's straight, don't worry." Just then, Maggie glanced at her own reflection and turned to each side trying to take in every angle.

The pink Laura Ashley dress complemented her rather full figure nicely. Like the rest of the Murphy women, Maggie was adding pounds as she got older. Her dark hair also was swept up in a bun, but with a single rose attached to a barrette holding it in place.

"What about me? Is my hair sticking up anywhere?" she asked frantically.

"No, your hair is fine," I assured her with a little laugh. "We're pathetic, aren't we?"

"Come on," she said chuckling. "We better get downstairs—it's almost time to leave."

I gave myself the once-over again in the mirror before turning on my heel and heading downstairs. Dad and Mom were waiting for us in the living room. Dad sat on the couch with his legs crossed, smoking a cigarette. His charcoal gray three-piece tux made him appear quite handsome. And Mom looked stunning in her mauve full-length dress, made of fine taffeta and soft velvet. As I entered, they both sucked in their breath.

Dad stood up. "Look at our little girl!" He beamed, stepping forward to reach for my headpiece. "It's a bit crooked," he said adjusting it.

"Anne, you look beautiful," Mom said smiling.

"There ..." Dad said looking me over again. "Now everything's perfect. Erin, isn't she gorgeous?" He turned to the photographer, who'd just arrived and was setting up his equipment. "Can you take a photo of just the three of us?"

After posing for photographs, we all stepped outside into the stifling air. The sun was hanging heavy in the sky.

"Ughh. It's so hot," Janine moaned. "Thank God this dress is light."

"I should have made the three of you wear heavy velvet," I teased. "Then maybe you'd be as hot as I am."

My gown, made thirty years earlier, contained layers of petticoats underneath, and the material seemed to weigh at least twenty pounds in the heat.

Shelley was already outside, smoking a cigarette.

"Hey, the limo's already here," she said, tossing the cigarette on the ground and snuffing it out with her heel.

"I'd like to take a few pictures outside first," I said to the photographer. "Let's take some with my parents and then some with the bridesmaids."

I even took a picture with my dog, Shannon. We finally piled into a silver stretch limousine, with the air-conditioning blasting, and headed over to Saint Elizabeth's. We waited until no guests were in sight before exiting the limousine and ascending the steep stone steps leading to the large white church.

*   *   *

Upon our arrival in the vestibule, Mom was quickly escorted to her seat by Brian. Janine, Shelley, and then Maggie, each in turn, made their way down the aisle to the reserved front row pew. As Dad and I stood at the top of the aisle, a pause came, in which everybody in the pews stood up erect, turned toward the center aisle, and craned their heads for a glimpse of the bride.

Dad took my arm.

"This is it," he said, pride emanating from his expression.

I flashed him a wide smile and nodded my head as the organist played Pachelbel's Canon. We slowly walked down the aisle, and all was surreal with everybody beaming and smiling as we passed. It was finally my wedding day, and I was floating down the aisle filled with the elation of soon becoming Matthew's wife. I saw him standing at the altar next to the priest; he looked handsome in his tuxedo as he watched me slowly walk with my father. My heart started beating faster when I realized we would soon be officially married. But Matthew had been right on the day he proposed, it felt like we'd been married the first time we saw each other. A smile spread across my face, as I remembered how he proposed on that hot Fourth of July day. Now we were marrying on another hot day!

My eyes briefly left Matthew as I scanned each pew, first seeing Aunt Lorraine dressed in a light blue dress sitting next to Uncle Ron, who was decked out in a three-piece brown suit. Grandpa was seated next to Mom and was dressed in his own black tuxedo and bow tie. All our aunts, uncles, cousins, and friends filled the pews on both sides of the aisle. Suddenly, a terrible sinking feeling was at the pit of my stomach—Jo was nowhere in sight. I didn't see her face in the crowd of smiling faces.

My eyes found Matthew again. His presence, along with the lopsided grin on his face, was enough to save me from worrying about Jo. His eyes were shining, and he looked like the happiest man alive.

He gently took my hand, and I squeezed his as we took our seats at the altar, and Father Brennan began the wedding mass.

"As we gather here today for this very special occasion—the union of Anne Marie and Matthew—let us reflect upon our own lives as we each strive to fulfill the teachings of Jesus Christ, our Lord."

It was just at that moment when from afar, I noticed a slender woman in a pink and black dress enter the church and slide inconspicuously into one of the rear pews. It was Jo, with Richard and Jessica. A great wave of relief broke over me. I took a deep breath while the mass continued.

"Do you take Anne to be your lawfully wedded wife?" Father Brennan asked Matthew. The three of us were at the altar, my train fanned out behind me.

Tears filled Matthew's eyes as he muttered, "Yes."

Now it was my turn. I said my vows never taking my eyes from Matthew's. He seemed to be more nervous than I was; his hands trembled when he slipped the matching golden wedding band on my finger. After I put his ring on his finger, we were declared husband and wife.

My heart soared, and we stood looking into each other's eyes at the altar until Father Brennan said that Matthew could kiss his bride.

We kissed and then embraced. Everyone pulled out cameras and began snapping pictures. It was hard to believe we were finally married and were going to live and be together for the rest of our lives. Matthew grabbed my hand, let out a big sigh, and led me down the aisle, through all the flashes and out of the church.

The photographer flashed a few more photos of us, and then we joined my parents and the wedding party for the receiving line, where for the next forty-five minutes, we greeted each guest as they left the church. I didn't see Jo in the line. Afterwards, Matthew and I found her on the side of the church, standing in the shade of a weeping willow tree, looking our way.

"Jo!" I cried, walking quickly over to them. "Thank you for coming." We embraced.

"We'd like you to be in some of our photos," Matthew said. "We're heading over to a nearby pond. Could you meet us there?"

Jo and Richard exchanged looks.

"Uh, I'm not sure if we can," Richard stammered.

"It'll only take a few minutes with the photographer," Matthew promised. "And only Anne and I and the wedding party will be there."

I don't even think Mom realized Jo had been present. They must have slipped out past the receiving line.

Jo nodded and looked over at Richard. He sighed deeply and reluctantly nodded his head.

"The pond is nearby," Matthew said, taking a wedding program. "Do you have a pen?" he asked, patting his empty pockets.

Jo handed him a pen from her purse, and Matthew quickly scribbled directions on the back of a wedding program.

*   *   *

The sun was even hotter by the time we arrived at the pond. The photographer took several shots of me and Jo alone and then some of us with

Richard, Jessica, and Matthew. Before she left, I promised to show her the videotape of our first dance.

By the time we reached the reception hall, Maggie's face was flushed, and I wasn't sure if it was from the heat or all the champagne she'd been drinking in the limousine. The temperature outside was well over ninety degrees, and there wasn't a cloud in sight to shield us from the sun's rays. Although it wasn't what I'd anticipated for an early June wedding, like Dad said earlier, it was better than rain.

The wedding party had a private cocktail hour during which Maggie tried desperately to bustle the back of my gown. After several failed attempts at it, she decided to instead finish the last bit of wine in her glass and saunter away toward my two brothers. Janine took over, quickly bustling my dress, and shortly thereafter, the maitre d' was announcing the names of the wedding party.

When it came time for our announcement, I grabbed hold of Matthew's hand and squeezed tightly.

"This is it," I whispered. "Are you ready?" He didn't seem a bit nervous about our first dance while my insides were fluttering wildly.

"Just remember, let me lead."

"And now, for the very first time, I would like to announce Mr. and Mrs. Matthew and Anne Marie Bauer."

Matthew grabbed my arm and led the way across the empty dance floor. The band began playing "Somewhere My Love," and as if a magic wand had been waved over the two of us, we immediately stood erect, tilted our heads slightly back, and began to waltz around the dance floor.

Everybody looked dumbfounded as they watched, but the shocked expressions were soon replaced with oohs and ahhs as we twirled round and round. Every so often, Matthew would spin me which made the crowd get even louder.

"Fred and Ginger!" my uncle Ron called out as we waltzed past his table.

We were floating on air, and when the final notes played, he spun me one last time and we embraced to a thundering applause from the crowd. The tone for the reception was set, and our parents joined us on the dance floor, and other couples followed suit as the band played Elvis's "Can't Help Falling in Love."

We danced for at least thirty minutes before the band took a short break. Our first course, a mesclun salad with cranberry vinaigrette dressing, sat tantalizingly at the tables. The floating minstrels came out and wandered by each table playing "Take Me out to the Ball Game," and other oldie favorites.

I looked over at Mom, glowing next to Grandpa at her table. The photographer clicked a picture of them together, Grandpa's arm dangled around her shoulders.

After dinner was served, Matthew and I made our customary rounds, making small-talk and thanking our guests for coming. Finally, we made it back to the head table, where the bridal party sat. Matthew slipped into his seat, and I plopped myself on his lap and wrapped my arms around him.

"Ugh," he groaned, pretending to be alarmed by my weight.

"What? She's only like ninety-eight pounds?" Thomas joked.

Matthew laughed and kissed my cheek. Maggie was sitting close by, halfway on her chair, with beads of sweat on her brow.

"Are you all right?" I asked, slipping into an empty seat beside her. I was beginning to worry about all the wine she drank earlier.

"I'm fine," she answered, nodding towards our grandfather. He got up from his seat and started dancing with Kayla, one of our younger cousins. "I wish Grandma was here," she said frowning. "Grandpa tried to convince her, but you know how stubborn she is."

I nodded, knowing fully that once Grandma made up her mind, there was no changing it. Our eyes moved from our grandfather towards the head table where we saw our mothers sitting with their heads practically glued together.

"Who do you think they're talking about?" I asked.

Maggie just laughed and shook her head.

After cake and coffee were served, I found Grandpa hanging off his chair surrounded by my cousins. His bald head gleamed in the candlelight.

"Coffee money?" he said, reaching into his trouser pockets. His glassy eyes were half open.

"Grandpa," I said in a low voice, leaning in towards him. "Don't you think you should have some coffee yourself?" I motioned for the waiter to bring the pot over, and a fresh cup was poured.

"Ah—nothing in here," he said turning his pockets inside out. "The devil invented Scotch whiskey to make the Irish poor."

The photographer took a last round of photos, and the evening abruptly ended. We said our farewells and left for a midnight flight to England and Ireland. Our wedding was everything I'd imagined it would be.

Part Four

"Not to have felt pain is not to have been human." —Jewish Proverb

Thirty-One

Venturing Beyond

Grandma once told me that a woman's emotional state during pregnancy affects the personality of the child. In her opinion, this was the reason I did so many crazy things when I was young, like pulling out my hair. She thought my birth mother must've been sad during her pregnancy.

The minute we returned from our honeymoon, a home pregnancy test confirmed it: I was pregnant. And this time, there was no mistake. The color was positive. It radiated a deep blush pink. I had my suspicions: nausea and fatigue, things I'd rarely experienced before. The symptoms gradually increased as we avidly toured London, lazily drove through the rolling English countryside, and then sailed across the Irish Sea to my ancestral homeland. By the time I was climbing the steps of Blarney Castle, severe queasiness had set in. Luckily, I still managed to kiss the Blarney Stone unwittingly passing on the promised gift of eloquence to my unborn child.

Mom and Mrs. Bauer initially reacted to our news by silently counting the months on their fingers to the due date; February 22 hovered on the nine-month mark.

"Yes, it's a honeymoon baby," I assured them laughing.

It was amazing how quickly I adjusted to being pregnant. Besides the initial queasiness and morning sickness, plaguing me for two months, my overall appearance actually improved.

Mom said it was hormonal and couldn't believe how clear my complexion was. She reminded me to take my prenatal vitamins every day, the nurse in her coming out. Jo too had her presumptions and said I simply glowed in the same way she did during all four of her pregnancies. Mrs. Bauer's only observation was that it was most likely a boy—the reason for me looking even better. Grandma agreed; she said girls made you have lots of pimples and expanded the waistline.

All in all, everyone was thrilled with the news, and there was another surprise while we were honeymooning, Shelley too was expecting and was due on New Year's Day!

Mom was beside herself—two weddings and now two babies. I'd never seen her happier until Shelley called one morning toward the end of the summer, frantic and crying. Thomas had left for work three days earlier and still hadn't returned. She thought with a baby on the way, he'd quickly abandon his bachelor ways including the disappearing for days on end. Dad and Shelley contacted every one of his friends, checked the local bars he frequented, and called his job, but nobody knew where he was.

It took Dad, along with Shelley and a private investigator, over a month to find him. He'd lost his job and was living in a run-down basement apartment in an old house in Irvington. If that wasn't bad enough, he was rooming with a beautiful dark-haired girl from Peru who worked as a stripper at a nearby go-go club.

Upon hearing the news, Mom was beyond comfort.

I too found it difficult maintaining the blissful atmosphere. Matthew and I were so happy being married and absolutely thrilled about our expected arrival. We planned to buy a house soon after the birth and in the meantime, began looking into setting up a college fund. We spent many weekends browsing through baby furniture stores looking for the perfect crib. Shelley, however, didn't have her husband to do these things with.

"You need to let it go," Matthew said, grabbing my hand. We were standing in line waiting to pay for a stack of infant drawstring gowns I couldn't resist buying. All the little gowns were in different pastel shades of yellow, white, and pale green. I told him I'd give a few to Shelley.

"We all knew this would eventually happen," he said looking into my sad eyes. "He took off right before his own wedding. It was only a matter of time."

"I know ... but it's just Shelley—and Mom. And I really want to just scream at Thomas!"

He had everything going for him: a beautiful house, a doting wife, and a new baby on the way. Most men would kill for his lifestyle, but not Thomas!

"I don't want you anywhere near him unless someone else is around," Matthew said with a serious look on his face. "We don't know where's he's been or exactly what he's been up to."

Matthew's suspicions were valid; none of us knew exactly what was going through Thomas's head.

"I just don't understand why he'd give up so much," I said, sighing deeply. I thought about the conditions of his current apartment; Dad said it was a dump.

None of us could understand his actions. Thomas insisted he loved the Peruvian girl named Rose and planned to remain with her. My parents didn't know which way to turn: Support their son's decision, even though they strongly disagreed, or denounce him completely for doing such a cruel and selfish thing to his pregnant wife? Shelley remained at their house, living alone. The Carters, who were last to know of Thomas's disappearance and his whereabouts with Rose, wouldn't talk to any of us. This was precisely the sort of thing Mom tried to avoid at all costs: the embarrassment of her family. Slowly, she gained back most of the weight she'd lost.

For the next couple of months, I tried cheering Mom up the best I could by visiting her practically every single day. She'd stop by my apartment as well, and we'd talk for hours about my pregnancy, the things needed for the baby, and she'd mention ideas about where I should hang pictures and how to arrange my linen closet. This was all so new because before I moved out, we'd never shared any intimate conversations and certainly never spent this much time together. For some reason, Mom felt more comfortable around me now that I was married.

Jo stopped by my apartment as well, usually once a month, and Matthew and I went for a few more dance lessons at the studio until the pregnancy made it uncomfortable performing twists and turns in high heels. Mom knew about our continued relationship. She turned her nose up slightly at the mention of Jo, but it was nowhere near what her reaction had been half a year earlier. Mom had seen the wedding pictures taken with Jo, Richard, and Jessica at the pond after the ceremony, and none of it seemed to bother her anymore. Her only comment was that she didn't like Jo's dress.

"Really, Anne," she said with much dismay. "Hot pink? I'd never be caught dead wearing that color at my age!"

Mom would never change, but I'd never want her to. I was enjoying our newfound relationship with each other. Like a faithful adopted daughter, I made sure Mom came first, and by the warm smiles I received when we were together, I'm sure it finally sank in that I never had any intention of replacing her as my mother.

*   *   *

The holiday season was upon us again, my favorite time of year, and the radio was playing "Jingle Bells" while we decorated our first tree with garland and ornaments. We wanted to make our first Christmas together special and splurged on a fresh seven-foot blue spruce tree. It was so tall that the top brushed against the ceiling, making it difficult to place the hand-painted porcelain angel that Mom gave me at the top.

The baby was just beginning to show, and my once slender figure showcased a small spherical swell. Jo said she carried the same way, a small bulge in the front, hardly visible. However, my middle was getting bigger every week, and the baby did acrobatics inside at every possible moment.

After the last of the decorations were hung, the telephone rang. Jo's voice was on the other end.

"You'll never guess where Sara and Armando are going tomorrow."

"Where?" I asked curiously, placing an empty box of ornaments on the floor and sinking into the couch. The mention of my half sister Sara quickly got my attention.

She had recently begun teaching ballroom dancing at a Steven Knightly studio in Tampa along with Armando, much to the delight of Jo and Richard.

"You know Matt was in contact with his grandmother several years ago? They wrote a few letters back and forth," she continued.

"He was the reason she knew where you were living," I reminded her.

She sighed heavily.

"I think about that a lot. If it wasn't for my mother, you may not have found me. Honestly, Anne, I hate to even think she played a part in our reunion. I know it's hard to understand, but what she did to me back then, with my pregnancy ... And she wouldn't attend my wedding to Richard or even acknowledge him!"

"I remember," I said softly.

"Anyway ... I don't know what came over her, but Sara is up for a short visit with Armando and out of the blue decided to call her and arrange a meeting for tomorrow afternoon."

I was stunned. My natural grandmother, I hadn't even considered trying to visit her. The thought never crossed my mind. Thus far, finding Jo had been enough.

"Sara said you could come along too if you want."

"I'd love to!" I said enthusiastically.

"I'm not going," she said firmly, before I even had a chance to ask.

"Jessica wants to go too. I really can't deny her the opportunity to meet her grandmother. The poor thing never had one. Richard's mother died years ago when Sara and Matt were very young."

*   *   *

This time around, Matthew wasn't upset that I was meeting yet another stranger that just happened to be a birth relative. Upon hearing the news, he shook his head and chuckled.

"Never a dull moment with you," he smirked.

Armando and Sara swung by my house at noon the next day. They were both dressed up for the occasion. Sara wore a tight pair of black leather pants and a low-cut, mauve silk blouse, and Armando was decked out in designer jeans and a grey blazer.

"We're going out afterwards," Sara explained when she saw me eyeing their outfits. I was wearing my usual plain attire: a pair of jeans and a simple crew neck sweater.

Outside, the air was sharp and cold even though the sun hung brilliantly in a cloudless sky. I sat in the rear along with Jessica, who happily chatted the entire time about how she was going to meet her grandmother.

"Will I be able to call her Grandma?" she asked excitedly. Her sparkling blue eyes danced with delight.

Sara looked over her shoulder at me from the front seat and shrugged her shoulders.

I shrugged my shoulders too.

"Mrs. Cusack," I finally suggested. Since none of us had ever met her before, *Grandma* sounded way too intimate.

Sara didn't respond. I leaned back and sighed. It still felt uncomfortable calling Jo by her first name, and I felt an uneasiness around Sara. We didn't say much to each other. She busied herself talking with Armando in the front while I chatted with Jessica in the back.

By the time we reached Bayonne, after a twenty-five-minute ride, Jessica was beside herself with anticipation. We quickly found the address and slowly drove by a two-story, dilapidated wood-frame house set back about a hundred yards from the curb.

"Could it be that one?" Armando asked, turning the car around.

"It is." Sara pointed to the mailbox, which was hanging practically upside down. "Number four."

We all held our breath as we stared at the house. It looked like nobody had lived there for years. The front yard was bare, only clumps of weeds were scattered amongst old rotting newspapers. Most of the screens in the windows contained holes, and the gutters, those that weren't hanging off the house, showcased miniature trees growing inside the wells. The steps leading up to the front door were crumbling.

"I can see why Mom never looked back," Sara said with a half laugh.

"Let's get this over with," Armando said impatiently. It was obvious he wasn't too thrilled with the prospect of this visit. "Don't forget we're meeting up at four with my cousin Marguerite and her new boyfriend."

We slowly made our way up to the front of the house, and Armando banged on the rickety wooden door with his knuckles.

A middle-aged woman dressed in baggy jeans and a worn blue sweatshirt opened the door. She had jet-black hair that was pulled back into a bun.

"Hi, I'm Tammy," she said smiling. "I take care of Mrs. Cusack."

She motioned for us to come inside and led us down a dark hallway; the worn, sloping hardwood floor was thick with dust and cobwebs. At the end was a badly dented steel door. Tammy quickly opened it and led us inside. We all moved carefully into the middle of the room, taking care not to knock into the various folding chairs and snack tables set haphazardly about when suddenly we all shuddered at once. There, sitting in bed propped up by several pillows, was our grandmother. She sat in a quiet, dreamlike state.

We all noticed her hands first, which were resting on top of the covers. Her fingers were crooked and bent inwards, and her nails were thick, long, and curling. I stared closely at her face. It was mottled gray with a fair amount of wrinkles, especially around the mouth. Her hair was stark white and was sticking up all over her head. Her clear blue eyes were large, round, and slightly bulging and seemed to be the only things that retained their luster. There was a ratty green shawl thrown over her shoulders.

Our eyes all seemed to move in unison as we first took in the sight of her; then we scanned the perimeters of the room, which was rather large and seemed to be the main living area of the house. The room was stuffy and cluttered. There was an area rug on the floor that was practically worn down to its matting, and the walls looked dark and dank. Thank goodness for a window on the other side of the room. It was slightly open, allowing the entrance of some light and a small breeze. As I looked around, a horrible thought flashed through my mind: If Jo had kept me and lived at home, this was where I would've been growing up.

The baby inside my belly turned a somersault, as if it too sensed my uneasiness.

Tammy went over and flipped on a lamp that was perched on a small wooden table next to the bed, but the room still remained quite dark, not to mention extremely dirty.

It looked and felt like a scene out of *Great Expectations*. My maternal grandma was like Dickens' Miss Havisham. She was currently peering at us through eyes that didn't seem to be looking at us, but rather through us.

"These are Jo's kids. Remember … they wanted to stop by and meet you," Tammy said.

Our grandmother slowly looked at each of us in turn.

"Oh …" she finally said in a bored voice. "I remember Jo's son wrote me some time ago, and I wrote back."

There had been a lot more spunk in her voice last year; now there was something not quite right with her affect, almost as if she was in another time period. I chalked it up to old age and thought she was probably starting to go a little senile.

"It was … oh, what was his name?" she asked, glancing up at Armando with her great blue eyes, looking a bit confused. Armando was from Columbia and had brown skin with dark straight hair and almost black eyes. Remembering what Jo had told me about her father being dark and how her mother tried to pass him for being dark Irish, maybe she thought this was Jo's son and couldn't believe her eyes that the dark Irish existed.

Sara must've had the same thought, because she said, "No, that's not him. This is my boyfriend Armando. My brother Matt isn't here; he had to work."

"Oh, I know Jo has a son," she said matter-of-factly, averting her eyes from Sara and Armando.

"Yes," Sara said, stepping forward. "And she has daughters."

Taking a step forward next to Sara, I pulled Jessica close to me.

Our grandmother seemed to understand, because she again looked at us each in turn, nodded curtly, and returned her attention to the wall on the other side of the room. Poor little Jessica, who had initially bounced into the room, now stood perfectly straight, a confused look on her face as she scanned the surroundings of the room until her eyes settled again on Grandmother Cusack. Jessica waited to be acknowledged. It wasn't so much that Jessica expected attention; the fact was Jessica had beautiful dark red hair that fell to her waist and drew attention from everyone no matter where she went. It was all the little girl knew, especially when meeting someone for the very first time. Jo told me that her hair color was always the initial topic of conversation.

Grandmother Cusack stared across the room, seemingly lost in thought.

"And this is Jessica," I said loudly, drawing the old woman's eyes over my way for a brief moment before they settled again somewhere on the other side of the room. "Isn't she absolutely adorable?"

"Oh, yes," piped in Tammy. "Irish red hair—huh?"

"My father had red hair," Grandmother Cusack said proudly. "It was referred to as *strawberry blond* back then." She rambled on about her father and how he was a fireman for the town of Hoboken and how he lived on Willow Avenue. "And now Jo's son has strawberry blond hair too," she said proudly. "He sent me his picture." For some reason, she seemed only interested in her male relatives. It would certainly explain the strained relationship she shared with Jo.

"Could we see some pictures of your parents?" I asked.

"Tammy, go and get me the photo albums."

Tammy disappeared into a room off the kitchen. We stood stock still waiting for her to return with the photos. I was haunted by visions of Jo prowling these dark and dusty rooms while I lay curled up inside her womb. She did, in fact, reside here for the majority of her pregnancy with me, save the last six weeks that she spent in the maternity home run by the nuns. We all stood together, not quite sure what to say, and listened politely as she told us more about her younger years living in Hoboken. She never bothered to ask us any questions.

Once the albums were fetched, our grandmother began slowly flipping through them while we all caught sight of a portable toilet seat along with many bottles of medicine lined up on a small table next to the bed. I also spied a rather large ashtray filled to the brim with old cigarette butts and ashes.

Tammy must have seen me eyeing the medicine.

"She's been very sick," she explained, coming to stand beside me. "She had cancer in the colon and underwent surgery six months ago. She needs to wear a bag all the time; that's why she can't get around much."

"Oh ... I'm sorry," I said sadly. "Do you live here with her?"

"No, I only come for a few hours a day to make sure she eats and is washed."

I glanced at Grandma Cusack. Her attention was focused on a picture sitting atop a table across the room. I looked too and saw that it was Jo.

"Is that my mom's high school graduation picture?" Sara asked, eyeing the photo as well.

"Graduation!" Grandma Cusack hooted loudly. "Jo never graduated from high school. She dropped out when she was sixteen."

Armando and I said, *"Oh,"* at the same time. Sara stood there with her mouth half hanging open as if she couldn't believe what she'd just heard.

"You didn't know?" Grandma Cusack asked. A smirk ever so slowly crept across her face.

We looked at each other, half surprised, half outraged. Although it was shocking to learn this news about Jo, it was more shocking to see this old woman enjoying herself with the divulgence of this little tidbit of information.

"No, Jo wanted to work—make money," Grandma Cusack continued. "I told her it was important to get a high school diploma, but she wouldn't listen."

Sara looked exasperated. She didn't know what to say, and Jessica kept looking from face to face trying to figure out the reason for all the tension. My baby kicked, and I instinctively caressed my belly and saw Grandma Cusack eyeing my motions. She knew I was pregnant. You couldn't miss my prominent waistline, and yet she ignored it, like poor little Jessica. No, she wasn't interested in us; it was obvious. And furthermore, I was convinced that she was completely sane. There was no dementia present as I had briefly considered when we first entered the room. One thing was for sure—she wasn't anything like my grandma who would, at the very least, smile warmly at Jessica.

Our visit didn't last much longer. Having already gone through the five or so photo albums and having heard the news about Jo's lack of education, there seemed to be nothing further to gain from visiting with this old woman who just happened to be our maternal grandmother.

Sara cued our imminent departure by announcing that we needed to get back by three in order to get Jessica to a birthday party. And as the four of us said our good-byes and marched past Grandma Cusack, there was no hint of protest or even an inquiry on her part if we would ever stop by again.

Jessica sat silently in the car during the ride home. Her eyes welled with tears.

"Jessica," I whispered, pulling her closer. "Did you know that in a couple of months, you're going to be an aunt?"

"And I'm only six years old," she said, her eyes lighting up. "I mean next week I'll be six years old!"

"What would you like for your birthday?" I asked.

"Oh, I want the new sparkle Barbie doll."

I promised to buy that, and she smiled and happily chatted about her Barbie collection.

Sara's only comment on the ride home about the visit was she could hardly wait to tell her mother that she knew she didn't graduate high school.

"Can you believe it?" she said turning to Armando. "Mom never graduated! And she gave *me* a hard time about staying in school."

Thirty-Two

Bundles of Joy

Christmas arrived and was as festive as ever. All the standard traditions were kept. Matthew and I started the holiday on Christmas Eve, partying it up at Aunt Lorraine's, then Christmas morning together for the first time in our apartment. It was bittersweet as we exchanged our gifts under the Christmas tree.

"You know, this will be the only time it's just you and me," Matthew said pulling me into his arms. We gently embraced, being ever so careful of the expected bundle of joy I was carrying. "Next year, we'll be three."

"I know," I said, looking into his dark green eyes. For a moment I forgot everything that had occurred over the past year ... forgot finding Jo, the arguments with my parents, and especially Thomas's recent behavior. I only remembered that Matthew and I were together, that we loved each other, and that we were finally husband and wife.

"I'm so happy we didn't wait to have a baby," I said opening up my first gift, a pair of stretch maternity blue jeans. "You know, I want at least six kids!" I laughed when I saw the bemused look on his face.

"Six!" he moaned. "I'll have to get a second job." He looked at me more seriously. "However many you want will be okay with me, as long as we're together."

A flush of warmth pulsed through my body. I could never be reminded enough of how lucky I was to have Matthew.

I opened three more boxes containing maternity blouses, each a different color; a smaller gift bag containing a bottle of Anaís perfume; and another small package containing a new red leather wallet. I presented Matthew with a pair of Nike sneakers, a shirt and tie for work, and a new pair of Levi's.

We left for my parents' house in time to open up gifts under their tree. Dad had prepared a huge breakfast which was spread on the dining room table, complete with scrambled eggs, bacon, home fries, and toast. We all grabbed a plate and sat, chatting in the family room. Brian, Matthew, and I sat together on the couch, with Shannon at my feet, while Mom and Dad lounged in their twin recliners. Soon, Thomas and Rose strolled in carrying two shopping bags filled with presents.

Mom was coming out of her fury and embarrassment with the present Thomas situation and was beginning to get used to the idea of Rose. She didn't like what Thomas had done, but she couldn't turn her back on her own son either. So Mom talked to Thomas when he telephoned, sat with him when he stopped by for a visit, and even invited them both for Christmas morning. This was the first time I had met Rose, and I was taken in by her tall, slender, almost too perfect figure. She looked at each of us with her dark, almond-shaped eyes while clinging to Thomas's hand.

"Hallo," she said nervously with a thick Latin accent. She was breathtaking which made me pause as I looked at my expanded waistline sticking out from under the red turtleneck dress I was wearing. I looked back up at her. She was dressed simply in black, from her three-inch spiked heels to her tight black denim skirt and cashmere sweater.

"Anne, Brian, Matthew ..." Thomas said putting his arm around Rose's shoulder. "This is Rose."

"Nice to meet you," the three of us said at the same time.

Brian and Matthew quickly returned their attention to their plates. I expected some goggling from them, but, like Mom, they seemed to be tolerating her presence, not taken in at all by her voluptuous appearance.

I, on the other hand, felt a horrible mixture of anger and pity as I watched them settle onto two chairs brought in from the dining room. *What was he doing with her?* Ripples of cold waved through my body. I wanted to shout out to Thomas, to tell him to wake up and return to Shelley and the wonderful life he was turning his back on. It was hard not feeling some resentment towards Rose. She was the one who stole my brother away from his pregnant wife. However, none of us were sure if Rose actually did the luring. Thomas explained that she'd only been in the country for six months, and her English wasn't very good. She suddenly looked so vulnerable sitting there, nervously looking around and trying so hard to look like she belonged here with my family.

She looked our way, eventually fixing her uneasy eyes on mine. My face softened. I couldn't blame her. Something stirred deep inside me, hinting that she was merely a pawn in Thomas's world. In that instant, I saw a scared, dependent girl who seemed to be clinging to Thomas for support and guidance.

Matthew and I stayed another hour then headed over to the Bauers' for Christmas dinner and the traditional gift exchanging with his family. The following day, we exchanged presents and had a big turkey dinner with all the usual trimmings with Jo and her family at their house in Mountaindale.

By the time the New Year rang in, I was exhausted! As my due date drew closer and closer, I arranged my leave of absence from work to begin the second week of February. I planned to return in August, only part-time, wanting to spend as much time as possible at home with my new baby. Matthew and I signed up for Lamaze classes at the hospital, which were to start in three weeks. It was a tense time, not just with my family and planning for the baby, but the news warned of impending war with Iraq. It was all everyone was talking about.

Snow finally started falling, and on January 8, Shelley had her baby, a little girl named Brittany. Mom and I went together to the hospital to visit, stopping first by the newborn nursery window.

"There she is," I said pointing to the third baby from the right. "Oh my God, look," I said, quite taken aback. "She looks exactly like Thomas!"

The baby's face was a miniature version of my brother's. She had the same nose, cheeks, and chin. She even had red blotchy cheeks like Thomas did as a child.

Mom peered closer.

"She does." Tears started to form in her eyes. "I just hope we get to see her."

*   *   *

Not even a month had passed before I too went into labor. But my due date was still five weeks away. While I lay in the hospital bed with Matthew at my side, the doctor explained that the baby would be born shortly and would be premature. It was too late to stop the contractions.

Earlier that morning, I had inspected two restaurants. Perhaps the activity induced labor early. I brought this to the attention of my obstetrician, Dr. Manila.

"Annie," he said, shaking his head. "Like I told you before, I think you have a uterus that's shaped differently." He laid his hand on my belly. "You see the way the baby is lying across and not with the head down. After the birth, we'll do a test to see if this is the case. In the meantime, hopefully the baby will turn from the force of the contractions; otherwise, we'll have to do a cesarean."

A strong contraction hit, sending pain in ripples from the base of my spine all the way round to the top of my belly which was as hard as a rock. When the contraction ended, I asked for pain medication.

He shook his head. "I'm trying to avoid medication. It could affect the baby's lungs."

No medication and I didn't even have Lamaze! Our classes were scheduled for the coming weekend. The thought of going through labor without any pain relief was bad enough, but my anxiety further escalated with the news of the Gulf War that had started the previous day. We watched a live broadcast from Iraq nervously on the television.

"What a night!" I sighed, looking over at Matt. His attention was on the prisoners of war currently being paraded by Iraqi soldiers. "Our country is at war in the Middle East, and I'm going to have a premature baby. What else could go wrong?"

"Try not to worry," Matthew said, taking my hand. "The baby will be fine." Even though his words were comforting, his face showed despair. Seeing me in so much pain was torturing him. After standing next to my hospital bed for nearly an hour, he finally pulled up a chair, sat down, and leaned his head close to mine and began doing what Matthew does best to reduce stress; he quietly sang the theme song to an old cartoon, *Magilla Gorilla*, which we had both watched when we were young.

"Magilla Gorilla?" I asked, sucking in my breath as the next contraction hit. My abdomen quickly jerked into a spasm. "The pain … need something." The words barely came out. "Please get the doctor." I squeezed his hand till it ended and then turned to my side and closed my eyes. "No more cartoon songs, sing me something from *The Sound of Music*."

Matthew returned a minute later along with the nurse who started changing my IV bag.

"I'm sorry, Dr. Manila said no medication. The baby will be here soon, and the drugs can get through," she explained.

Another contraction, this one stronger than the last, doubled me over. All I could do was moan and run my fingers through my hair.

"Perhaps I can ask him again," she said, looking sorry. She came back a few minutes later and injected something into my IV tube. Within a few minutes, I started drifting off to sleep but awoke for every contraction—and the pain only got worse.

After an hour of this, the nurse checked my cervix, making me wince and squirm.

"I'm sorry," she apologized. "You're fully dilated, and good news ... the baby turned. I can feel the head." She quickly left the room, returning a moment later. "I talked to Dr. Manila, and it's time to push, but only during contractions."

When the next contraction came, I swore I was going to split wide open.

"There's no way this baby's going to fit," I whispered, practically out of breath.

"Push ... push," the nurse chanted anyway. I wanted to scream for her to shut up! But exhaustion took over, and I could only lie there and writhe in pain.

When the next contraction ended, I took a mouthful of ice chips and finally caught my breath. My attention returned briefly to the television and the videotape of Israel being bombed. It was reported that a hospital had been hit. Oh my God! There had to be women in labor there, and I couldn't imagine being in this state with bombs dropping all around. I felt so lucky to be here, safe in a hospital, out of harm's way. Another contraction started as Dr. Manila entered the room fully garbed in scrubs and a facemask.

"It's almost time, Annie," he said, sitting on a stool at the foot of the labor bed.

"Already?" I asked, hardly getting the word out. I didn't think the baby would be born this soon. There were so many horror stories telling of hours after hours of hard labor; sometimes it lasted a day or two. I arrived at the hospital at ten that evening, and now it was only about one in the morning.

"Okay, Annie, give me one more push ... really hard this time," he instructed.

I didn't even have to try this time because my body seemed to take over, and my lower half convulsed along with the strongest contraction yet.

"Okay, this is it," Doctor Manila said. "Only a little push now. No, that's too hard. Push gently for the shoulders."

Finally, there was a big splash, and I looked down to see my beautiful baby. It was a boy—Connor.

"What a relief," I said, gazing at him for the longest moment, taking in all of his features at once: His thick crop of black hair, his wet, wrinkled skin, and his large, round eyes that intently stared back into mine. It felt as if time stood still, and a great sense of peace completely consumed me.

They quickly dried him and placed him under a warmer. My eyes wouldn't leave him. He was absolutely beautiful. Matthew came to my side and held my hand. Our eyes met briefly, and then we turned them together on Connor, who was still being worked on by the doctor and nurse. After a few minutes, they swaddled him in a hospital blanket and brought him over to me.

"I'm sorry, but you don't have time to hold him. You can give him a quick kiss," the pediatrician said in a rushed voice. "We have to get him over to the NICU. It's a special nursery for preemies. We're concerned about his temperature right now."

"Of course," I murmured, my heart pounding. I kissed Connor's cheek. "Please, take care of my baby," I whispered. Tears welled in my eyes.

The pediatrician nodded, and his serene expression told me he would be in good hands.

"You can come along," he said motioning to Matthew.

Matthew bent over and kissed me on the cheek.

"Connor will be okay," he said. "I'll let you know what's going on."

Tears slid down my cheeks as I watched Matthew and the pediatrician leave with Connor. *He's going to be just fine,* I told myself repeatedly. *Matthew's with him.*

It was eight o'clock in the morning before I had a chance to see my baby again. Matthew took me to the NICU, and we were comforted by the pediatrician who said he'd be just fine. His lungs were slightly immature and needed some oxygen therapy; otherwise, he was perfect. Connor's condition wasn't unusual; in fact, it was quite common for premature babies to have underdeveloped lungs.

We found Connor lying on his side sleeping soundly amidst the shrill of the alarm sounds from the numerous monitors and machines. There had to be at least a dozen other babies. Most were a lot smaller than Connor and had more tubes and lines attached to their fragile little pink bodies. Both of us stood motionless, staring at our baby, tuning out all the loud noises.

"Matthew," I finally said, peering closely at Connor. "Who does he look like?" Already, I could tell from his features that he must resemble somebody. His complexion was slightly darker than ours. His eyes were shut tight, still covered with the antibiotic ointment.

"I see you."

I smiled. *Finally someone who looks like me,* I thought. But I knew there was another person lurking in those features—my birth father. *Someday, I'll search for him too.*

I looked at Connor under the warmer and reached out to touch his face. My fingertips gently started at his temple and slowly, tenderly, worked down in an inward curve and found a resting place just under his little chin. He stirred, and I knew my touch penetrated enough to reach in and warm his heart.

An image of Jo in her hospital bed flashed in my mind. The covers were pulled up tightly around her shoulders; in the distance, a baby was crying. How could she not come and see her own baby? I shivered at the thought of not going to comfort Connor. There wasn't anything that could've kept me from this room at the moment. I'd walk through fire and back again for my child.

Matthew caught my gaze, and our eyes locked. Without speaking words, I knew we shared the same thoughts. Nothing could keep us from providing our child with all the love, warmth, and happiness he so desperately needed—the things most vital in a child's life.

Thirty-Three

Life Goes On

Mom and Dad showed up later in the morning, and after viewing Connor in the nursery, they strolled through the door to my room with armloads of shopping bags.

"He's absolutely beautiful," Dad said, kissing me on the cheek.

Mom shook her head in agreement, but she looked terribly upset.

"I'm so sorry, Anne," she said, trying not to cry. "I planned the baby shower for the second Sunday in February. I thought it would be more than enough time, because everybody usually goes past their due date! I shouldn't have waited till February."

"It's okay. We didn't know Connor was going to be premature. The doctors said this morning he's doing great. Later, they're going to let him come to my room, and I can feed him."

I looked at all the bags.

"Where did all of this come from?"

"We just spent the entire morning at Macy's buying out their entire newborn department," Dad said grinning. He sat down on the chair at the foot of my bed.

Mom just stood there.

"I feel so awful. You should have had your shower already," she said hanging her head.

"It's no big deal," I said motioning for her to sit in the chair next to my bed. "I have some things anyway. I've picked up a couple of outfits over the months, and Matthew's at the pharmacy right now picking up diapers, pacifiers, and a whole bunch of other stuff."

Matthew hadn't slept since before Connor was born. He had stayed up the rest of the night after the birth and then went out to the store to stock up on baby necessities.

"Well, these should help," Mom said, bringing over the bags. "Take a look inside."

I spent the next hour opening all the bags, quickly realizing there wasn't much more that we needed. There were onesies, more drawstring gowns, a couple of newborn outfits in blue and green, blankets, hooded towels, and a whole basket full of baby bath items.

"Oh, and one more thing. Bob," she said, motioning to the door. "Go and get the car seat."

Dad brought in a huge box containing a brand-new hunter green Century car seat.

"Thank you so much!" I sighed, shaking my head in disbelief. "You two must have spent a fortune."

"Anything for you," Dad said. There was a sad look in his eyes. "We may never get to know our other grandchild."

Mom and Dad looked at each other. So far, since Shelley went home with Brittany last week, they hadn't been invited over yet to see her. It was tearing Mom's heart to threads.

"You'll always have Connor," I said warmly. "You don't ever need to worry about that."

Jo and Richard showed up just as Mom and Dad were leaving. They were all cordial enough, it being the first time they'd seen each other since the meeting nearly a year earlier at the house.

So far, every time Jo planned to stop by my apartment for a visit, I made sure Mom or Dad weren't expected. It was an unspoken request that I fulfilled for Mom's sake, because none of us really needed anymore drama in our lives.

"Anne, he's so tiny!" Jo crooned, once Mom and Dad were long gone. There was an absolutely ecstatic look on her face. "Richard and I bought a cradle for the baby. Here's a picture," she said pulling out a circular from J. C. Penney. "We'll put it together for you. All of my babies were in a cradle for the first three to four months. I hope you like it."

"Yes, I love it," I said looking at the picture. It was golden oak and had carved spindles. It was adorable!

"And it rocks too," Jo added, beaming. She kept on for a good hour talking about how she couldn't believe she was a grandmother already. I found it hard to believe too. She barely looked a day over thirty.

When Connor was three weeks old, I brought him along to my baby shower. Mom decided to have the shower as planned at her house, and it was welcoming to receive, unlike most baby showers held before the birth, all the little outfits, blankets, and other items all in blue. There were absolutely no pink items at this shower! Not surprisingly, Jo wasn't present; I didn't have the heart to inquire if she was invited when Mom looked so happy. Even Grandma attended, showing up in her wheelchair without the slightest bit of embarrassment. I placed Connor, swaddled in his receiving blanket, in her arms.

"Oh ... Annie," she said, gazing down at Connor. "You ... were ... this ... small too ... when ... we ... took ... you ... home."

"But he's a lot quieter," Mom pointed out laughing.

Connor rarely cried. I think it was all the breast milk he received. Mom, my mother-in-law, and just about every aunt present couldn't believe that Connor was fully nursed.

"Don't you slip him a bottle now and then?" Aunt Lorraine asked. "I used to add a tablespoon of rice cereal to Maggie's formula so she'd sleep better."

Unfortunately, Maggie couldn't make the shower; she'd gotten a job bartending and had to work. She sent along a beautiful navy blue diaper bag from Land's End.

Just when we were sitting down for cake, Shelley strolled through the front door with Brittany. Shelley had dressed her completely in pink from her soft homemade knit cap to her brushed cotton blanket. Mom breathed a sigh of relief when she saw the two of them. Although Mom would have preferred Thomas and Shelley together, her day was still complete. And everyone spent the remainder of the shower swooning over the two little bundles of joy, a boy and a girl. Mom couldn't have been happier.

*   *   *

Just as the pediatrician promised, by the time Connor reached three months, he was physically and developmentally caught up with the other babies his age. Another milestone occurred: Thomas left Rose and returned home. Shelley immediately took him back. We were all flabbergasted. I couldn't help but feel for Rose, imagining her sad eyes when she learned her new boyfriend was leaving. Mom, however, didn't want to hear anything about the stripper who caused so much turmoil. She was just elated that things were beginning to return to normal.

"Life goes on," she simply said.

According to Mom, their problems were in the past and were private matters to be settled between Thomas and his wife. She was more concerned with her two new grandchildren. They were like a gift from heaven, and she wouldn't let anybody detract from her current state of joy.

As for Shelley and Thomas, they went on as if Rose never existed. They set up Brittany's nursery, complete with a beautiful white crib with a matching dresser and adorned the walls with pink–and–green striped wallpaper. Their house, located in the town adjacent to Mom and Dad's, was proving too close for Thomas. They unwillingly enjoyed early visits from our father almost on a daily basis.

"He always has an excuse," Thomas told me.

Once a week, I'd stopped over during the day with Connor for a visit. Shelley wasn't home, working her usual shift at the hospital, and Thomas, not yet able to find another job, minded baby Brittany.

"And then he starts pointing out everything out of place in the kitchen or on the dining room table," he added, his face flushed in anger.

"That's Dad." I laughed.

"Anne, you don't understand ... I can't take him anymore. He's driving me mad. There's something about the way he walks right in thinking it's his house."

I nodded my head. Although Dad's temper wasn't what it used to be, he still lacked any sense of boundaries.

"I just can't shake the memories of him. Every time I look at him, I see the same angry face we saw every day when we were younger." Thomas looked away, lost in his thoughts.

"Thomas, that was in the past." I sighed. "You have to let it go. Dad isn't anything like he used to be. Now he's just annoying, but in a funny way," I said smiling, hoping to lighten up his mood. "Just try to ignore his comments or be like Brian and shrug your shoulders when he starts going on about something." Our father was really so vulnerable on the inside. Lately, his obsessive-compulsive nature went from being something I once feared to something I now found quite amusing. The truth of the matter was that our father was completely harmless. But Thomas still looked quite agitated, and I swore there was a hint of fear in his eyes whenever he mentioned our father. "He could never hurt you," I added gently.

Thomas shrugged his shoulders and looked away. I glanced at Connor in my arms. He peacefully sucked his pacifier.

"Did you find a house yet?" he asked. It was obvious he wanted to change the subject. I only hoped he'd listen to my advice about Dad. There was an overwhelming feeling that this was the root of his problems.

"Yes, we put an offer on a cute little colonial a few houses down from Mom and Dad," I said excitedly. Matthew and I, having both worked full-time over the past three years, had finally saved enough money for a down payment. After viewing at least two dozen different homes in the area, we settled on one in my old neighborhood, a few houses away from my parents', in similar fashion as my parents did years ago with my grandparents.

Thomas didn't seem to share in my enthusiasm because he looked at me like I was crazy.

"Do you know Dad will be at your house every day at six o'clock in the morning?" There was a half-exasperated look on his face as if he couldn't believe all the needling and tormenting we endured over the years wasn't enough.

I shrugged my shoulders.

"You'll never get rid of him," he said waving his hand in disgust.

*   *   *

True to Thomas's warning, Dad began visiting my house on a daily basis. He'd show up at all hours. Six in the morning, noon, seven in the evening, it didn't matter to Dad, and for some reason, it didn't matter to me. Even Matthew, for my sake, put up with my father. Matthew and I agreed: Dad was Dad, and as long as he kept his temper at bay, we didn't mind the constant drop-ins, the constant meddling in what needed to be done around our house, and the way he loved to take over home improvement projects we were working on. Despite this, it was nice having him and Mom around. We all grew closer and closer as each day went by.

Thirty-Four

New Problems

In the fall, I learned that we were expecting again, and the following June, I gave birth to another baby, a daughter, whom we named Rebecca Anne. Rebecca's birth was a lot different than Connor's. For one thing, there was no longer a war going on; secondly, we knew she was going to be born early.

After running tests, Dr. Manila informed me that my uterus was abnormal. It was T-shaped and typical of daughters born to mothers who took a drug called DES during their pregnancies to prevent miscarriages.

"You have the classic signs. Most women with this condition are infertile," he explained. "Did your mother ever take DES during her pregnancy?"

I was at a loss for words as my mind searched what Jo had told me.

"I'm adopted," I told him. "But luckily, I recently found my birth mother, and she claims she didn't see a doctor till her fifth month. I doubt she ever took this DES."

Dr. Manila wanted me to ask her anyway, just in case, because he was convinced I was a classic DES daughter, as this syndrome was called. Jo was shocked and denied taking anything more than prenatal vitamins prescribed after she went for prenatal care in her fifth month.

"Perhaps there's something genetic on your father's side," Jo suggested. "All my babies, including you, were born around their due dates, and I know of nobody else in my family who had problems."

The only logical conclusion was that something was lurking in my birth father's genes. I thought about Matthew and our conversation several years earlier; indeed, knowing your medical history was proving quite necessary. Although we still didn't know the origins of my condition, we did know that I couldn't carry a baby to term, and we prepared for another early delivery.

Rebecca decided to make her entrance into the world even earlier than Connor, a full six and a half weeks before her due date. During labor, she wasn't able to turn to the traditional head-down position for birth, so a cesarean was announced two hours later. Mom popped by after we heard the news. She'd just finished her shift on the floor above. As she sat there beside my bed, something came over me; Mom should be present for the baby's birth.

The color drained from her face when I mentioned this.

"Oh, Anne ... I don't know ... I'd be too nervous."

"But, Mom, you're a nurse!"

"They may not even allow me in the room!" she said, half exasperated.

"You can take my place," Matthew offered, a grin on his face.

I shot him a dirty look, although I knew he was joking.

"I don't think so." I turned back to Mom. "Wouldn't you like to experience the birth of one of your grandchildren?"

I don't know why I hadn't thought of it earlier. Even though she had attended births before during nursing school, she hadn't experienced the exhilaration of watching a member of her own family being born.

"That would be nice," she said, her eyes glancing up as if she too were considering this a possibility.

"And you've seen this before since you're a nurse," I pointed out. "So don't worry about passing out."

The nurse finished going over instructions with Matthew about remaining in his seat behind me during the operation. She explained that every so often, a husband faints, and if he's sitting down, it's less likely to occur.

Just then, my doctor came in.

"All set, Annie?" he asked, flipping through my chart.

"Would it be all right if my mom could also be present during the cesarean? She's a nurse here at Valley. Look," I said pointing. She was still sitting on the chair, her chin resting on one of her hands.

"What floor do you work on?" Dr. Manila asked, eyeing her name tag hanging from a blue cord around her neck.

"Fourth floor ... orthopedics."

"Sure, of course. Your mother should be there." He turned to the nurse who had just finished my IV line. "Evelyn," he said, glancing once more at his notes in my chart. "Can you get Annie's mother a pair of scrubs; she's going to be present in the section room."

"It's settled then," I said smiling at Dr. Manila.

*   *   *

Mom talked about Rebecca's birth for weeks on end. She told the second-to-second details about how worried she was when Rebecca was pulled out completely blue and how they needed to administer oxygen right away.

"I kept saying to myself that they better hurry and do something for that baby. She was as blue as the shirt I'm wearing," Mom explained, embellishing a bit on the details, but it was obvious her heart swelled with happiness at having experienced the birth of her granddaughter.

Rebecca, like Connor, caught up physically and developmentally in leaps and bounds. And what surprised us all the most was her flaming red wavy hair! It was the exact same shade as Jessica's and was complemented by fair skin and sparkling blue eyes. Jo continued visiting at least once a month. She'd come by late in the afternoon, along with Jessica, who had just started the first grade. And Mom and I, only living two doors apart, saw each other every day.

I never returned to work after Rebecca's birth, having given in my resignation. I didn't want to be a health inspector anymore—I wanted to be a nurse. My recent urge to change my career stemmed from all the time spent in the NICU after the births of Connor and Rebecca. I had felt at ease amidst all the vulnerable newborns and anxious mothers and felt a calling to this area of nursing. And what also helped were the more flexible hours available to work, including weekends when Matthew would be home and able to watch Connor and Rebecca.

This sat well with Mom who said she could always see me being a nurse.

"I told you, Anne, years ago to pursue nursing in college." There was a satisfied look on her face from finally having gotten this one right. I let Mom have her moment, because she was right. I always did like biology but was clueless at seventeen when I entered college. I saw nursing at that time as only taking care of sick old people.

I enrolled at Fairleigh Dickinson University, twenty-five minutes from my home, and was immediately accepted into their evening accelerated nursing program. Mom and Dad watched Connor and Rebecca for a few hours in the evening until Matthew arrived home from work. Things were going smoothly for everybody, and life couldn't have been happier.

*   *   *

On Connor's second birthday, I held a big celebration at my new house. Everybody was invited. It was the first time Jo and her family were going to mingle directly with all of mine. I laid low with this issue for a while, not wanting to push either side, but felt it was time for both sides of my family to try to tolerate the other's company. Little did I know at the time that this event was the beginning of a major turning point in my relationship with Jo. What didn't help matters that day was that Thomas, Shelley, and Brittany were present along with Matthew's older brother, Adam. For some reason, my brother and Adam never hit it off very well. They barely tolerated each other's company, throwing snide comments back and forth over the dinner table at many family gatherings. By the time dinner was being served, they were in a heated debate about a combination of things, especially the Giants and their potential to win in the Super Bowl this year, and somehow, politics and Bill Clinton got weeded into the argument. Soon enough, Dad and Mr. Bauer joined in, and before you knew it, Mom was pleading with them.

"Will you all please stop it!" she cried with her usual fed-up look plastered over her entire face.

For the first hour, things had seemed to be going fairly well—Jo and Richard blended in easily with my parents and my in-laws, making small talk and munching on chips and dip. But soon after Thomas and Adam got going, Jo and Richard sat silently together on the couch, miserable frowns on their faces.

The kids didn't seem to mind the distraction. Jessica was busy reading little picture books to Rebecca and Brittany in the back kitchen. Connor, however, kept switching between the dining room and the living room as he talked and performed his favorite scenes from the latest Disney movie, *Beauty and the Beast*, keeping his interest on the heated argument. Connor was a natural when it came to socializing; even at his tender age of two, he knew how to work a room and be the center of attention.

Richard uncomfortably watched Connor, an exuberant child in action. I pretended everything was fine switching my attention from Jo and Richard in the living room to serving and clearing food from the table. Surprisingly, even Mom came over several times and sat and talked with them. She was coming along when it came to Jo, but there was a hint of resentment still present. The little green monster within couldn't help but show from time to time. Mom also wouldn't accept the fact that Connor and Rebecca looked like me, as if somehow admitting that fact would be admitting my biological side of the family. Even though Rebecca had the same color hair as Jessica, Mom pointed out how Matthew's aunt had the same color and that was where Rebecca got her red hair from. There wasn't much she could say about Connor and Rebecca having my eyes. No one on the Bauer side had anything close to my size or color, but she casually brushed that feature under the carpet and instead focused on any quality that could be attributed to the Bauer side of the family.

It was a subtle unspoken warfare being waged against my genes, and everybody seemed to be involved in the battle—my parents, the Bauers, and even at times, Matthew. Nobody admitted that my children looked anything like me. If Mom could have wiped away the similarities my children shared with me, she'd have done so in a heartbeat.

However, nobody realized that ignoring my genes was ignoring me. As in my childhood, the theme set by everyone took precedence, and I learned quickly not to point out how Connor and Rebecca resembled anybody on my side of the gene pool. I wondered why it was always the adopted child, now even as an adult, who still suppressed feelings and natural tendencies in order to make the adoptive parents feel better. There was definitely something wrong with the picture.

Soon after everyone had finished eating, Jo came to help out in the kitchen. Before long, Richard strolled in, looking over our shoulders and hovering about for a few minutes. He motioned for Jo to join him in the hallway off the back kitchen where they talked in hushed tones and an occasional, "I know … I know," could be heard coming from Jo. They eventually joined me in the living room; her head was hanging low as she informed me they had to get going.

Even as she said it, I felt unnaturally anxious.

"So soon?" I asked. "But I'm just about to serve the cake."

"Thanks for having us," Richard said, bending over to kiss me on the cheek.

I wanted with all my heart to say, "Please stay," but somehow, the simple plea wouldn't rise from my lips.

Without so much as a blink of an eye, the two of them quickly put on their coats, said their farewells, and disappeared out the front door with Jessica trailing behind.

Since that birthday party, things quickly changed between Jo and me. First of all, she no longer wanted to share celebrations along with my family. She preferred to have something separate on another day when they weren't around. Second, the dinner invitations to her house starting dwindling considerably until we were over once every other year. I never questioned Jo about the sudden change or asked for more. I knew the gathering for Connor's birthday couldn't be the decisive factor, but it did serve as a convenient reason to excuse themselves from the presence of my family, and over time, slowly from me.

However, Jo and I still got together at my house a couple of times a year. Although I missed the initial closeness we once shared during the first couple of years, I didn't want to ruin things by pressing for more and resigned myself to being grateful for the little time we spent together.

The following year, Sara moved back to New Jersey along with Armando, and a wedding was planned for the following summer. Matthew and I were invited, but during the reception, we sat alone at a table with people we hadn't met and weren't asked to be in a single photo along with Jo's family.

The silence that day seemed to become, all of a sudden, much deeper. It wasn't as if she was trying to hide who I was, everyone knew our relationship. However, it was crystal clear where I *didn't* stand within Jo's family. Why was she treating me this way? My heart ached to be included in some way. Being in a picture or two would have been enough. My not having an active role in Sara's wedding was understandable; we weren't close and only saw each other from time to time, but it hurt that Jo didn't bother to invite me to be included in anything that day. It was as if I were nobody to her now, even though I took up residence inside her womb. Having children of my own and knowing in my heart I could never do such a thing to them only made things worse.

I tried to enjoy myself at Sara's wedding, but the entire time, I was constantly battling tears that kept creeping up in my eyes, and Matthew, sensing my sadness, kept squeezing my hand. I didn't need to tell him what was bothering me—he knew.

"It's okay, Anne; we have Connor and Rebecca back at home."

I never did bring up my disappointments to Jo about Sara's wedding, deciding again to brush it under the carpet, never understanding why she wanted me excluded. I was just happy that she was still in my life, even if it was only for brief moments. It was better than nothing.

*   *   *

By early fall, I finally graduated from nursing school, with high honors again. In November, I took and passed my state exams and became a licensed registered nurse. Wanting to continue with part-time hours, I found a position at Wayne General Hospital working three nights a week in their labor and delivery room and newborn nursery.

My parents became more and more an integral part of my daily life. Over and over, Dad commented how lucky he was to have my family in his and Mom's life. Brian, who decided to return to college after meeting his new girlfriend Tina, finally moved into an apartment of his own. And Thomas, exactly as Matthew predicted, took off again.

This time, Shelley refused to take him back. Thomas's life was like one long roller-coaster ride, filled with ups and downs and danger at every bend. Shelley filed for a divorce when she learned that he'd found someone else, this time an older woman who had a six-year-old son of her own. Thomas moved in with them and refused to see or speak to any of us, including his own daughter. The next year, Shelley remarried, bought a new house with her husband, and was expecting a baby.

Although devastated again, Mom got over it quickly this time around. She turned her attention to my family and to Brian, who finished college, earning a degree in finance. Brian and Tina eventually moved in together and began planning to someday get engaged—but they were in no rush. We were all just glad that he finally decided to get his life together. And my parents— like my grandparents—were becoming an important part of the daily lives of my children. My mom was known as Mimi and my dad as Pop-pop. Our front doors became revolving, and I was so happy that my children shared a close relationship with their grandparents in the same way I had done years ago with mine.

Thirty-Five

Grandma

It was a bitter cold day in March, several years later, when I heard the news about Grandma. My belly was just beginning to swell with yet another child. Mom called and told me through tears that Grandma had died early that morning. Instead of remembering what Grandma looked like on my last visit, I tried visualizing her sitting in her favorite armchair, a mug of hot tea nearby while she happily watched her game shows on TV. It was hard to keep this image alive when she suffered so much over the last decade, confined to the wheelchair which she hated. She died peacefully after being in the hospital for a bout with pneumonia. Initially, the doctors thought it would be a short hospital stay once the intravenous antibiotics kicked in. She never did get to return home.

We all arrived at the hospital in time to say our farewells. She was semiconscious for the most part, looking ghostly beneath the IV lines and tubes attached to her sallow, puffy skin that stretched till it gleamed. The pneumonia quickly turned septic, and she was too weak to fight off the illness. During our last moments together, I sat solemnly beside her for the longest time, sipping a cup of lukewarm tea while the machines and monitors beeped eerily. As I was getting ready to leave, I held her pale, cold hand.

"Grandma," I whispered, "I'm pregnant again."

I could have sworn I felt her ever so slightly squeeze my hand, but it was probably wishful thinking. She slept soundly, her breathing sporadic, and her once-vivid aura that emanated and warmed my heart was nearly gone. I silently left the room and the presence of the one soul who truly loved me beyond belief.

The despair in Mom's voice as she told me of Grandma's death couldn't be missed. Not only did she have to deal with Grandma dying, but she had to deal with Thomas's absence. And Brian, like always, kept mostly to himself, rarely visiting. "I don't feel comfortable around Dad," was all Brian commented when I asked why he barely came around.

Dad's take on the situation concerning his sons was he thanked God he and Mom had me.

"You know, Anne," he said, as we were getting ready to leave for the wake. Mom was still upstairs getting dressed. "Your mother and I are so lucky to have you and your family. I don't think either one of us would be here today if it wasn't for you."

I'd heard this so many times lately—each time making me feel awkward.

"Oh, Dad," I muttered. "Of course you both would still be here."

"No, I don't think so. You're the reason we stay together. If we didn't live so close and I couldn't see you and the kids every day, I'd be gone, either dead or living somewhere else."

I thought again about my two brothers.

"And Thomas and Brian, they just have problems. Brian actually seems to be getting his life together lately."

"He could care less about your mother and me. It's like we don't even exist. And your brother, Thomas ..." Dad added. It was funny how he referred to Thomas as my brother whenever he had something nasty to say about him. "I don't even know what to think anymore about him. He has no idea his grandmother is dead. Do you know how that will hurt your mother?"

Mom was beyond words. We didn't mention Thomas's absence, and when we arrived at the funeral home, seeing Grandma lying in her coffin was worse than hearing about her death. I couldn't stop thinking about how much I was going to miss her. She'd been such an important and influential part of my life. If it weren't for her amusing views—which seemed rather dubious to others—that rubbed off on me, I might never have found the courage to break through the walls of guilt and blame pertaining to my adoption.

Grandma had two viewing sessions at the funeral parlor and burial the very next day. Matthew and I, along with Connor and Rebecca, drove to the wake with my parents. At first, Mom felt it was inappropriate for young children to be present at wakes and funerals, but due to the look on my face, she quickly gave up any attempts to dissuade me. My long history of having suffered from hiding facts proved that it's much more beneficial to be completely honest with children, keeping the information brief, but truthful.

When we arrived, we were met by Grandpa, Aunt Lorraine, Uncle Ron, and my cousins. Maggie attempted to smile when she saw me but was unsuccessful and large round tears began rolling down her cheeks. She rummaged in her purse for a tissue.

"I can't believe she's gone," she said with a hiccup.

Grandma was buried in a Catholic cemetery located in her hometown of Chester. It reminded me of the Irish countryside I saw on my honeymoon with Matthew. The tombstones were all arranged in neat little rows up and down the slopes in similar fashion to the ancient rock boundary lines in Ireland. The serenely blue sky above contained white, wispy clouds slowly floating by, and there was a peaceful calm that seemed to generate through us all as we stood side by side as her ivory coffin was lowered into the freshly dug pit. Grandma now, like her ancestors, had her little plot of land on her rolling hill. The priest from Grandma's parish recited her favorite Irish prayer:

May the road rise to meet you.
May the wind be always at your back.
May the sunshine warm your face, the rain fall soft upon your fields.
And until we meet again, may God hold you in the palm of his hands.

We each in turn tossed a long-stemmed red rose on top of her coffin and solemnly watched as the first shovelful of fresh earth was placed on top of her coffin.

"And from dust we came and to dust we return," the priest recited as we turned and quietly left the cemetery.

Afterwards, as was the Murphy family custom, we all gathered at Aunt Lorraine and Grandpa's house. As we pulled up their long driveway, we saw a dim light emanating from a downstairs window.

"That must be Grandpa," I said. "I bet he's got the sauce already on the stove."

Sure enough, we found Grandpa already home and standing in front of the stove, an apron tied tightly around his slim waist as he stirred a large pot of tomato sauce. He was so pale that his balding head seemed to shine, even in the dimly lit kitchen. When Grandpa was upset, he cooked; he only drank when he was happy. Grandpa must've had a happy life because he sure drank a lot.

Mom sighed when we entered his kitchen. She was worried about his health, due to a combination of his excessive drinking, Grandma's death, and the fact that he still commuted to work in New York City every day.

But as my Aunt Lorraine pointed out to everyone as we gathered around the dining room table, the air thick with cigarette and cigar smoke, "You can never take the New Yorker out of him. Even though he's seventy-six years old, he'll keep going to New York and making his rounds at the pubs on the way home, and the day he stops doing this will be the last day he's on earth."

*   *   *

I gave birth to a baby boy later that year in October 1997. We named him Michael. Unlike his siblings', his premature labor was halted with special medications, and he was actually born in the month he was due. Our newest little angel was the spitting image of his father, complete with chubby cheeks and blond wavy locks in similar fashion to Matthew when he was young. The only feature Michael shared with me were his piercing cerulean blue eyes that became a popular topic of conversation in the family, not so much for their sleepy or mysterious appearance as mine had been, but more for the sharp way his eyes looked at you whenever he was angry.

My adoption status was a topic that now, Matthew and I talked about with our three children. Early on, I explained to them about Jo and the special relationship she had to all of us. I simply told them that she was unable to raise me when I was born so my parents did instead. They knew she was one of their grandmothers and referred to her as Jo, as I did. They thought it was so cool that I actually had two mothers. To them, there were no baffling questions that couldn't be answered, and they even got to see this special other grandmother. It seems that simply telling the entire truth right from the start diffuses any possibility of problems arising later on.

As for Sam, my birth father, I told them what little I knew and showed them the three pictures from Jo.

"Don't worry, Ma," Rebecca told me after she finished looking at the pictures. "I'm sure you'll find him."

Rebecca's comment gave me hope and the spark to start searching. I knew my birth father had served in the army, and I remembered reading in a genealogy magazine that military information was available to family members. So I sent for a form from the National Personnel Records Center in St. Louis and requested military records for my father, stating I was conducting genealogy research and wanted precise service dates for my data. The reply came six weeks later; they were unable to locate a military service record from the information provided. Maybe they needed more than just a name and a possible birth date. The only other option was to try to locate his birth record, and once again, I sent out requests, this time to every state in the country. It cost a small fortune in search fees and postage. Some responded; others didn't. In the end, I simply couldn't find him.

*   *   *

Each year, I met another person touched by adoption. And every story, although unique for each person, carried similar themes. Of the half a dozen or so adoptees I came across, all wanted to search but felt that they would be disloyal to their adoptive family in doing so. A girl I knew, Nancy, was no different.

That summer, we both attended a neighborhood barbecue, and the topic of adoption came up. We quickly learned we were fellow adoptees. That familiar sense of adoptee kinship instantly formed between us as I relayed my story about how I searched and found my birth mother eight years earlier.

"Anne, that's just amazing." Nancy's eyes widened with wonder. "I could never do it," she said, looking over her shoulder. Her parents were at the barbecue, sitting directly behind us. "You have no idea how they'd react," Nancy said, after leaning in closer towards me. "My mom gets all crazy whenever I mention the topic."

"Mine weren't happy," I said, lowering my voice. "Today, they tolerate it. They don't yell anymore, but I can tell deep down, they don't like the idea of me having contact with her."

"How often do you see each other?" Nancy asked.

"Every once in a while. You should really think about searching. Finding Jo and knowing her story, which is also my story, have helped me tremendously. That whole aura of secrecy is gone."

"I'd like to know too." Nancy sighed. "But … I just can't go there. Sorry, but I don't want the drama in my life."

Thirty-Six

The Argument

That fall, Connor started grade school. He attended Saint Peter's, a Catholic elementary school, keeping in tune with the Murphy educational standards—although I made sure there were no nuns teaching at the school before enrolling him. Actually, there wasn't a single nun in the whole parish, which suited me fine. The school was small and had a warm, close-knit atmosphere which I considered essential in a child's school environment. The next year, Rebecca also attended Saint Peter's, and in the meantime, I continued to work one or two weekends a month at the same hospital.

It was at this time when Jo told me about her plans to have a special thirty-year wedding anniversary celebration for herself and Richard. She excitedly told me about the hotel where it was going to be held, the music, and the menu arrangements. She always ended the conversation by saying I was the only member on her side of the family who was attending. Her mother had died without notice or comment the previous year. Jo's brother made the call to her a week after the event. Besides her brother, whom Jo didn't see, there was nobody else.

As her anniversary party drew nearer, I sensed this event wasn't going to be enjoyable. Visions of me being left out at Sara's wedding haunted me, and I didn't want to go through that experience again. Jo practically insisted that I come, so we secured a babysitter, and after buying a new dress, I reluctantly agreed to attend—for Jo's sake.

It was a big gala affair at a grand hotel with a live band, a photographer, and fresh flowers for the tables—the usual wedding traditions. We arrived during the cocktail hour and were instantly met with Jo and her family posing for professional photographs. Jo, Richard, Sara, Armando, Matt, and Jessica all dressed in long, flowing evening gowns and tuxedos, posed for at least a dozen shots along with Richard's siblings and their spouses. Matthew and I stood off to the side—waiting—but again, Jo never came over and asked us to be in a single photo. Those old feelings quickly returned. *Why couldn't I be included in at least one photo?* I thought as my stomach turned over.

Over and over, I kept telling myself that it didn't matter; it was just a picture. But another part of me knew it was more than just a photo; it was the meaning—a snapshot of the present broadcasting that Jo, to this day, still didn't consider me a part of the family.

My half brother Matt was watching us from across the room. When the photographer finished, he strolled over.

"Anne ... Matthew," he said shaking Matthew's hand. He bent over and kissed my cheek. "Good to see you both." He still kept his shoulder-length auburn hair swept up in a ponytail, reminding me of the very first time we met in Jo's living room. That day seemed liked eons ago.

We made small talk for a minute or two while my brother Matt curiously looked me over.

"Don't worry," he finally said. "You didn't miss anything great. It wasn't always roses growing up with them."

His statement took me by surprise, and I just stared at him. He knew. He could see how upset I was, and for some reason, he sensed my pain at being excluded. Why couldn't Jo?

We didn't talk to him again. He joined a group of his cousins while Matthew and I stuck to our table and watched everyone dance the latest moves. Even though Matthew and I were seasoned dance students, the majority of the guests in attendance far surpassed our skills, and we watched everyone on the dance floor with awe. I couldn't get Matt's comment off my mind; his words and his kind gesture—as small as it was—meant the world to me. Throughout the remainder of the party, whenever we saw Richard, we were met with awkward gazes, and it all was too much to bear a second time. That same strange detachment I felt at Sara's wedding and a cold chill running up and down my spine hinted that I didn't belong here. They saw me as an outsider, and I wondered why Jo even bothered inviting me.

Through the remainder of the evening, visions of Jo, Richard, and Jessica posing for pictures on our wedding day flashed through my head. I even proudly displayed one of the photographs on my bookshelf alongside other family portraits. Why did Jo want to keep me this way? I was no threat to any members of their family. Having me around in no way took anything away from any of them. When would everybody realize that excluding people is the worst punishment that could be inflicted on them?

We left the anniversary party early.

When we arrived home, I went straight upstairs to the bathroom, stripped off my clothes, and stood for the longest time under the steamy water in the shower. The events of the evening replayed in my mind like a broken record—Jo leaving me out, once again, and the overwhelming feeling of being considered an outsider.

Instead of feeling sorry for myself, I decided to confront Jo. It was necessary; she needed to realize that her indifference was deeply upsetting. It wasn't as if I wanted to be a big part of her family or step on anyone's toes. I merely wanted every now and then to be included. The strong possibility that my gripes may drive a wedge between what little we had between us almost made me change my mind, but in the end, I couldn't let it go. My insides were being ripped to pieces.

Later, as I sat in my bedroom, my children already snug in their beds, I leafed through the few precious objects from Jo that were stored carefully away in a large gray envelope: the letter from the adoption agency, the photos she gave me, and the torn-out piece of notebook paper containing the heartfelt letter she had written. I reread her words again, noticing how she referred to herself as my mom several times. My thoughts tumbled inside my head. *Where was the person who years ago painstakingly wrote this letter? How can she consider herself my mother and then treat me as if I were nobody?*

I could almost feel the once-familiar dread of uncertainty envelope me again. What would happen when I confronted her? There was the likelihood she may never want to see or speak with me again. *It was a valid possibility*, I thought, remembering how she cut out her own family entirely from her life after I'd been born. Would she treat me any differently?

I couldn't be sure how it was going to be played out. For eight years, we had each held up an invisible barrier which didn't allow us to get too close in fear of hurting our families. It was more like a safety net built out of fear and desperation just in case the other decided to end the relationship. Why did we feel all of this was necessary? Can any relationship withstand so much? There was also the impediment of everyone around us. There wasn't only the initial disapproval of my parents, my in-laws, and Richard, but society as well. There was so much frowning when we only wanted to know each other. It was actually remarkable that through all the opposition, we still continued a relationship—a weak one, but it was something.

The following day, Matthew took the morning off from work and played catch with Connor in the backyard. Our new Labrador puppy, Shelby, was jovially romping in the yard along with Rebecca. I stood off to the side holding Michael, marveling at how Matthew was so wonderful with the children, much different than my own father had been when I was a child. It was so nice that I was so close now to my parents. It was funny, but ever since I found Jo, the relationships I had with my parents only strengthened. I wondered what my childhood would've been like if all the secrets pertaining to my adoption were open right from the start—just imagine.

The next day, it poured. I stared out the window watching the rain pound the pavement as Matthew's car slowly pulled away from the curb. He waved several times as he zoomed out of sight. Reluctantly, I went and found the portable telephone and dialed Jo's number.

I knew I couldn't put this off any longer. She picked up after the second ring.

"Hi, it's Anne."

"Oh … hi," she said cautiously as if she knew what was coming. She shared the same sixth sense I possessed, that ever-present sense of foreboding.

We were both silent until I said, "I need to talk with you about what happened at your anniversary party the other night." The words reluctantly left my lips as we had never so much as disagreed before. Although it was extremely uncomfortable, it was necessary. It had gone on far too long, and the pent-up hurt and anger, normally kept at bay, was gnawing at me from within.

"I've kept it to myself for all these years," I started, trying to keep an even tone in my voice. "After I first found you, we saw each other quite often. It may have been because we just met and it was intense, but even after the initial year, the second was the same. Matthew and I still came for dinner at least once every other month and then … something happened." I paused.

"Nothing happened," she said with a hint of desperation in her voice.

"Something must have happened," I went on, "because now its nonexistent … Initially, you visited so often, then suddenly, after Connor's birthday party, you pulled away. I know you're busy with Jessica and I'm busy with my children … but something changed."

"No, nothing changed," she vehemently denied.

"Yes, Jo, *something* changed," I repeated with emphasis. "I don't know exactly why, but you did a complete turnaround." I paused again, waiting for her to respond, but she didn't say anything. It was precisely the silence that told me I'd struck a chord. "I can almost pinpoint it to Connor's birthday party."

She sucked in her breath.

"You and Richard left in such a hurry, it seemed you two wanted to be anywhere but at my house that day. I understand if you feel uncomfortable around my family … Believe me, I know they're not the easiest people to get along with. But why pull away from me because of them?"

"But, Anne … your parents. It's not fair to them. They raised you … I didn't. Richard pointed out how involved they were in your life, and he feels I'm stepping on their toes."

"Richard?" I asked. "Richard is concerned about *my parents?*"

"Umm, no, I feel that way too," she said quickly, as if she realized what she'd just admitted to.

"Do you really think Richard cares so much about my parents?"

"Oh, Anne … what about Richard … I just …" She broke off.

I didn't want to believe what I'd heard. But I hung on every word … *What about Richard* … those three words told me more than a thousand words could. Richard didn't want to share his wife with me. Why couldn't Richard and everyone else who had frowned upon our reunion and relationship acknowledge that we had needs too? Jo had a need for her own child, and I had a need to know my own birth mother. We were not asking our families to give anything up. We were not trying to replace anybody. We were only asking for everyone to open up their hearts and find room for another person. Was that really asking too much? Apparently, it was, and now Jo was siding against me.

It was all too much to bear. I closed my eyes, not wanting to feel the chill that ran wildly through my body. At that moment, I didn't want to feel anything.

"Anne, you have to understand, we can never have the same relationship I have with my other three children … They all have a history with me … We don't have that."

Her statement stung.

"What about the last eight years?" I asked, fighting back tears. "Eight years isn't a good start?"

"It's just not the same. Your parents raised you … I didn't."

I thought about the last eight years with my parents. This time period had been the most important part of our relationship. Before that, it was practically nonexistent—save for the rantings and ravings. If the last eight years could be a fresh beginning for my parents and me, why couldn't Jo do the same?

My stomach clenched into a knot as we went back and forth. Jo's words about us not having a history hurt beyond belief. I thought about her practically every day while growing up. Didn't she think about me? If she didn't, then yes, there was no history for her, but if she did as she claimed to—eight years ago, when we first met—then we did indeed have a history. It was just a different type, one that existed in our hopes and dreams—but it was real nonetheless. I don't know what came over me, but words started to spill out of my mouth.

"Jo, you need to know about my childhood and what it was like."

She needed to know the truth, even though deep down, I suspected she somehow had to have known all along that there were things amiss during my childhood. There was something in the way she flinched the few times she was in the presence of my father. She never looked comfortable around him. Her body would become as rigid as a board, and she tried to avoid his gaze.

"I know you met my father and got along great, but there's more to him than what you've seen, a side that still affects my brothers to this day." She suspected, I was sure of it, but she never asked me a thing, especially about my childhood—The subject was never discussed.

"You see ..." I took a deep breath and quickly divulged the details. She was silent through my story, and in the end, Jo was at a loss for words. There was only the sound of her soft breath on the other end of the line. And for once, I didn't feel sorry for her. For once, my sympathies rested solely with myself. They were certainly not with my adoptive parents anymore, who made the decision as adults to raise children borne from another, and not with Jo, for having to endure the pain of giving up her newborn baby, a choice she too freely made as an adult. But for once, the sympathies lay with me, the adopted child, who made no decisions and merely had to endure a life full of secrets, guilt trips, and seclusion from both families, adoptive and natural. This was the reason there were so few adoptees who voiced their concerns. How could we speak out about our pain when deep inside we knew we'd be seen as nothing but ungrateful?

I decided to stand up for myself, to stand up for the adopted adult I was now and for the adopted child that still remained.

"I'm sorry, Jo, but I cannot allow you to continue to treat me like I'm an outsider. You can't allow me into your life and treat me like a daughter for nearly two years and then suddenly stop and treat me like I'm just some distant relative. I have feelings too."

There was silence for almost a full minute until Jo finally muttered a few words.

"Anne ... I'm so sorry." Her voice was barely audible.

I was silent too. A part of me seemed to take a deep breath, releasing not only the burden taken on to protect Jo from learning the truth, but the burden of ignoring my own needs. Again, like with my parents, I felt the need to suppress feelings in order to make Jo feel better. I was nothing less than a sacrificial lamb, once again. How sad that the adoptive child's needs are always second best.

"I had no idea," she said slowly. "I always pictured you as an only child. A little girl smothered with love and affection from your parents who couldn't have children of ... of their own." Her voice cracked. "You're right ... it was my job to include you in my family pictures. I promise I'll do better. I'll make sure next time. Of course you should've been a part of those moments with Sara, Jessica, and Matthew."

"Thank you," I whispered. Jo's apology was enough to sustain me.

"Anne," she said sadly. "I don't want to lose you. I want us to continue seeing each other." She sounded so desperate, so afraid that I was going to end it on the telephone that day. And all along, I thought it would be the other way around. "I have an idea," she said sighing deeply.

"I'm listening."

"Why don't we set aside a day each week, you know, special time just for the two of us? We can start over, talk more, and I'd like to get to know your children better."

"*Your* grandchildren," I reminded her.

Her voice cracked.

"Yes, they're my grandchildren."

"Jo, you've known Connor, Rebecca, and Michael from their births, and yet, you keep them at such a distance."

"I was only thinking about your parents."

"Why can't my children have more than two sets of grandparents? You have three children; do you ignore Jessica because she's the third?"

"No, of course not. But Richard thinks we should step back."

"Have I ever treated my parents like they were back burner, second rate to me and my family?"

"No."

"Have you seen me exclude my parents from special events or flaunt you around as the real grandmother?"

"No." Her answer was barely audible.

"I've treated my parents with more respect and dignity than I received from them and more than I received from you and Richard."

"Anne ... you're right," she said weakly.

I paused and caught my breath. I had to get used to this sudden acquiescence. With my parents, I was never right.

"I like the idea about getting together each week. Wednesdays or Fridays after school work for me; the kids don't have any activities on those days."

"Wednesdays would be better for me," Jo said on a brighter note.

It was settled, and before we hung up, Jo apologized again.

"The adoption agency ... they were supposed to screen the parents ... they promised me."

Thirty-Seven

My Father

When Connor was in the fourth grade, a chance conversation with his teacher, Mrs. Bradforth, sparked my interest to search for my birth father. Connor was doing a school genealogy report and had to list his relatives.

It was precisely this sort of project routinely done in schools that caused anguish for adoptees, having no choice but to fill in the names of their adoptive family's ancestors on the chart. My grandparents' names made sense because I knew them, but somehow, I couldn't make the connection to the great-grandparents and beyond. Something in the back of my mind reminded me that they were not my lineage, as teachers so blatantly taught was a direct bloodline. And now my son was getting a taste of it too. He wanted to list everybody—all six of his grandparents!

His teacher instructed that he needed to choose for the maternal side, natural or adoptive. The teacher's directions didn't make sense to Connor. A child's mind, so simple and instinctively in tune to such matters, only wanted to do what felt right to him. "But I can't leave anybody out; they're all my grandparents. Why can't I list them all?"

Would a mother, or a father for that matter, leave out one of their children if they had more than four?

Since Connor's data proved quite complicated, his teacher discussed the matter with me one day after school and I told her about my search for Jo.

"What an amazing story," she said quite flabbergasted. "But tell me ..." she said leaning in. "I bet your parents were upset?" Her usually soft eyes widened expectantly.

I stood there stricken. It was so unexpected to hear her ask that question ... at that moment, and yet, I'd heard it a thousand times already. *I bet your parents were upset.* Her words felt like arrows ripping through me, tearing up old wounds. I had been so sure, so absolutely confident that the guilt so heavily laid upon me from the time I was a child was gone. It had been put to rest, especially after the events at Jo's anniversary party several years ago. I was confident that no one would ever again make me feel ungrateful.

But now, here was Mrs. Bradforth dredging up old wounds. Does every adoptee go through this? Sensing ambivalence on my part, she quickly added, "I'm only asking because a close friend of mine adopted a little girl from Korea, and she's said many times that it would break her heart if someday her daughter wants to find her natural mother."

"Why is that?" I managed to say, feeling my heart quicken.

"Hmm ... why is what?" she asked, taking a step closer.

Why does everybody assume it would naturally cause adoptive parents grief? Why can't everybody assume instead that most adoptive parents are nothing but happy and supportive? Mrs. Bradforth's comments struck a chord, but it wasn't my own guilt that she flared up, it was the guilt of every adoptee who ever searched. The outrage vibrated through me, telling me that other adoptees were going through the same thing.

"Yes ... my parents were very upset when I found my birth mother ..." I slowly answered. "And it was probably one of the worst times emotionally in my life."

"Oh, my ... I had no idea," she said tilting her head to the side. "It affected you as well?" she asked, a look on her face as if she couldn't believe such a thing was possible.

Imagine ... a child with feelings.

"Everybody made me feel like I did the most horrible thing to my parents ... All I wanted was to know where I came from, to know my story ... And when I found out what my story was and didn't hate my birth mother for giving me away ..." I hesitated, the memories from that time seemed so far away, and yet, at that moment, they suddenly came flooding back in again. "They screamed at me, my parents—everybody. Nobody could forgive me ... for forgiving her."

Mrs. Bradforth stared at me in disbelief.

"I still see her till this day," I went on. "We get together a couple of times a month. I can't see how everyone can feel that once reunited, I should then shut her out of my life because she didn't raise me. To me, she's my mother as well—my other mother."

She fumbled with the buttons on her sweater. "What about your father ... I mean, you know, your birth father?"

I told her what little bit I knew.

"What about the Internet?" she asked. "I hear many people are locating long-lost friends that way."

I sighed deeply; we had finally just gotten a computer for the home. We joked that we were probably one of the last families in America to have one.

"I feel kind of funny ... he doesn't even know I exist."

She shook her head.

"The man has a daughter. He should know about you and the fact that he has three grandchildren. He would love to know Connor because he's such an amazing and entertaining child. The things he comes up with in class are remarkable."

*   *   *

Later that night as the lights from the Christmas tree twinkled, I sat at the computer, surfing the Web. I can't say with any great certainty that Mrs. Bradforth renewed my quest for my birth father. It was rather a ruling impulse, present from my very conception, propelling me ever forward in his pursuit. The very idea of him both excited and frightened me. As much as I yearned to be reunited, and to learn of the other half to my gene pool, I feared his rejection just as much.

As for my search, this time around, there were so many more resources available—and right at my fingertips. There were online search and reunion registries—there had to be a least a dozen different sites—as well as online forums where adoptees, birth parents, and adoptive parents posted comments and others responded. As I browsed through all the Web sites, I realized adoption had come along in some ways. There was much more information and support available, but still there was a long way to go as forty-six states still sealed records. However, Oregon and Alabama had both recently reversed their sealed records laws and now allowed adult adoptees access to their own records.

The majority of adult adoptees in America wishing to search still had to rely on my pre-computer ways, making phone calls and sending out requests to health departments in order to obtain information if they couldn't initially find each other on one of the online registries. And what was most surprising was that many adoptees still searched in secrecy. Guilt trips were being laid heavily on adoptees who wanted to search and especially on those who were reunited. Sadly, adoption hadn't gone anywhere in regards to the legal and emotional needs of adoptees.

Mrs. Bradforth's comment also gave me the drive to start writing my story, but the priority was finding my birth father. The glare from the computer monitor was starting to give me a headache, and yet I still scrolled, looking for the name Kohlpann. Nothing. Over the next few days, I kept looking online for any mention of his name. The New Year rang in, 2001, and again, all went by smoothly, the gloomy predictions about catastrophes and the end of the world that many predicted would come to be in 2001 when 2000 showed up nothing were quickly put to rest. Finally, I found a white pages search engine and typed in his full name, Sam Kohlpann; it wasn't listed but other people with the same surname were.

Why not call them up in every state and ask if they know a Sam in the family? I could tell them he's about fifty-six years old, was once in the army, and had been a dance instructor at the Hoboken Steven Knightly studio in the 1960s. Sadly, this was the only information I knew. There was nothing to lose except some dignity from an occasional disconnect. It would take more than that to keep me from trying.

The first name on the list was of someone who lived in Oregon. I picked up the telephone and dialed the number. No answer. Three more residences were called, and all picked up—they'd never heard of a Sam Kohlpann. Maybe I should just give up or perhaps hire a private detective. Our finances were a lot better than they were eleven years earlier. I looked at the next name on the screen, a residence in the state of Utah. I dialed the number, and a woman quickly answered.

"Hello, I hope you can help me," I began. "I'm trying to locate an old friend of my mother's for a thirty-five-year reunion. The man I'm looking for is named Sam or Samuel Kohlpann, and he's about fifty-six years old. In the phone book, you share the same last name, and I was hoping that maybe he was a relative of yours."

"Yes, all the Kohlpanns are related in some way or another."

"They are?"

"Um-hum, there was a genealogy done on the family name."

"This is interesting. Do you know the original nationality of the name?"

"The family came from Germany. It's a Jewish name."

"Oh … do you know a Sam?"

"No, I'm sorry. Not the way you spelled the name. Wait a minute. I could check the genealogy. It lists every Kohlpann right up to the present day."

She took my name and phone number and promised to call back. Patiently over the holiday weekend and the days following, I waited for a return call from the Kohlpanns in Utah. It never came. I considered calling her back but first tried a few more numbers listed.

The next two calls I made were to Kohlpanns with thick Southern accents, and neither had heard of him. Then there was a Stephanie from Minnesota. A young man answered the line and knew no Sam. He suggested calling his father who knew everybody in the family and gave me his unlisted phone number. A woman answered.

"Hello, I'm looking for a Sam or Samuel Kohlpann. He's about fifty-six years old and once lived in the New York City area during the late 1960s."

"Why are you looking for him?" she interrupted.

"He was a very close friend of my mother's. They worked together. I'm trying to arrange a reunion with all of the people they worked with. They were dance instructors with Steven Knightly."

"Why haven't you been able to find him?"

"I've checked just about every phone listing in the United States, and he's not listed. So I thought I'd try to contact a family member instead." I hesitated. "Are you able to help me?"

"Well … I just don't know." It was obvious she wasn't buying my story.

There was a long silence, and I thought for sure she was going to hang up, but she seemed to be waiting for me to say something more.

"To tell you the truth," I went on, taking a deep breath. There was an overwhelming feeling telling me to be up front. "… he did work with my mother as a dance instructor, but also … he's my father."

"Oh."

"I was put up for adoption and am trying to locate him." I held my breath as I waited for a response. My heart was beating faster as I anticipated the sound of a click at the other end.

Instead, I received something very different. "Oh my … yes … I do know him. He lives in Mexico."

"Mexico?" I asked in disbelief. "The *country* Mexico?"

"Yes, in Guadalajara. I can give you his phone number. Hold on. I'll get my address book … Wait, here it is. But I think I'll give you his cell phone number instead—because of the circumstances," she added with a small chuckle.

To be polite, I chuckled too, but I was sitting on the edge of the seat of the recliner in the living room, holding my breath, praying she had the right Sam. She told me his number, and I jotted it down, thanking her profusely for her generosity.

"Oh, by the way, there was an extensive genealogy research done on the family."

My heart raced. This must be some research. How I would love to have access to that data!

"I'm actually in the process of tracing back all the family branches for my children."

"This branch is done," she said matter-of-factly. "The researcher went all the way back to the fourteen or fifteen hundreds."

My heart leapt with joy. "Do you have a copy of that information?" I gently asked, not sure if she was willing to share such information with a stranger, claiming to be a long-lost family member.

"I sure do. I can mail you a copy if you give me your address."

After telling her my address, I thanked God for such luck.

On my lap was the photo album where photos of Jo and her family were stored. Flipping through the pages, I located the lot Jo gave me eleven years earlier and found the photo of Jo and Sam dancing together. I stared at his picture, seeing those all too familiar eyes, so much like mine. I took a deep breath. *Yes, this is worth it,* I told myself, and then quickly dialed the cell phone number in Guadalajara.

Much to my surprise, a distant voice said hello after two rings.

"Hello, can I please speak with a Sam Kohlpann?"

"Yes ... speaking."

My heart raced. Again, I hadn't rehearsed anything to say.

"Uh ... is your name Sam or Samuel?" I asked, tucking my legs under me in the chair.

"Ye ... es," he answered in a shaky voice.

"Can I ask you if you ever worked for a Steven Knightly dance studio in Hoboken, in the 1960s?"

"Yes, I did."

"Did you know a Jo Cusack who worked there in 1965 and 1966?"

"... Yes."

"Then you must be the one—you're my father," I said bluntly, sitting straight up in the recliner.

There was a thick silence, even the sharpest knife would have difficulty cutting. After a moment, I continued talking.

"Jo became pregnant—by you. She never told you about it. She wasn't able to care for me at the time so she gave me away for adoption immediately after I was born. Another couple raised me. I found Jo eleven years ago and have been unable to find you." I swallowed, a thick lump in my throat. I was talking so fast, similar to when I was a little girl. "That is—until now," I added.

"I ... uh," he began to say something and then stopped.

"You can't deny it. I have a picture of you, and we look a lot alike," I said defiantly. So far, I had no idea what to make of this man—who happened to be my father. It was obvious he wasn't buying my story.

"No ... no ... I'm ... I'm not trying to do that," he said warily.

The conversation didn't seem to be going well, and I wasn't sure what to make of him. Did he actually believe he was my father? Or did he think he had some lunatic on the other end of the line? I could only imagine what he must be thinking.

"I know this must be a shock to you," I said cautiously.

After another long moment, he agreed, "Well ... Yes, it is."

I decided to give him more details. *Maybe that would help,* I thought, even though I was convinced this conversation wasn't going to last much longer.

"After I found Jo," I began. "I looked for you too, but over the years, I only came up with dead ends. Eventually, I gave up. Recently, I've been doing genealogy research and realized it was important to know the other half of my ethnic background."

"Uh-huh." From the sound of his voice, I assumed he wasn't too thrilled with my announcement, a thirty-four-year-old daughter! He wasn't saying much, and I couldn't tell whether he was happy or angry with this telephone call. If anything, it was wise to extract as much information as possible while I still had him on the line. I sat back and readied my pen. "May I ask where you were born and when your birthday is?"

"I was born in New York City. My birthday is in June on the twelfth. When is your birthday?"

"In November. I was born in New Jersey. I'm married now and have three children."

"Wow, three children!"

This was a lot better. He sounded at least a bit interested in me.

"Yes, two boys and a girl," I answered happily. "How long have you lived in Mexico? Jo told me she thought you were from the state New Mexico."

"I've lived here most of my life, except for three years when I was in the military and lived in New Jersey. I was a food inspector for the three years I was in the army, and I also worked at the dance studio."

"You were a food inspector?" I asked with a jolt.

"Yes."

"How very odd ... I used to be one too."

"Really?"

"Yeah ... I worked in that field for about three years after graduating from college. My job title was health inspector, and I worked for the Edgewood health department. A few years ago, I went back to college, and now I'm a nurse. I work part-time because of the children."

"That's so wonderful. Three children."

There was a chill in the air. I pulled the afghan hanging on the back of the recliner around my shoulders while I told him a little bit about Connor, Rebecca, and Michael.

"And are you married?" I asked.

"Yes, to a Mexican girl—and we have two daughters."

Daughters! That meant I had more sisters.

"We all live in Guadalajara."

"So are you Mexican?" I asked.

"No, actually I was born in New York. I lived there for the first seven years of my life. After my mother died, my father took my sister and me to Mexico."

"Oh," I muttered. *So that explains it,* I thought. He didn't look Mexican in the pictures. "So I assume you're fluent in Spanish?"

"Yes, I'm fluent."

"I've been trying to learn Spanish for the past few years," I said, chuckling. "You see, at the hospital where I work, all of the patients come from Paterson and speak only Spanish." I paused. "May I ask your ethnic background and religion?"

"I come from a mostly German background, and I'm Jewish."

"I thought the name was Jewish," I said more to myself. "So your whole family is Jewish?"

"Yes. And what's your religion?" he asked.

"I was raised Catholic—in a big Irish family. My two eldest, Connor and Rebecca, go to a Catholic elementary school, but we're not very religious," I explained.

"Oh."

"It's a great school, very small, and everybody knows each other. We're very involved there. My husband coaches their basketball teams, and I'm currently the secretary on the school board. Keeping the minutes from the meetings is a busy job!"

"Oh, uh … I'm on a board also. It's with the temple I belong to, and I'm also the secretary."

"What a coincidence," I said, though I didn't believe in coincidences. Nothing in life happened merely by chance. For everything, there was a reason, and there was something peculiar about him, something I couldn't quite put my finger on.

"Could I have your address and phone number?" he asked. "Also e-mail address if you have one."

I gave him the information, and he gave me his e-mail address.

"Would you like me to send you a picture of myself? I have a photo of you—it's more than thirty years old, but we look very much alike."

"Yes ..." he said eagerly. "Could you send it now?"

I quickly got up from the recliner and made a beeline to the computer in the other room. I frantically opened up my picture file and selected a shot of me sitting on the family room floor with Michael in my lap. I was so eager for him to have a picture of me, his long-lost daughter. I could only imagine how I'd feel if someone called me out of the blue with similar news. I knew I'd be like a madwoman, wanting to immediately see my unknown child. I uploaded the photo and sent it off, quickly getting back on the line.

"It's on its way—my e-mail's pretty fast. It should get to you in under a minute." I plopped myself back in the recliner.

"Here it is," he said after a moment. There was a lot more pep to his voice, and then, "Oh ... my."

"Did you see it?" I excitedly asked.

"I ... uh ... there won't be any need for a blood test, now will there?"

We both laughed. It was still so hard to believe that I'd finally found him. He had seemed so distant and out of reach for so long, and then like magic, he suddenly appeared in my life. The search for him was a whole lot easier than the one for Jo had been. It was as if the universe finally rearranged itself and felt the time was right for us to be reunited.

He promised to mail some pictures of his family and that he'd either call or e-mail me soon. It was all too much as I sat motionless for the longest time, considering the conversation I'd just shared with my birth father. The strange feeling that had washed over me earlier lingered. I curled up in the recliner, afghan pulled tightly around me. This was the first time we'd spoken, and yet he seemed so familiar. How could that be?

It hit me at that moment, portable phone still clutched in my hand and images of Jo and Sam dancing together swimming in my head. The search for my birth parents wasn't all about gaining information, which is the only thing the social workers and psychologists think adoptees need. Facts alone couldn't fill the void in my heart. Yes, finally, I knew where I came from and the reasons behind my adoption, but was merely knowing the details about my origins the remedy? No, it wasn't.

My adoptive family, the courts, and the social workers all claim that it's not necessary to know anything about my beginnings. Throughout my life, it was expected of me to feel that my other parents didn't matter, that being adopted was no big deal. The existence of my other parents was a mere fact, and once divulged, it was supposed to be forgotten. But how does one ever forget such a thing as having another family, a mysterious family that you know exists but that you're never allowed to see or even talk about? The whole adoption setup struck me as institutionalized brainwashing.

Unfortunately, those who don't walk in the footsteps of an adoptee can never understand how painful the path is. There was such a need for everyone to know just how difficult it is to be cut off from your own beginnings. Just then, a commercial came on the television for the upcoming Sunday evening movie of the week, *The Sound of Music.* The theme song played in the background giving me that all-too-familiar feeling of contentment and hope.

I shivered, pulled the afghan tighter, and snuggled into the chair. The sound of Matthew's footsteps could be heard outside, bringing me back to reality. *Just wait until he hears my news about Sam,* I thought as he came through the door.

Afterword

Everyone thinks adoption has come a long way. Today, only six states allow adoptees to view their original birth certificate—only six. In the other forty-four states, adoptees must petition the courts and show good cause for access to their own birth certificates—and still there are no guarantees that they'll get permission. Every United States citizen enjoys the right—the liberty—to have full access to their own public records, including birth certificates.

Why are adoptees treated differently?

Even as a legal adult, to this day, in the state of New Jersey, I can't view my original birth certificate.

And everyone thinks adoption has come a long way.

Today when you hear the word *adoption*, you think of the little Asian girl the neighbors adopted from overseas or the African-American child here in the United States that would've been raised in foster care. So much care and attention is taken to ensure that these children grow up with a sense of their heritage and pride in their genetic culture. They know so much—not only where their ancestors came from, but some even have ongoing contact with the birth parents. Society has accepted this fact and realizes how crucial it is to the healthy development of these adopted children.

However, this way of thinking needs to extend to those children placed for adoption that aren't of a different race from their adoptive parents, the ones who may look similar on the outside—the same eye color, the same fair complexions. Beneath the skin, down to the very depths of their heart and soul, they need to be reached and given the same courtesy of having their own genetic heritage acknowledged as well.

The current army of psychologists says the adoptee should know some information about the birth family but remain separate from it. According to this thinking, the adoptee can't possibly be close to the birth parents because they didn't do the raising; they weren't present during childhood.

What the psychologists don't know is that the birth parents are *indeed* present throughout an adoptee's childhood. As a child, I was keenly aware of the fact that I had another mother and another father floating somewhere out there in the world. I may not have known what they looked like, but nonetheless, they were real to me, and they became a part of who I was and am now. These phantom parents were with me every day, every minute, every second of my life.

Secrets are still a reality for many adopted individuals. When will the secrets end? If children are to be told that they're adopted, then society needs to embrace the full consequences of the truth and remove the series of obstacles that prevent adoptees from not only finding their birth family but also from establishing an ongoing relationship with them. I'm hoping this memoir will serve as a reminder to the entire adoption community that when children are kept in the dark regarding their origins, nobody wins.

Appendix

These organizations serve individuals touched by adoption. Many advocate for fair and ethical adoption laws and practices. They also provide useful aids for those who are searching for relatives and support for all family members separated by adoption.

Concerned United Birthparents (CUB)
> Concerned United Birthparents, Inc.
> P.O. Box 503475
> San Diego, CA 92150-3475
> 800-822-2777
> www.cubirthparents.org

American Adoption Congress
> 1000 Connecticut Ave., N.W., Suite 9
> Washington, D.C. 20036
> (202) 483-3399
> www.americanadoptioncongress.org

International Soundex Reunion Registry (ISRR)
> P.O. Box 371179
> Las Vegas, NV 89137
> (775) 882-7755 or (888) 886-ISRR
> www.isrr.net

Adoption Crossroads
> www.adoptioncrossroads.org

About the Author

Anne Bauer was inspired to write a true account of her life as an adopted individual in the hopes of raising awareness of civil rights of adoptees and instigating reform in the current laws pertaining to adoptee records. She lives in northern New Jersey with her husband and their three children.

Please visit Anne at:
www.adopteesvoice.com

Printed in the United States
216573BV00002B/10/P

9 780595 520305